THE ART OF NAVIGATION IN ENGLAND IN
ELIZABETHAN AND EARLY STUART TIMES

The research for this book and its publication
have been made possible by the generosity of
Mr. Henry C. Taylor of New York.

I. The Father of English Navigation. Sebastian Cabot (?1470–1557).

The Art of Navigation
in England in Elizabethan and
Early Stuart Times

BY

DAVID W. WATERS, FSA, FRHistS, FRIN

Deputy Director, National Maritime Museum

Part One

Modern Maritime Classics Reprint No. 2

*Published by the Trustees of the National
Maritime Museum, Greenwich*

Second Edition with revisions 1978

IBN 0 905555 13 9

ISSN 0140 9042

Produced in England by Her Majesty's
Stationery Office Reprographic Centre, Basildon

To the memory of

ENG.-LIEUTENANT WILLIAM WATERS, R.N.,

H.M.S. *Formidable*, 1 January 1915

and

LIEUTENANT-COMMANDER WILLIAM ERSKINE WATERS, D.F.C., R.N.,

H.M.S. *Illustrious*, 13 January 1943

who

'wonne that honour that no Sea can droune,
no age weare out'.

PURCHAS HIS PILGRIMES

FOREWORD

by

THE EARL MOUNTBATTEN OF BURMA

FOR the past four thousand years the Art of Navigation has been one of the most important contributions to the development of civilization; for perhaps the greatest achievement of man in the ancient world was his realization that he could explore new territories as a source of new materials. But the caravan routes that he established entailed large initial outlay for roads, and a vast output of energy in carrying loads; so trading along these routes was mostly confined to luxury articles (such as spices, silks, and jewels) whose value was very high in relation to their weight or bulk.

The invention of sailing, which was man's first attempt to replace the labour of slaves or animals by the harnessing of natural forces, introduced for the first time the prospect of importing and exporting goods in bulk, and of developing a way of life that would to some extent be dependent on materials produced elsewhere.

With the introduction of sailing the need immediately arose for navigational calculations; for the stars provided the primitive seafarer with his only means of finding his way when land was no longer in sight. The beginnings of calculation are to be found in the earliest civilizations of Egypt, Sumeria, and Babylon; though the results were mainly used for the building of temples and pyramids. But these techniques spread along the great trade routes, down to and beyond the Mediterranean, where the Semitic peoples began to trade in tin and dyes.

Already by 2000 B.C. the Semites of Asia Minor had established colonies throughout the Mediterranean world; Carthage was founded in the ninth century B.C. by the Phœnicians; and three centuries later Hanno was able to coast along West Africa as far as Sierra Leone—to within 8° of the equator. The Phœnicians found out very early how to navigate by the position of the stars in the Little Bear; but scientific geography can really be said to have begun with the determination of latitude, which probably ante-dates Greek civilization.

In the sixth century B.C. Thales of Miletus, a merchant of Tyrian parentage, founded Greek geometry and astronomy; and soon in the city states of Greece calculation became a fashionable pastime. Indeed, Plato taught that geometry was the highest exercise to which human leisure could be devoted. But its practical uses were considered secondary; and it was

not until the famous school of Euclid was founded three hundred years
later—in Alexandria, which at that time was becoming a centre not only of
commerce but of learning and research—that geometry really came into
its own.

In the second century B.C. Hipparchus, the founder of trigonometry,
devised a method of fixing terrestrial positions by circles of latitude and
longitude. But for some centuries after this no significant navigational
advances were made; since, so long as a large part of the world (as it then
seemed) could be explored by sailing close to the coast, the ancient
techniques of star-lore were found adequate.

When the Dark Ages engulfed Christendom, the Alexandrians kept
astronomy alive in the first instance. Later the Moslem civilization combined the techniques of the Greeks and Alexandrians with the new methods
of handling numbers which the Hindus had developed; for the latter had
invented number-symbols that made simple calculation possible without
the use of mechanical aids. And when the conquering Moors swept across
the Straits of Gibraltar they established universities in Spain in which this
new arithmetic was taught. Jewish scholars from the Moorish universities
in Spain brought the new arithmetic along the trade-routes of Southern
Europe, and soon seafarers took to carrying Jewish astronomers who
could use the star-maps which Arab scholarship had prepared from the
ancient star-maps of Alexandria.

When the Renaissance of learning began to spread across Europe,
coasting began to give place to ocean voyages, and the need for improved
navigational methods became urgent. In A.D. 1543 Copernicus, in his *De
Revolutionibus*, attacked the premises of Ptolemaic astronomy, still
currently held—which assumed that the whole universe revolved about
the earth—and boldly defended the doctrine of Aristarchus, who had
taught exactly the opposite, eighteen centuries before!

It is at this point that Lieutenant-Commander Waters—a retired naval
officer, an Admiralty historian, and a member of the Society for Nautical
Research—takes over. His book, which I consider a true *magnum opus*,
tackles a period in the development of navigation which has until now
remained singularly neglected. It describes, in scholarly detail, the first
Elizabethan era, and the problems of oceanic navigation which had suddenly assumed a vital urgency in that New Age of merchant enterprise.

Lieutenant-Commander Waters explains how seamen like Hawkins,
Drake, Hudson, and Baffin were navigationally equipped to undertake
their momentous voyages; and he fills in the gaps in our knowledge of the
tremendous advance that took place within some 80 years (1550–1630).
His book must become a standard work on this subject; it also holds a
particular interest at the present time, when the advent of the Nuclear
Age is providing a challenge to our navigators and scientists comparable
with that which faced our ancestors four centuries ago.

For we are on the threshold of intensive deep-sea navigation; and in addition to looking upward to take celestial observations, and horizontally for bearings of objects on shore, we shall in future be directing our attention downwards as well. The navies of the world will be sending their nuclear-powered submarines on missions that will preclude their surfacing to take sights or obtain radio-fixes—yet these submarines must be able to fix their positions with great accuracy while submerged. Since it appears, moreover, that large tankers and cargo vessels could be propelled at a high speed far more economically, if totally submerged, the same navigational problems will face the merchant navies also, if it proves feasible to operate such craft.

If this happens, much greater accuracy in the charting of the ocean-beds and sea-mounts will become necessary, and considerable hydrographic work in this field remains to be done. An entirely new 'inertial' system of navigation dependent solely on the rotation of the earth is now being developed by which the navigator will be able to determine his position without coming to the surface. As we enter, so to speak, a new dimension, the development of the Art of Navigation in the First Elizabethan Era—which this book so graphically describes—can provide an inspiration to our navigators and scientists in the Second.

MOUNTBATTEN OF BURMA

CONTENTS

APPENDICES

ILLUSTRATIONS

Plate

VIII CIRCULAR TIDE-TABLES FOR PORTS WITH ESTABLISHMENTS OF
SOUTH-SOUTH-EAST AND SOUTH (High Water on days of full and
change at 10.30 and 12.00), Brouscon's Tide-Tables and
Almanac of *c.* 1548 (*see Appendix* 3). *By courtesy of the Master
and Fellows of Magdalene College, Cambridge* **facing page 32**

IX A NOCTURNAL OF 1545. *By courtesy of Henry C. Taylor*
between pages 32 and 33

> From *The Arte of Navigation* (1561). Martin Cortes was the first writer on
> navigation to publish an illustration of a nocturnal.
> The Nocturnal was used for finding the time of the night by means of the
> Pole Star and its Guards.
> The Nocturnal was made of a disc of wood or brass, from 5 to 7 inches in
> diameter, with a handle on one edge (not shown by Cortes) and a pointer
> diametrically opposite it. The days of the month were engraved around it, the
> 28th October in line with the handle, the 19th April in line with the pointer,
> these being the dates when the guards of *Ursa Minor* transited respectively
> south and north at midnight by solar time. The hours were engraved on 'a
> lesser roundle' from twelve noon to twelve midnight, a pointer engraved
> 'Time' on the edge of this lesser roundel marking midnight. To find the
> time the pointer or 'tooth' on the lesser roundel marked 'Time' was set to the
> day of the month then 'holding the instrument by the handle with your owne
> hand right before your face, leave not to put that hand forward from you, or
> to bring it backwards towards you, until you may see with one eye, winking
> with the other, the North Starre through the hole of the pen, [about which
> the lesser roundel and hour index pivoted] which is the centre of the instru-
> ment: and so soon as you see the North Starre, lift with your other hand the
> index up and down [the Horn in Cortes's diagram] until you see also at that
> instant the North Guard of the Loadstar on the outside of the instrument
> appearing even with the fiduciall line or inward edge of the said index. Then
> staying the index there, look upon what houre it falleth, for that shall be the
> houre of the night.' Blundeville's *Exercises* (1594).
> The nocturnal depicted shows that the time is 3.45 a.m. on 25th June.

X A TRAVERSE BOARD. *By courtesy of the Trustees, The National
Maritime Museum, Greenwich* *between pages 32 and 33*

> The circular portion was used by the helmsman for recording with a peg the
> mean course steered each half-hour of his four-hour watch.
> The rectangular portion of the base was probably not provided before the
> first quarter of the seventeenth century when knotted log-lines and half-
> minute glasses began to come into use. The distance sailed was pegged each
> half-hour of the watch.

XI THE RULE OF THE NORTH STAR, DISTANCE TO RAISE OR LAY
1° OF LATITUDE AND THE ALMANAC FOR JANUARY AND FEBRUARY,
in Brouscon's Tide-Tables and Almanac of *c.* 1548 (*see Appendix* 3). *By courtesy of the Master and Fellows of Magdalene
College, Cambridge* **facing page 33**

XII THE PTOLEMAIC WORLD SYSTEM. From William Cuningham's
The Cosmographical Glasse (1559), the first English book on cosmography. *By courtesy of the Trustees of the British Museum*
facing page 56

> This beautiful woodcut illustrates the Ptolemaic world scheme (modified
> to suit Christian dogmas), the popular explanation of the universe until well
> into the eighteenth century and the one adhered to by navigators throughout
> the sixteenth and early seventeenth centuries.

Plate

XIII, XIV and **XV** DECLINATION TABLES, 1545–1688. Folios xxiii(a), xxv(a) and xxvi(a) of Cortes's *The Arte of Navigation* (1561). *By courtesy of the Trustees of the British Museum*
between pages 56 and 57

XVI DECLINATION TABLE FOR 'ABRIL–MAYO–JUNIO 2ND YEAR' AFTER A LEAP YEAR. Folio lv(b) of Medina's *Arte de Navegar*, Valladolid, 1545. *By courtesy of Henry C. Taylor   between pp. 56 and 57*

The straightforward declination table for mariners. Contrast it with the three tables (Pls. XIII, XIV and XV) and with the calculations necessary to find the declination of the sun in Cortes's tables, taken from Eden's translation.

Until Bourne published his *Rules of Navigation* in 1567 English mariners had no printed simple declination tables like Medina's. The French and Italians had them in 1554 when Medina's work was translated into French and Italian.

It will be noticed in these tables and in Cortes's that there is an apparent error of eleven days in the declination. In Medina's table the sun's maximum northerly declination occurs on 12th June and is given as 23° 33′. In Cortes's table the sun is on the equinoctial on 13th September. Today the summer solstice occurs on 22nd June, the autumn equinox on 23rd September. The difference arises from the tables having been drawn up for the Old Style or Julian Calendar. The New Style or Gregorian Calendar was adopted from 1582 in various continental countries. In England it was not adopted until the eighteenth century.

Medina's declination tables were drawn from those prepared about 1475 by the Spanish astronomer Zacuto, edited by the Portuguese astronomer Vizinho, and published in 1496 (*Almanach perpetuum*, Leiria).

Cortes's declination tables were based on the astronomical tables of Regiomontanus, Johann Müller of Königsberg, whose *Tabulae directionum profectionumque*, first published in 1475, contained tables of the position of the sun and whose *Ephemerides*, first published in 1474, included in the 1498 and later editions the declination of the sun. Before this edition, published in Venice, Regiomontanus's tables were suited only to astronomers. Zacuto's *Almanach perpetuum* was the source of all the earliest nautical declination tables.

XVII TAKING A POLE STAR SIGHT WITH A CROSS-STAFF. From Medina's *Regimiento de Navegacion*, Sevilla, 1552. *By courtesy of Henry C. Taylor*
between pages 56 and 57

XVIII TAKING A MERIDIAN ALTITUDE OBSERVATION OF THE SUN WITH AN ASTROLABE. From Medina's *Regimiento de Navegacion*, Sevilla, 1552. *By courtesy of Henry C. Taylor*
between pages 56 and 57

XIX(a) SPANISH SEA-ASTROLABE OF 1545. From Cortes's *Arte of Navigation* (1561). *By courtesy of Henry C. Taylor*
between pages 56 and 57

Made from sheet brass, this type of astrolabe was developed from the medieval planispheric astrolabe introduced from the Middle East, where it had been invented in the sixth century. By the 1500s the cast ring-type of sea-astrolabe had come into use amongst mariners.

XIX(b) SEA-ASTROLABE OF THE CAST-RING TYPE, DATED 1555. *By courtesy of the Curator of the Albert Institute, Dundee*
between pages 56 and 57

Discovered in Dundee, this is one of the oldest known dated sea-astrolabes. The scale is remarkable in that it is engraved for zenith distances. This suggests that it is of Portuguese workmanship, though its large size suggests that it is of English design. It measures 8 inches in diameter and weighs 6 lb. 6 oz.

Plate

tunate Islands—the Canary Islands, the various stars placed on the globe to aid position-finding. Of the latter *Humerus Pegasi* and *Crus Pegasi* in Longitude 340° are examples.

The Horizon Circle shows the Signs and Degrees of the Zodiac—the Ecliptic can be seen on the globe crossing the Equator at the Prime Meridian; the days and months of the year; the fixed feast days; and the Rhumbs of the Winds.

This is the first globe known to have rhumb lines drawn in. It was the favourite marine globe for over half a century—until superseded by the Molyneux globe of 1592 and 1603, and the Dutch globes of the early seventeenth century.

XXVI CHART OF NORTH-EAST ATLANTIC in Brouscon's Tide-Tables and Almanac of *c.* 1548. *By courtesy of the Master and Fellows of Magdalene College, Cambridge   between pages 72 and 73*

This large chart folds into the book. The two top right-hand sections contain the coasts of Holland and Denmark and the name 'F. Drak' on the otherwise blank fly.

XXVII and XXVIII THE FRONT AND BACK OF THOMAS GEMINI'S UNIVERSAL PLANISPHERIC ASTROLABE OF 1552. *By courtesy of Henri Michel, of Brussels   facing page 73*

Gemini was one of the foreign instrument-makers, engravers and printers, who started the English instrument industry and raised the standard of English book production and illustration in the middle of the sixteenth century. This magnificent astrolabe, engraved with the arms of the Duke of Northumberland, Sir John Cheke and Edward VI, and dated 1552, reflects the measures taken for the development of the art of navigation in England in the 1550s, and particularly the preparations for the voyage of 1553 to the North-East. These included the provision of astrolabes. Foreign pilots, the Portuguese Pinteado, and the Frenchman Jean Ribault, were employed on preparing charts.

Until about 1550 the planispheric astrolabe had on the front a stereographic projection of the heavens, usually from the North Pole to the Tropic of Capricorn, for a particular latitude. The circles included the equator, the two tropics, the meridian of the place, the azimuth for the latitude and the almucantaras for the same latitude. Rotating above this fixed plate was the net, the projection of the celestial sphere on which was given the ecliptic and the principal fixed stars.

In 1556 Gemma Frisius published a description of a universal astrolabe or *Astrolabum Catholicum*. Known to Iberian astronomers in the thirteenth century, it was suitable for all latitudes, and thus of particular value to seamen, being a stereographic projection of the sphere on the colure of the solstices, the centre of the projection being the vernal point.

In 1550 de Roias, a pupil of Gemma Frisius, published a variation of the *Astrolabum Catholicum*, an orthogonal projection of the sphere on the colure of the solstices. It was fitted with a diametrical rule and a cursor analagous to those also fitted on the *Astrolabum Catholicum*.

On the back of these types of astrolabe it was usual to include, as on the one illustrated, a zodiacal calendar, an altitude scale, a conversion scale for equal and unequal hours, a scale of *ombra recta* and *ombra versa*, and an alidade.

XXIX THE HAVEN OF DEATH, 1553. The penultimate page of Sir Hugh Willoughby's Journal of 1553. *By courtesy of the Trustees of the British Museum   facing page 120*

The last lines of the journal end abruptly on the other side of this page. It would seem from the marginal entry on this page that Sir Hugh knew they were doomed. He and all his crew perished, frozen to death. (*See Appendix 5.*)

Plate

XXX and XXXI TIDE TABLES AND RULES FOR THEIR USE in Leonard Digges's *A Prognostication everlasting of right good effecte* . . . (1556). *By courtesy of the Trustees of the British Museum* facing page 121

In the last half of the sixteenth century and first half of the seventeenth century this was one of the most popular English almanacs covering a period of years. First published in 1555, it was kept up to date by new editions.

XXXII SIR THOMAS GRESHAM, ?1519–1579. Attributed to A. Key. *By courtesy of the Trustees of the National Portrait Gallery, London* facing page 136

Founder of Gresham College, London, the 'Precursor of the Royal Society,' and of all scientific institutions in England; and, by virtue of his munificent endowment, father of the scientific development of navigation in England.

XXXIII(a) A REGIMENT FOR THE SEA (1574). Title-page of the earliest edition. *By courtesy of the Bibliothèque nationale, Paris* facing page 137

The sea-astrolabe is of typically English design, the design is plain and economical, the vanes fairly widely spaced. In his *Rules* of 1567 Bourne included a somewhat similar illustration. However, only the upper left-hand arc was graduated (for altitudes), the vanes were wider spaced and had only one (sun) pin-hole.

XXXIII(b) A REGIMENT FOR THE SEA (1577). *By courtesy of Boston Public Library, Massachusetts* facing page 144

Title-page of the second and apparently unauthorized edition, showing the large English warship of the early 1570s on the verso of the title page of the 1574 edition. Note the top-sails of the mizzen- and bonaventure mizzen-masts and the top-gallant sails on the fore- and main-masts. The fore-sail and main-sail are set, the fore-sail with a drabbler laced on; reef points were not used at this period. The bowlines for controlling the set of the sails when close-hauled are clearly seen. Ten ships of this type were amongst the royal warships that, a dozen years later, fought the Spanish Armada in the English Channel.

XXXIV TITLE PAGE OF DIGGES'S *A Prognostication everlastinge* (1576). *By courtesy of the Trustees of the British Museum* between pages 144 and 145

This was the first English book to contain an illustration of the Copernican theory. It also contained notes on errors in navigation, and a discourse on variation. (*See Appendix 11.*)

XXXV DIGGES'S DIAGRAM OF THE COPERNICAN SYSTEM from *A Prognostication everlastinge* (1576). *By courtesy of the Trustees of the British Museum* between pages 144 and 145

XXXVI SIGNED AND DATED MS. CHART OF 1576 OF THE N.W. ATLANTIC BY WILLIAM BOROUGH. Original size 33½ × 27 inches. Signed: 'The first of June 1576 By W: Borough.' *By courtesy of the Marquess of Salisbury* facing page 145

This chart has four endorsements on the back. '1578, Marty furbushers Navigatio. 98', and 'North West furbishers Voyage'; these are in Lord Burghley's handwriting; the other two in a later hand both read: 'A Sea Carde of S^r M^tine furbushers voayadge'. Note in particular the arrows indicating the amount of variation observed at various points on the voyage. (*See Appendix 10A.*)

Plate

XXXVII A PAGE FROM HALL'S JOURNAL of 1578. Harleian MS. 167.
By courtesy of the Trustees of the British Museum   facing page 152

'Ye account of the third Voyage to Meta Incognito, made by Mr. Christopher Hall, M. of the Ship Ayde, and now Pilott in the ship Thomas Allyn.' (*See Appendix 13.*)

XXXVIII TYPICAL PAGE OF ROBERT NORMAN'S *The Safegard of Sailers* (1590). *By courtesy of the Trustees of the British Museum*
facing page 153

XXXIX THE MARINERS MIRROUR (?1588). Title-Page of *The Mariners Mirrour*, the (1588) translation by Anthony Ashley of Wagenaer's *Spieghel der Zeevaerdt* (1585). (See Pl. III.) *By courtesy of the Lords Commissioners of the Admiralty* facing page 168

The mariners are in English dress; the ship, despite its flags (which have been changed like the mariners' dress for this English edition), is a Flemish carrack.
Included are quadrants, astrolabes and cross-staves for shooting the sun or stars; hour-glasses and sounding leads and lines; terrestrial and celestial spheres. The leads and lines are repeated in the motif of the mariners, who are holding the lines correctly palm downwards, to ensure their running freely when cast. This repetition emphasizes the importance of the lead and line, so does the prominence given to the two sea-compasses and the beautifully wrought compasses 'for pricking the card'.

XL 'THIS VPPER HALF CIRCLE'. Diagram from Wagenaer's *The Mariners Mirrour* (?1588). *By courtesy of the Lords Commissioners of the Admiralty*   between pages 168 *and* 169

Diagram to show '*Distance to Raise or Lay a Degree*' and '*Distance run East or West*' in raising or laying a degree on different rhumbs, incorporating a circular tide-table showing the establishment of various important ports or points on the coast of N.W. Europe, with the establishment, in the outer circle, of the tides off shore. This diagram could be used in conjunction with tables following it for finding the time of High Water on any given day of the month at the places indicated on the diagram.

XLI 'A GENERAL CARTE, & DESCRIPTION OF THE SEA COASTES OF EUROPE AND NAVIGATION IN THIS BOOK CONTAINED.' The first chart in Wagenaer's *The Mariners Mirrour* (?1588). *By courtesy of the Lords Commissioners of the Admiralty* between pages 168 *and* 169

It shows distinct *portulan* characteristics which the remainder do not.

XLII 'THE COASTES OF ENGLAND, FROM THE SORLINGS [SCILLY IS.] BY THE LANDES END TO PLYMOUTH WITH THE HAVENS AND HARBOURGHES.' From Wagenaer's *The Mariners Mirrour* (?1588). *By courtesy of the Lords Commissioners of the Admiralty facing page* 169

Probably published in 1588, but too late for the Armada campaign, they were the first printed charts generally available to English seamen.

XLIII POCKET DIALS BY HUMPHREY COLE, DATED 1569. *By courtesy of the Trustees of the National Maritime Museum, Greenwich*
facing page 184

They are traditionally described as having belonged to Sir Francis Drake. (*See Appendix 7A.*)

The columns are: Moneth; Dayes; Houres [since last entry]; Course [made good]; Leagues [distance sailed]; Eleuation of the pole [latitude in] Deg and Min.; The winde; The Discovrse. [Remarks or Journal.]

The Discovrse of 31 July reads: This 31 at Noone, coming close by a foreland or great cape, we fell into a might rase, where an island of ice was carried by the force or the current as fast as our barke could sail with lum [*sic*] wind, all sails bearing. This cape as it was the most Southerly limit of the gulfe which we passed over the 30 day of this month, so was it the North promontory or first beginning of another very great inlet, whose Southe limit at this present wee saw not. Which inlet or gulfe this afternoone, and in the night, we passed over: where to our great admiration we saw the sea falling down into the gulfe with a mighty overfal, and roring, and with divers circular motions like whirlepooles, in such sort as forcible streames passe thorow the arches of bridges.

The Discovrse of 1 August reads: The true course, etc. This first of August we fell with the promontory of the sayd gulfe or second passage, having coasted by divers courses for our safeguard, a great banke of ice driven out of the gulfe.

The Discovrse of 13 August reads: This day seeking for our ships that went to fish, we strook on a rock, being among many iles, and had a great leake.

The Discovrse of 14 August reads: This day we stopped our leak in a storme. The 15 of August at noon, being in the latitude of 52 degrees 12 min. and 16 leagues from the shore, we shaped our course for England, in God's name, as followeth.*

The Discovrse of 17 August reads: The true course, etc. This day upon the Banke we met a Biscaine bound either for the Grand Bay or for the passage. He chased us.

The Discovrse of 24 August reads: The true course, etc. This 24 August observing the variation. I found the compass to vary towards the East, from the true Meridian, one degree.

The Discovrse of 5 September reads: The true course, etc. Now we supposed our selves to be 55 leagues frõ Scillie.

The Discovrse of 15 September reads: This 15 of September we arrived at Dartmouth.

At the foot of the page the note reads: Vnder the title of *houres*, where any number exceedeth 24, it is the summe or casting vp of so many other dayes and parts of dayes going next before, as containe the fore sayd summe.

The first edition (second edition, 1603) of the first English celestial globe which was also the largest manufactured up till then for sale. This globe and the companion terrestrial globe were constructed by Emerys Molyneux. The gores were engraved by the Dutch engraver, Hondius. The manufacture of the globe was financed by William Sanderson.

The first English terrestrial globe (first edition, 1592), the largest globe manufactured for sale up till then. A smaller, cheaper edition of both globes was sold for students. Note the rhumbs and the tracks of Drake's and Cavendish's voyages of circumnavigation. A terrestrial globe of the first (1592) edition was recently found in the library of Petworth House, Sussex.

Plate

This was the first backstaff in its original form. While it incorporated Hood's principle of observing the sun's shadow it incorporated also a new one—that of observing the sun indirectly by back observation. This had the advantage of eliminating parallax arising from the eccentricity of the observer's eye, and of avoiding dazzle from the horizon beneath the sun.

LV   CAPTAIN JOHN DAVIS'S 90° BACKSTAFF OR QUADRANT. (*The Seamans Secrets*, 1657, a reprint of the 1595 edition.) *By courtesy of the Lords Commissioners of the Admiralty*
between pages 208 and 209

The staff had a horizon vane and was graduated for the upper, and longer, 'cross', and for the shorter and lower one. The latter was also graduated and carried a sight-vane, omitted from Davis's illustration. The shadow cast was not sharp owing to the distance of the shadow 'cross' from the horizon vane. The upper cross was a chord of a circle, the lower an arc.

LVI(a)   HORIZONTAL PLANE SPHERE BY HUMPHREY COLE, DATED 1574. *By courtesy of the Trustees of the National Maritime Museum, Greenwich*   *between pages 208 and 209*

One of the instruments which Frobisher took on his 1576 voyage was a Horizontal Plane Sphere made by Humphrey Cole. John Davis considered it one of the navigator's necessary instruments (*The Seamans Secrets*, 1595). It was used for fixing positions by bearing and distance, or, if the navigator was a skilled surveyor, for triangulation survey work. This one is interesting for its outer graduation dividing the circle into 360°, its inner graduation dividing each quadrant into 90°, its innermost graduation of the rhumbs of the winds, and those of 'The Geometricall Square' used in survey work.

.The geometrical square was a primitive scale for finding distances. Even after triangulation was introduced in the middle of the sixteenth century, surveyors continued to be chiefly interested in distances and heights rather than angles. A quadrant, or quarter of a geometrical square, will usually be found upon quadrants intended for use in survey work, and a double quadrant on the lower half of the back of planispheric astrolabes. The sides of the quadrants are usually divided into 12, 60, 100 or 120 divisions, the more numerous sub-divisions being a refinement of the instruments of the sixteenth and seventeenth centuries. They correspond to imperfect tangent and co-tangent scales.

This planisphere forms the base of Humphrey Cole's Theodolite of 1574 which was derived from Waldseemüller's holimetrum of 1512 with the addition of a nautical compass, a development probably first made by Gemma Frisius about 1530. He used a separate compass. In Cole's instrument the compass forms an integral part of the instrument about which the vertical semi-circle rotated.

LVI(b)   ARMILLARY SPHERE BY HUMPHREY COLE, 1582. *By courtesy of the Department of Natural Philosophy of the University of St. Andrews*   *facing page* 209

Inscribed '*Humfrey Cole fecit*–1582', it measures 18 inches over-all height. In the centre of the base support is a ring for a plumb-bob (missing). The compass box is engraved in the interior with the four quadrants of the compass and contains a rod-type compass needle with a brass capital. The planisphere is on the projection of de Roias (1550). Frobisher's instruments for the voyage of 1576 to the North-West included 'a great instrument of brasse named Armilla Tolomei or Hemisperium' by Humphrey Cole. (*See Appendix 10B.*)

LVII   LUKE FOXE'S CIRCUMPOLAR CHART OF 1631. *By courtesy of the Trustees of the British Museum*   *facing page* 224

'I have also placed a Polar Map or Card, that this Discoverie may be the better understood, and for that I did desire to give satisfaction by Demonstration of all treated of in the Booke; for, otherwise, another proiection could not have contained it but at vnreasonable diversity, and because I cannot des-

Plate

cribe all the Names in Frctum Hudson, of Capes, Ilands, and Bayes at length in Letters, in respect of the smallnesse of the Degrees of Longitude, I have inserted them in a table by the letters of the Alphabet, as thou shalt find, beginning with A, b, c, d, and tracted my owne way and discovery forth and home in small prickes. Luke Foxe. *From* Kingston *upon* Hull, *this first of* January, 1635.' This chart projection shows admirably the reason for the 140-year attempt of the English to find either a North-West or a North-East Passage to the Orient—it would be so much shorter and quicker than by way of the Cape of Good Hope. Note the typical way in which Foxe's track is pricked on the chart.

LVIII   EDWARD WRIGHT'S CHART OF THE N.E. ATLANTIC ON MERCATOR'S PROJECTION from *Certaine Errors of Navigation* (1599). *By courtesy of Henry C. Taylor*   *between pages* 224 *and* 225

This is the earliest printed chart on Mercator's projection. It should be compared with the Hatfield MS. chart of the same area, also on Mercator's projection, with which it has much in common. (Pl. LXI). The Course of the Earl of Cumberland's ship in 1589 is pricked off on the chart. This chart should also be contrasted with Hood's plane chart of 1592 covering the same region. (Pl. XLIX.) (*See Appendix 18B.*)

LIX   THE FIRST PRINTED TABLE OF MERIDIONAL PARTS FOR EVERY 10 MINUTES OF LATITUDE. From Wright's *Certaine Errors of Navigation* (1599). *By courtesy of Henry C. Taylor*   *facing page* 225

'A correction of Errors.

'Till the Printer had thus farre proceeded, I was purposed to haue published the whole Table before mencioned, in such sort as I had made it, (supposing a Meridian of the nauticall Planisphaere to be diuided, beginning at the aequinoctial) into such parts whereof a minute of the aequinoctial containeth 10,000. and setting downe by which of these parts euerie minute of latitude is to be drawne, till you come within a minute of the Pole.

'But vpon further aduice it was thought more meet to abrdige the same as followeth, to euery tenth minute, & to cut off throughout the Table the three first figures towards the right hand, meaning not at this time to trouble thee with more then mought be of vse, for the true diuiding of the Meridian in the Sea Chart into degrees, and sixt parts of a degree, without sensible error which may be sufficient for the greatest sort of Sea Charts or Maps, that hitherto hue beene commonly vsed.

'This Table is diuided into two columnes, whereof the first containeth degrees, and tennes of minutes, of the Meridian of the nauticall planisphaere, beginning at the aequinoctial. The second columne containeth aequal parts of the same Meridian, beginning likewise to be numbred from the aequinoctial: (of which parts euery minute of the aequinoctial is vnderstoode to containe 10.) and sheweth how many of these parts are answerable to any degree or Decade of minutes of latitdue, in the nauticall Planisphaere or Sea Chart.'

LX   MERCATOR'S PROJECTION as described by Edward Wright in *Certaine Errors* (1599). *Drawn from a sketch by the author*   *facing page* 232

'Suppose a sphericall superficies with meridians, paralels, rumbs, and the whole hydrographicall description drawne therupon to bee inscribed into a concave cylinder, their axes agreeing in one. Let this sphericall superficies swel like a bladder, (whiles it is in blowing) equally always in every part thereof (that is as much in longitude as latitude) till it apply, and joigne itselfe (round about, and all alongst also towards either pole) into the concave superficies of the cylinder, each paralel upon this sphericall superficies increasing successively from the equinoctial towardes eyther pole until it come to be of equal diameter with the cylinder, and consequently the meridians still widening them selves, til they come to be so far distant every where ech from other as they are at the equinoctiall. Thus it may most easily be understoode how a sphericall superficies may (by extension) be made a ... plaine ... superficies ...'

Plate

Of *The Log or Table of Courses* Sir Thomas wrote: 'The 6: of March $\frac{1614}{15}$ at
7 in the morninge: ye Lizard Bearing N.W.b.N.5 Leaugs off: I begann this
Course.' *The Journal of Obseruations according to ye Table of Course* was an
expansion of summary entries in the log. (*See Appendix 21.*) Not all masters
kept such excellent journals as did the accomplished amateur navigator Sir
Thomas Roe, first English plenipotentiary to India. Captain Peyton's
journal of the voyage (B.M. Addl. MS. 19, 276) had a margin for comments,
a narrow column for dates, and a wide one for all courses, observations, winds,
etc. These were logged in narrative form across the page. Roe's longitude was
estimated from the meridian of the Lizard, as far as the Cape of Good Hope.
Then the Cape of Good Hope became the prime meridian.

LXIX FOUR SEA ASTROLABES. SIXTEENTH AND EARLY SEVEN-
TEENTH CENTURIES. *By courtesy of the Trustees of the National
Maritime Museum, Greenwich, of the Department of Natural
Philosophy of the University of St. Andrews, and of the Curators
of the Albert Institute, Dundee and the Museum of the History of
Science, Oxford*

About thirty mariner's astrolabes are known, a score have come to light –
many from wrecks – in recent years. In 1958 only these were known: *1.
Dundee, Albert Institute, 1555. (Portuguese?) *2. Greenwich, N.M.M., *c.* 1585.
(Spanish?) 3. Denmark, Kronborg Museum, 1600. (French?) *4. Oxford,
History of Science Museum, *c.* 1600. (Spanish?) 5. New York, Hoffman
Collection (Decd.) 1603. (French?) 6. Japan, Tenri University, *before* 1610.
(Portuguese.) *7. St. Andrews University, 1616. (English.) 8. Sweden,
Skokloster Castle, 1626. (French?) 9. France, Caudebec-en-Caux Museum,
1632. (French.) 10. Portugal, Coimbra University, *c.* 1650. (Portuguese.) The
earliest illustration of a cast astrolabe is dated 1517 (Albuquerque, L. de,
Curso de Historia da Nautica (1972), 185). The St. Andrews specimen is, by
its great weight and size, and its precision, the peer of all known examples; its
maker, Elias Allen, was the finest instrument maker of his day. Asterisk (*)
indicates those shown in this plate.

LXX IVORY PRESENTATION BACKSTAFF OR DAVIS QUADRANT OF
c. 1695. *By courtesy of the Trustees of the National Maritime
Museum, Greenwich*

Though made of ivory and dating from the last decade of the seventeenth
century it is typical in design and detail of wooden Davis quadrants of the
first quarter of the century. Observe the sighting vane with sighting hole on
the large 30° arc, the horizon vane with horizon slit, and, on the 60° arc, the
shadow vane. The arcs are graduated, as was common by 1630, with a Zenith
Distance—complement of the altitude—scale. The 60° arc is graduated to
degrees. For use the shadow vane was set to within 15°–20° of the estimated
meridian Zenith Distance. The observation was completed by the adjustment
of the sighting vane. The diagonal scale enabled readings to be taken accurately to within 2'. If the shadow was cast by the upper edge of the shadow
vane 16' was added to the observation to allow for the sun's semi-diameter,
if the lower edge cast the shadow 16' was substracted. The small radius of
the 60° arc brought the shadow vane close to the horizon vane and so
ensured that a sharp shadow line was cast. The direct reading of the Zenith
Distance simplified the computation for finding latitude.

LXXI EVOLUTION OF THE NAUTICAL CROSS-STAFF DOWN TO 1631
Drawn from a sketch by the author

LXXII THE DIAGONAL SCALE AND THE NONIUS SCALE. From
Captain George Waymouth's MS., *The Jewell of Artes*, of 1604.
By courtesy of the Trustees of the British Museum

The diagonal scale was probably devised by Richard Chancellor about
1550; the nonius was devised by Pedro Nuñez about 1540. The nonius was
not a practical scale for seamen as its readings had to be converted into
minutes. The diagonal scale seems to have been adopted by them fairly
generally from the end of the sixteenth century when improved instruments

Plate

and declination tables came into use and tables of corrections for height of eye and refraction were prepared. It enabled much more accurate readings to be taken than hitherto. A general rule for reading a diagonal scale: First count how many concentric circles there are. There are usually 6 or 10. Then see how many diagonal lines are drawn within the limits of one degree. There are usually 2 or 3. Then multiply the number of concentric circles by the number of diagonals in 1°, divide the product into 60 (the number of minutes in a degree). The quotient gives the number of minutes that each intersection increases by and is more than the preceding one. The nonius is often erroneously referred to as a vernier, but Vernier published his invention in 1631, Nuñez his in 1542 in *De Crepusculis*. By drawing a series of arcs (Nuñez drew 44) inside and concentric with the arc of a quadrant, and by graduating the outermost arc into 90 degrees and the inner ones into progressively fewer equal divisions (Nuñez divided his into 89, 88, 87 and so on, the 44th inner arc being divided into 46 equal divisions), it was possible to ensure that the alidade would cut, more or less accurately, one of the 45 arcs. The resultant reading was either in degrees, exactly, or in arcs and equal divisions of arc. Conversion to minutes and seconds was not really difficult, but it was a task few navigators, if any, were prepared to tackle. If, for instance, the alidade on a full nonius cut the arc divided into 55 equal parts at the 45th

division, the angle measured was $\frac{45}{55}$ of $90° = 90° \times \frac{9}{11} = \frac{810°}{11} = 73° \frac{7°}{11}$

$= 7 \times \frac{60'}{11} = \frac{420'}{11} = 38'\frac{2'}{11} = \frac{2'}{11} \times 60'' = 11''$.

Answer 73° 38′ 11″. On nonius scales with fewer divisions the same method of conversion was employed.

LXXIII Title-Page of Edward Wright's *Certaine Errors in Navigation*, second edition, 1610. *By courtesy of the Trustees of New York Public Library*   *facing page* 313

   Note the illustrations of Edward Wright's Quadrant, Universal Rings for finding variation, and his World Chart on Mercator's projection. The chart, it will be observed, includes 'Terra Australis' and 'The South Land Yet Vnknoune', features omitted in the World Chart of 1600. The possibility of a N.W. Passage is evident beyond Hope Sanderson and west of Fretum Davis. To the North-East the advantages of a N.E. Passage are clear from the supposed shape of China. A Dip-circle, Sea-Astrolabe, Cross-staff, Compasses, Armillary Sphere, Rutter and Astrolabe are clearly delineated.

LXXIV Title-Page of the Second Part of *The Mariners Mirrour* (1605). *By courtesy of Henry C. Taylor*   *facing page* 328

   The title-page of the first part of this edition is identical with that of the English edition of ?1588, except for the elimination of the reference to the exploits of Howard and Drake, and the substitution of *Jodocus Hondius excudit ann.* 1605. Two copies only of this edition are now known.

LXXV Frontispiece of *The Light of Navigation* (1612), Willem Jantszoon Blaeu's English edition of his Dutch waggoner of 1608. *By courtesy of the Trustees of the British Museum*
                           between pages 328 *and* 329

   This superseded Ashley's translation of Wagenaer's *The Mariners Mirrour* (?1588), the second English edition of which, that of 1605, had Dutch letterpress and English charts. This frontispiece gives a lively picture of instruction in the art of navigation in Holland in the first decade of the seventeenth century. In the foreground from left to right are a compass, running-glass, various charts (including a paradoxal one), another 'wagonner', a universal astrolabe. The men on the left are discussing a sea-astrolabe, those behind are measuring off a distance from a chart in a 'waggoner'. At their feet is a rutter; a celestial globe is in front of them, and next to it is a terrestrial globe on which a master-pilot is demonstrating. A mariner measures off a distance on it, watched by another. Behind them two more mariners are poring over a plane chart. On the right a cross-staff with three crosses is being explained to two boys.

Plate

Cross Staff (17th century) (with 60° Cross)		Brass Quadrant (17th century)
(5°, 15°, and 30° Crosses)	Battery of ½ Hr. Glasses (17th century)	
Two Pairs of Circular Compasses (17th century)	MS. Waggoner of Caribbean Charts (17th century)	Dial Watch (16th century)
	Gunter's Scale (17th century)	

The Mercator's Globes though obsolescent by 1631 might well have been carried. They measure 16 inches in diameter. The Mariner's Astrolabe too, was obsolescent, being superseded by the Davis Quadrant; like the brass Quadrant it was useful when the horizon was obscured. The quadrant is seventeenth century. The Cross-Staff and Davis Quadrant are of late seventeenth century manufacture and are in ivory, being a presentation set. They are, however, otherwise similar to pear-wood instruments of the early seventeenth century. (See Pls. LIII and LXX.) The Battery of Running Glasses is of the seventeenth century. It will be noticed that the glass on the left has got out of step with the rest. The navigator would therefore take the mean time of the other three. The Circular Compasses are seventeenth-century and for use with the globe. The MS. Waggoner is actually one of fifty years later, but it is a typical seventeenth-century production. Indeed on Drake's last voyage of 1595–6 a similar Waggoner was compiled and survives, in Paris. The Waggoner shown is *Description of the South Sea by B.S. Made by William Hack, Wapping, 1684.* It is often known as the *Buccaneer's Waggoner.* There is a copy (Sloane MS. 44) in the British Museum as well as at Greenwich. Page 34/70 is opened. It depicts the Gulf of Vallona on the Caribbean Coast of Panama. On the right-hand page is inscribed: 'On this Banck was the Almirant of the King of Spaine Castaway in the year 1631.' The Charts of paper or parchment were normally kept rolled. As the Gunter's scale has been included Gunter's Sector, which preceded his scale with its logarithmic lines, has been omitted.

LXXXVI   CAPTAIN JAMES'S CHART OF HIS VOYAGE FOR THE DISCOVERY OF THE N.W. PASSAGE IN 1631–32. *By courtesy of the Trustees of the British Museum*   *facing page* 488

Unlike Foxe's chart of this region James's is on Mercator's projection. The distortions in higher latitudes caused by this projection can be clearly seen by comparison with Foxe's circumpolar chart on a zenithal equidistant projection (See Pl. LVII). He called the distortions 'unreasonable diversity'. The names of the headlands, bays and islands reflect the hopes and frustrations of the N.W. explorers and commemorate their names and those of the merchants and nobility who financed their voyages. The mythical Buss I. and Friesland between England and Greenland will be noticed. As in James's chart Cape Farewell is charted several degrees too far to the southward, evidence of the difficulty of accurate navigation in northern waters. None of the explorers hitherto had been able to *observe* the latitude of the Cape, few besides Davis had seen it; knowing its presence they had preferred to give it plenty of sea-room.

LXXXVII   SIGNIFICANT ENGLISH VOYAGES OF THE SIXTEENTH AND EARLY SEVENTEENTH CENTURIES. *Drawn from a sketch by the author*   *facing page* 489

DIAGRAMS

The *Coxon hath*   3

The *trumpeter hath*   4,

The *Sailers, two or one & a half*

The *Boyes a single share.*

The *Lievetenant what the Captaine will give him, or as they can agree.*

They ufe to appoint a certaine reward extraordinary to him that firft defcries a Sayle if they take her, and to him that firft enters her.

For to learne to obferve the Altitude, Latitude, Longitude, Amplitude, the variation of the Compaffe, the Sunnes Azimuth and Almicanter, to fhift the Sunne and Moone, and to know the tydes,

tydes, your roomes, pricke your card, & fay yonr Compaffe, get fome of thofe bookes, but practife is the beft.

Mr. Wrights *errors of Navigation.*

Mr. Taps *Sea-mans kallender.*

The *Art of Navigation.*

The *Sea Regiment.*

The *Sea-mans fecrets.*

Wagganour.

Mr. Gunters *workes.*

The *Sea-mans glaffe for the skale.*

The *new attracter for variatiõ.*

Mr. Wright *for the ufe of the Globe.*

Mr. Hewes *for the fame.*

E3   Good

II. Pages 52–53 of Captain John Smith's *An Accidence* (1626).

INTRODUCTION

IN the year 1626 Captain John Smith, sometime Governor of Virginia and Admiral of New England, published in London a slim quarto volume called '*An Accidence or The Path-way to experience Necessary for all Young Sea-men, or those that are desirous to goe to Sea. . .*'.[1]

It was not the first book from his pen. Virginia, settled successfully in 1607, owed its permanency to the skill, resolution, valour, and energy with which he had nursed it through the first years of settlement. When he had left in 1609, the colony, more than once in the throes of death, was convalescent. Three years later Richard Pots, Clerk of the Council at James Town, Virginia, and W. Phettiplace, Gentleman, wrote of Captain Smith's departure: 'What shall I say? But thus we lost him that, in all his proceedings, made Justice his first guide, and Experience his second, that loved actions more than words, whose adventures were our lives, and whose loss, our deaths.'

Since then Captain Smith had spent his enthusiasm and boundless energy in advocating with his pen as well as by word of mouth the colonization of the New World by the English. Yet he was essentially a practical man. An outstanding man of action himself, his motto for others was 'Practice is best.' Advising those lacking experience but desirous of learning to be seamen, he wrote, 'to be a good gunner you must learne it by practice'; and again, 'to learne' navigation 'practice is the best'.

Advocacy of the cause for colonization was one activity, but it was typical of the man that in 1614, on a voyage to the territories known as New England, finding the charts of the coastline 'no more good then so much waste paper' he should chart it anew himself and publish it, and so make straight the crooked way for those he hoped would follow after—as six years later the Pilgrim Fathers did.

Similarly the aim of the *Accidence* was essentially practical.[2] It was to be

[1] Captain Smith's advice to would-be seamen is also contained in: A Sea Grammar, WITH THE PLAINE EXPOSITION of SMITHS Accidence for young Sea-men, enlarged. Diuided into fifteene Chapters: what they are you may partly conceiue by the Contents. Written by Captaine IOHN SMITH, sometimes Gouernour of VIRGINIA, and Admirall of NEW-ENGLAND. LONDON, Printed by IOHN HAUILAND, 1627.

[2] The full title of Captain John Smith's *Accidence* is: AN ACCIDENCE OR The Path-way to EXPERIENCE, necessary for all Young Sea-men, or those that are desirous to goe to Sea, briefly shewing the Phrases, Offices, and Words of Command, Belonging to the Building, Ridging, and Sayling, a Man of Warre; And how to manage a Fight at Sea. Together with The Charge and Duty of *every Officer and, their Shares*: Also the Names, Weight, Charge, Shot, and *Powder of all sorts of great Ordnance. With the vse of the Petty Tally*. Written by Captaine IOHN SMITH sometimes Governour of *Virginia*, and Admirall of New ENGLAND. *LONDON*; Printed for *Jonas Man*, and *Benjamin Fisher*, and are to be sold at the signe of the *Talbot*, in *Aldersgate* streete. 1626.

a manual to aid would-be colonists on the long sea-passage that they had to make in order to reach America; and it was to aid the 'many young Gentlemen and Valiant spirits of all sorts desirous to trye their Fortunes at Sea' in the war with Spain.

Captain Smith was a pioneer in more ways than one. He was persuaded to print the *Accidence* because, as he put it, it was 'a subject I never see writ before'. Conscious of professional jealousy, he was quick to add that he wrote it 'not as an instruction to Marriners nor Sailers . . . But as an introduction for such as wants experience, and are desirous to learne what belongs to a Seaman . . .'

When he wrote his *Accidence for Young Sea-men*, and later when he expanded it into his *Sea Grammar*, he eschewed the subject of navigation, contenting himself with the advice that 'to learne to obserue the Altitude, Latitude, Longitude, Amplitude, the variation of the Compasse, the Sunnes Azimuth and Almicanter, to shift the Sunne and Moone, and to know the tydes, your roomes [rhumbs], pricke your card, and say your Compasse, get some of these bookes, but practise is the best'.

'Mr. Wrights *errors of Navigation*.
Mr. Taps *Sea-mans kallender*.
The Art of Navigation.
The Sea Regiment.
The Sea-mans secrets.
Wagganour.
Mr. Gunters *workes*.
The Sea-mans glasse for the skale.
The new attracter for variatiō.
Mr. Wright *for the use of the Globe*.
Mr. Hewes *for the same*.
Good Sea Cards
Two paire of compasses
An Astrolabe quadrant
A crosse staffe
A backe staffe
An Astrolabe
An Nocturnall.'

It is from a study of the books and the instruments listed by Smith that most can be learnt about the art of navigation in Elizabethan and early Stuart times. And not least amongst the virtues of his own two books is to be counted the fact that they are the first English books to record what were considered to be, as indeed they prove to be, the most valuable manuals and accessories for the budding and the practising navigator of those days.

I undertook the work that follows because it deals with a subject which I had never seen treated before. Like John Smith, I have written it not as an instruction for mariners or sailors but as an introduction for such as are desirous to learn what belonged to a seaman in the days when Englishmen first ventured upon the ocean ocao, taking for their motto that brave one of Robert Thorne of Bristol, in 1527, 'there be no land unconquerable nor sea innavigable'.

What instruments, what books, tables, charts, and other navigational aids had they? We shall see. We shall see, too, what contributions they made towards the advancement of the art of navigation during Elizabethan and early Stuart times. We shall examine the conditions and influences under which their works arose. Remembering that their object was always practical, we shall consider why these works were called for, why they were produced, when and by whom; and, in order to assess their value, we shall first ascertain what was the common navigational practice in Europe up to the middle of the sixteenth century, when the English first took to oceanic navigation.

But we must not forget that the books they wrote and the instruments they wrought were the handiwork of men, for, as Richard Eden, the translator of the first manual of navigation to be printed in English, wrote: 'it is decent to commend those Citizens that by theyr industry of bodye or mynde have done greate affayres, and have wyllyngly obeyed good lawes'.[1] Many of them were men famous in their generation, whose names today are still remembered and revered, of whose lives much is known. But of others, only their works remain. Yet, like John Aspley, they held, 'We are not born for ourselves only, but . . . *those that traffique in the deepe, and have their business in great waters*, those that are unto this Island as a woodden wall, the Sea-chariots, and the horses of *England*; these, I say, may claime justly to the fruits of our labours. . . .'[2] Holding to that creed, they gave ungrudgingly of their best.

But what of the men who used the tools that they made and sailed the ships that they built? These men had for an example Richard Chancellor. He, in the year 1553, bound with Sir Hugh Willoughby on the first great voyage of discovery that was essentially English in inspiration and in execution, was met on his way by tales of the terrors and dangers of the Arctic Seas beyond the North Cape of Norway. But 'persuading himself that a man of valour could not commit a more dishonourable part than, for fear of danger, to avoid and shun great attempts, he was nothing at all changed or discouraged . . . remaining stedfast and immutable in his first resolution' to find the North-East Passage to Cathay.

Some there were like Captain John Smith (if that active, erstwhile Governor of Virginia ever indeed did relax) who could say:

> Sleepe after toyle, port after stormie seas,
> Ease after warre . . . doth greatly please.

[1] *The Arte of Navigation* translated 'out of Spanyshe into Englyshe by Richard Eden', 1561, from the *Arte de Navegar* by Martin Cortes, Seville, 1551.

[2] John Aspley's *Speculum Nauticum, A Looking Glasse for Sea-men* (1624). Dedicated to 'The Worshipfull The Master Wardens, and Assistants of the Trinity House in Deptford Strand'.

Some there were like Sir Hugh Willoughby and his enduring companions who left only their frozen bones to mark their resting place.

But of many more, Richard Chancellor amongst them, Hawkins, the illustrious Drake, John Davis, Henry Hudson, who gave his name to New York's teeming river, and a whole host unnamed, the poet of their age, Will Shakespeare, wrote the epitaph:

> Full fathom five thy father lies;
> Of his bones are coral made;
> Those are pearls that were his eyes;
> Nothing of him that doth fade,
> But doth suffer a sea-change
> Into something rich and strange,
> Sea-nymphs hourly ring his knell:
> Ding-dong.
> Hark, now I hear them—ding-dong-bell.

ACKNOWLEDGMENTS

SOME years ago Mr. Henry C. Taylor, of New York, suggested to me that the historical significance of the navigational books and manuscripts of the sixteenth and early seventeenth centuries in his library, particularly their contribution towards the successful colonization of America by the English, which formed the beginnings of the United States of America, would provide the theme for a short essay of considerable interest. From that seed this book has grown and taken shape. Its completion also is due, in the first instance, to the unfailing interest of Mr. Taylor in the progress of my researches, and to his ever-ready help and advice. Moreover, without full access to his remarkable library of books and manuscripts relating to the early colonization of America and the navigational techniques used and developed, the task of writing this book would have been both more difficult and less congenial.

To the late Mr. Bonner Smith, when Admiralty Librarian, and to the late Monsieur D. Gernez of Versailles, I am indebted for much practical encouragement in the pursuit of my earliest researches.

Without the skilful and painstaking assistance of Dr. Sylvia L. England, who read through the original manuscript and made numerous invaluable suggestions and criticisms and who has translated documents, transcribed manuscripts and title-pages, dealt with bibliographical questions and located rare copies of works on my behalf, this history could not have been finished so soon as it has, nor could its contents have been so complete. To Mr. René Hague, who has made many valuable suggestions in the course of preparing the manuscript for printing and who has compiled the comprehensive index I owe a special debt, as I do also to Mr. Michael W. Richey, Executive Secretary of the Institute of Navigation, London, for helping to see the book through the press. To Professor E. G. R. Taylor, Emeritus Professor of Geography in the University of London, who read through the whole of my manuscript I am grateful for much encouragement, and for invaluable comments. Dr. J. F. Scott, Vice-Principal of St. Mary's Training College, Twickenham, very kindly read through the passages relating to the mathematical developments in navigation in the early seventeenth century and made a number of most valuable suggestions for clarifying obscurities and for explaining the early history of logarithms. Dr. F. S. Ferguson has been of the greatest assistance on a number of occasions in solving apparently intractable bibliographical problems. I have received numerous courtesies from Mr. R. A. Skelton, Superintendent, Map Room, British Museum, and his staff. From Mr. F. C. Francis, Deputy Keeper of Printed Books, British Museum, and from Mr. Harry Sellers, late Superintendent of the North Library, British Museum, I have received never-failing courtesy and consideration. I am also very grateful to the present Superintendent of the North Library, Mr. D. Rhodes, and to the staff for their co-operation and help over what amounts now to many years of research.

Among those who have given me generously both of their time and their knowledge I should like to mention especially: Professor J. F. Allen, F.R.S., of the University of St. Andrews; Commander F. Barley, Historical Section, Admiralty; Professor C. R. Boxer, King's College, London; Mr. M. G. Brock, Librarian of Corpus Christi College, Oxford; Baron Rubin de Cervin, Museo Storico Navale, Venice; Dr. E. Crone, of Amsterdam; Mr. G. R. Crone, Librarian and Map Curator, Royal Geographical Society, London; Coronel Astrónomo de la Armada Salvador García Franco, Museo Naval, Madrid; Commander H. Oliver Hill, R.N., National Maritime Museum, Greenwich; Mr. C. H. Josten, Curator, The Museum of the History of Science, Oxford; Mr. Karl Kup, Curator of Prints, New York Public Library; Commander W. E. May, R.N., National Maritime Museum, Greenwich; Monsieur Henri Michel, of Brussels; Mr. G. P. B. Naish, National Maritime Museum, Greenwich; Dr. A. D. Vietor, Yale University Library; Mr. F. A. B. Ward, Science Museum, South Kensington; Mr. N. B. White, Librarian, Marsh's Library, Dublin; Dr. Louis B. Wright, and his staff, of the Folger Shakespeare Library, Washington, D.C.; Dr. Lawrence C. Wroth, Librarian of the John Carter Brown Library, Providence, R.I.

To Dr. James A. Williamson I am peculiarly indebted: it was through his writings on Tudor maritime enterprise that my interest in the Elizabethans and their navigational problems was first aroused.

D. W. WATERS

Jolyons,
Bury,
West Sussex.
1958.

ADDRESS TO THE GENTLE READER

'Excuse me, gentle reader if oughte be amisse, straung paths ar not trodē al truly at the first: the way muste needes be combrous, wher none hathe gone before. where no man hathe geuen light, lighte is it to offend, but when the light is shewed ones, light is it to amende. If my light may so light some other, to espie and marke my faultes, I wish it may so lighten thē, that they may voide offence. Of staggeringe and stomblinge, and vnconstaunt turmoilinge; often offending, and seldome amending, such vices to eschewe, and their fine wittes to shew that they may winne the praise, and I to hold the candle, whilest they their glorious works with eloquence sette forth, so cunningly inuented, so finely indited, that my bokes maie seme worthie to occupie no roome. For neither is mi wit so finelie filed, nother mi learning so largely lettered, nother yet mi laiser so quiet and vnincōbered, that I maie perform iustlie so learned a laboure or accordinglie to accomplishe so haulte an enforcement, yet maie I thinke thus: This candle did I light: this lighte haue I kindeled: that learned men maie se, to practise their pennes, their eloquence to aduaunce, to register their names in the booke of memorie I drew the platte rudelie, whereon they maie builde, whom god hath endued with learning and liuelihood. For liuing by laboure doth learning so hinder, that learning serueth liuinge, whiche is a peruers trade. Yet as carefull familie shall ccase hir cruell callinge, and suffer anie laiser to learninge to repaire, I will not cease from trauaile the path so to trade, that finer wittes maie fashion them selues with such glimsinge dull light, a more complete woorke at laiser to finisshe, with inuencion agreable, and aptnes of eloquence.

And this gentle reader I hartelie protest where erroure hathe happened I wisshe it redrest.'

This address is from Robert Recorde's *The Pathway to Knowledge*, London, 1551, the first English book on geometry. The address is no less sincerely that of the author of the present work, penned in these times when 'liuing by laboure doth learning so hinder'.

Author's note to revised edition

The executors of the late Mr Henry C Taylor have generously given permission for this work to be reprinted with revisions. As the substance of the book has stood the test of time I have confined myself to correcting a number of small errors of fact and of 'faults escaped in the printing' which have come to light with the passing years. My regret is that Mr Taylor did not live long enough to authorise and see the work revised.

I think it appropriate to advise readers here that ten years after the publication of the first edition I published, at Mr Taylor's suggestion, a detailed study of the first English and French sailing directions, with facsimile reproductions of the printed texts, under the title of *The Rutters of the Sea*. This considerably amplifies the history of the development of the rutter contained in this present volume and identifies *The Rutter of the Sea* as a translation by Robert Copland of, in all probability, *Le Routier de la Mer*, (1505-10), itself probably compiled by Pierre Garcie.

For those who wish to study the history of the development of navigation in England in Elizabethan and early Stuart times in greater depth and from the contemporary sources I have since compiled an exhaustive annotated bibliography, which is shortly to be published separately by the Trustees of the National Maritime Museum. It contains bibliographical descriptions, with reproductions of the title-pages of every surviving edition and issue of all the known works printed in English during the period which relate to the art of navigation, together with notes on the particular importance of each work. The bibliography also locates copies of the various books in Libraries in Great Britain and in the United States (and some elsewhere) accessible to students and scholars, and indexes the various libraries' holdings of them. As a guide to further reading on the subject, an up-to-date selective bibliography of secondary sources is also included.

Just as Mr Taylor defrayed the entire and very considerable cost of the research into and writing of this *Art of Navigation* so also did he most liberally finance the research, writing and publication of *The Rutters of the Sea* and the preparation of the manuscript of the bibliography of navigational books in English printed down to 1640.

All interested in the history of navigation will rejoice to know that the splendid library of navigational books and manuscripts that Mr Taylor formed during his life-time (and which inspired the writing of these and other books is now, through his generosity, preserved for posterity as a part of the library of Yale University, in New Haven, Connecticut.

D. W. Waters

National Maritime Museum
Greenwich   1977

Part I

THE DEVELOPMENT OF THE ART OF NAVIGATION IN EUROPE IN THE FIFTEENTH AND EARLY SIXTEENTH CENTURIES

'What can be a better or more charitable dede, than to bryng them into the way that wander: What can be more difficulte than to guyde a shyppe engoulfed, where only water and heaven may be seene.'

Martin Cortes, 1551. (Richard Eden's translation, 1561.)

Chapter One

THE ART OF PILOTAGE

'Gentle mariners one a boune vyage
Hoyce vp the saile and let God steer.
in yᵉ bonavēture making your passage
It is ful sea, the wether fair and cleer
The nepetides shall you nothing dere
a seeboord mates, S. george to borow
Mary & John ye shall not need to feer
but with this book to go safe thorow.'
Robert Copland, 1528–50?

THE Elizabethan scholar Dr. John Dee, one of the first, if not the first of English scholars to teach the art of navigation, defined it, in 1570, in these simple terms: 'The art of navigation demonstrateth how by the shortest good way, by the aptest direction, and in the shortest time, a sufficient ship . . . be conducted.'

It is a good definition, and it is as good a definition of the modern navigator's art as it was of the Elizabethan navigator's of 1570. It comprehends in a small compass all the factors of time and space, distance, direction, speed, and seaworthiness, which govern the calculated movements of a ship. But in doing so it leaves so much the more to the imagination or knowledge of the reader. Of what did the art of navigation consist? And how did the Elizabethans practise it? Again let us get brief answers to these questions from a contemporary author. This time it is not from an Englishman that we shall get the most succinct replies, but from the manual of navigation published at Antwerp, in 1581, by a Flemish teacher of the art,[1] Michiel Coignet, whose words are later paraphrased in one of the most popular English navigation manuals of the later seventeenth and early eighteenth centuries, Seller's *Practical Navigation or an Introduction to the Whole Art.*

'Nous appellons cōmunement l'art de nauiguer la science de bien et seuremēt gouuerner et diriger par reigles certaines le nauire de l'vn port à l'autre', wrote Michiel Coignet, following closely the definition of Dr. Dee. We can translate this definition freely as, 'We commonly call the art

---

[1] Coignet, M., *Instruction nouvelle des poincts plus excellents & necessaires, touchant l'art de naviguer* (1581). The full title will be found on p. 154.

The first navigation manual printed in English was a translation of the Spanish manual; Breue compendio de la sphera y de la arte de nauegar—con nueuos instrumentos y reglas—exemplificado con muy subtiles demonstraciones: compuesto por Martin Cortes natural de burjalos en el reyno de Aragon y de presente vezino de la ciudad de Cadiz: dirigido al inuictissimo Monarcha Carlo Quinto Rey de las Hespañas etč. Señor Nuestro. (Seville, 1551).

of navigation the science of well and safely steering and directing a ship by certain rules, from one port of call to another.' 'Cette pratique', he continues, 'est repartie en deux, a sçauoir en la nauigation cōmune et la nauigation grande.' As Seller put it a hundred years later, 'Practical Navigation . . . consists of two general Parts, *First*, That which may be called the *Domestick* or more *common Navigation* (I mean Coasting or Sailing along the Shore) . . . *Secondly*, That which may more properly bear the Name and principally deserves to be entitled the *Art of Navigation*, . . . that Part which guides the Ship in her Course through the Immense Ocean, to any part of the Known World. . . .'[1]

In short, the art of navigation in Elizabethan and Stuart times comprised the art of pilotage or coasting—Coignet's 'la nauigation cōmune'; and oceanic navigation—'la navigation grande'. Both were referred to indiscriminately as an art or as a science, and for the present we will leave open the question whether both or either practice deserved to be termed a science. Michiel Coignet adds a great deal more about pilotage; not so much about oceanic navigation.

'La nauigation cōmune', he continues, 'ne se sert d'autres instrumēs, que de l'experiēce, de l'aiguille, et de la sonde.' That is, 'Pilotage uses no other instruments than experience, the compass and the lead.'

'Car l'entière science de cette nauigation commune ne consiste en autre, qu'à bien et parfaictemēt conoistre tous les caps, ports, et riuieres, comme iceulx se montrent et s'apparoissent en mer, quelle distance il y a entre eux, quelle route ou cours ils tiennent, aussy a quel rumb de Lune la marée y est plaine ou basse, le cours & descente de toutes eaues, auecque la qualité, profondeur & fond d'icelles. Ce que principalemen (comme dessus est dict) s'apprend par experience, et instruction des anciens Pilotes bien exercitez.' Which we can render as, 'This is because the whole science of this form of navigation—pilotage—consists in nothing more than in knowing perfectly by sight all the capes, ports, and rivers met with, how they rise up and how they appear from the sea, and what distance lies between them, and what route or course, or rather bearing, they have one from another; also in knowing on what rhumb (bearing) of the moon high and low tide occur and the ebb and flow of the waters; and in knowing the depth and nature of the bottom. These are all principally things (as was said before) which are taught by experience, and the instruction of old and well-tried Pilots.' Whereas, 'La nauigation grande se sert outre les pratiques susdites, de plusieurs autres reigles fort ingenieuses et instrumens prins de l'art de l'Astronomie et Cosmographie. . . .' That is, 'Oceanic navigation on the other hand, employs, besides the above-mentioned practices, several other very ingenious rules and instruments derived from the art of Astronomy and Cosmography.' Or as Seller put it later, rather more precisely, coasting 'employs the Mariners *Compass* and *Lead*, as the chief Instruments', while 'the *Masterpiece* of *Nautical* Science' is

[1] Seller, *Practical Navigation* (1717) (first ed. 1669).

to determine 'in what place the Ship is at all times both in respect of *Latitude* and *Longitude*: this being the principal care of a Navigator. . . . To the Commendable Accomplishment of which knowledge, these four things are subordinate Requisites:

viz. $\begin{cases} Arithmetick \\ Geometry \\ Trigonometry, \text{ and} \\ Astronomy.' \end{cases}$

We may conclude, then, that by Elizabethan times navigation consisted of two fairly distinct arts, pilotage and oceanic navigation. One, pilotage, was empirical and depended primarily upon experience and the observation of terrestrial objects. The other, oceanic navigation, was fundamentally scientific and depended primarily upon calculation and the observation of celestial bodies. A pilot's ability was measured by the skill with which he conned his ship in coastal waters, from cape to cape, and by his knowledge of the off-shore soundings and sea-bed, and his familiarity with sea-marks and land-marks, tides and estuarine shoals. Of the navigator was demanded the same skill and, over and above this, the ability to direct the ship's course and fix the ship's position when far from land by instrumental observation of heavenly bodies and mathematical calculation.

Today, with his modern navigational aids and education, the ordinary navigator can both pilot and navigate his ship in all the waters of the world. The pilot is almost a rarity, his activities being confined to peculiarly treacherous waters in the approaches to important ports. Until the latter half of the sixteenth century the ordinary master of an English ship was still typified by Chaucer's

> 'A SHIPMAN was ther, woning fer by weste:
> For aught I woot, he was of Dertemouthe . . .
> A daggere hanging on a laas hadde he
> About his nekke under his arm adoun . . .
> . . . of his craft to rekene wel his tydes,
> His stremes and his daungers him bisydes,
> His herberwe and his mone, his lodemenage,
> Ther was noon swich from Hull to Carthage.
> Hardy he was, and wys to undertake;
> With many a tempest hadde his berd been shake.
> He knew wel alle the havenes, as they were,
> From Gootlond to the Cape of Finistere,
> And every cryke in Britayne and in Spayne;
> His barge y-cleped was the Maudelayne.'[1]

Nevertheless, from early in the sixteenth century the growth of the Royal Navy, the gradual increase in the size of merchants' ships, small though

---

[1] Chaucer, *Canterbury Tales*, Prologue (c. 1390), lines 390, with omissions, to 410, from Skeat, W.W., *The Complete Works of Geoffrey Chaucer* (1949);
  lodemenage = pilotage; Britayne = Brittany; barge = ship.

they still were, the silting up of many of the older ports, the growing importance of London as a port and naval base, and the consequent increased use of the wide shoal-infested, tide-tortured reaches of the lower Thames had led to the establishment of officially recognized bodies of licensed pilots. Although the distinction between port pilots and sea-going pilots can be traced back many centuries earlier, it can be said that from early Tudor times it was officially recognized that port pilots were properly those who, to quote an early seventeenth-century authority, '(upon coasts and shores unknown unto the Master), were employed for the conduction of ships into roads and harbours, or when they were to pass over bars or sands'; whereas 'the charge and duty of the Master of a ship was to undertake the conduction of her to the places and ports whither she was bound, and to shape all such courses as might best conduce there unto . . . .'[1] Thus in the first half of the sixteenth century we find strictly regulated port pilotage organizations established at Kingston upon Hull, Newcastle upon Tyne, and Bristol, as well as at London, whose pilots controlled the movements of ships within the respective port boundaries. In Elizabethan times, that is in the latter half of the sixteenth century, there developed two sorts of master: the master who was essentially a coastal and short sea-route pilot—like Chaucer's shipman—and the master who was an oceanic navigator. They were the practitioners of two distinct arts, though, unlike the master-pilot, who could not navigate in the ocean sea, the master-navigator could pilot his ship in the familiar waters off his native shores, and required a pilot only when entering or leaving harbour or off unfamiliar foreign shores. But by Stuart times—the first quarter of the seventeenth century—the master-navigator had become almost a specialist in oceanic navigation, at any rate in the view of at least one Elizabethan sea-captain. Comparing Elizabethan and Stuart masters Sir William Monson in his old age vowed 'that since I served in the Narrow Seas I find so great a difference betwixt the masters of that time and this that I may compare it to an ancient art, that in long continuance of time has been forgotten and lost for want of use. The masters in those days were either ignorantly adventurous, or in this Time providently cautious . . . because their breeding has not been to sail amongst sands, or in seas so narrow that . . . that wind which is secure upon one shore is death upon another; and tides that sometimes are advantageous to them, at other times may prove dangerous. . . .' To remedy this state of affairs Monson called for 'expert and skilful pilots that make the Narrow Seas their daily trade and practice'.[2] In short, by then the pilot, the coaster or channeller, and the navigator had

---

[1] *Boteler's Dialogues*, N.R.S., Vol. 65. For the employment of pilots by shipping engaged in the Bordeaux wine trade, see Williams, T. D., 'The Maritime Relations of Bordeaux and Southampton in the Thirteenth Century.' *Scot. Geog. Mag.*, Vol. 47. See also Farr, G., 'Bristol Channel Pilotage', and McGrath, P.V., 'Bristol Channel Pilots', *M.M.*, Vol. 39.

[2] *Monson's Tracts*. Vol. 4, N.R.S., Vol. 45, pp. 152–5, and on medieval pilotage, see Williams, T. D., *op. cit.*, pp. 152-5; Nicholas, N. H. *History*, II, p. 476.

become pretty clearly established as distinct types of seamen having
accomplishments peculiarly their own. It had happened in the space of a
lifetime. For whereas the pilot's art—in the broad sense of the word—
was immemorially old, in the sixteenth century the navigator's had only
a few score years of age.

The English seaman under the early Tudors traded in the waters of
north-west Europe as far as Iceland for fish, the Low Countries for fine
cloths and Rhenish wines, Bordeaux and the Biscay ports for woad, used
in dyeing, and fine French wines, and to Portugal and Spain for fruits, wax,
iron, and again wines. In exchange he carried wool and cloth, tin and hides.[1]
The great manufacturing centres of the world were the Lombardy plain in
Italy, and the Low Countries. The goods of the Italian craftsmen, and the
wines and silks of Italy were brought chiefly in foreign bottoms, those of
the Low Countries in French and Flemish as well as English ones. The
naval stores—timbers for masts and spars, hemp for rope, pitch and train-
oil for seams, bottom coating and grease—and grain came from the Baltic
in the ships of the Hanseatic League. English seamen rarely penetrated
the Baltic or extended their voyages to the Atlantic islands of Spain and
Portugal—Madeira, the Canaries, and the Azores—or to the Mediterranean. Theirs was essentially a home trade, a coastal trade. They were
practised in the art of pilotage only. Their ships were very small, mostly
under 100 tons, and were in the early years still chiefly clinker built, that
is with overlapping strakes. Although in the first half of the sixteenth
century the stronger Mediterranean carvel build, under the influence of
Italian shipwrights brought in by Henry VIII, displaced the clinker build,
the merchant ships, despite subsidies, did not greatly increase in size.
As late as 1626 an inventory of 'all the ships and barques, belonging to
the Port of Bristall' listed only four ships between 250 and 200 tons, and
twelve between 200 and 100 tons, compared with twenty-six between 100
and 20 tons.[2] Of the many others engaged upon the foreign trade but
captured by pirates in the preceding twenty-five years, most were under
100 tons. The smaller English merchant ships in the first half of the sixteenth century were single-masted and rigged with fore-and-aft sails—a
jib and a sprit sail—or a single square sail. Either rig was simple to work
and required only a small crew. The larger vessels were square-rigged only,
or 'cross-sailed' as it was termed, with three masts and a bowsprit. The
fore and main masts each carried a course and a top-sail, the bow-sprit
a sprit-sail; all these were 'cross-sails'; the mizzen mast carried a lateen-
sail. This rig remained typical of merchant ships well into the eighteenth

[1] Hunter H. C., *How England got its Merchant Marine*, 1066–1776 (1935), contains valuable summaries and extracts of English mercantile legislation designed
to build up the merchant and royal navies. The extent and volume of the English
carrying trade at various periods can be ascertained from this valuable work. The
standard work on the subject is Cunningham, W., *The Growth of English Commerce
and Industry* (1903).

[2] McGrath, P. V., 'The Merchant Venturers of Bristol and Bristol Shipping in
the Early Seventeenth Century', *M.M.*, Vol. 36.

century. The running rigging of these ships was coarse and clumsy by modern standards and heavy to handle. The result was that rather large crews were carried; numbers were also an advantage in the event of a struggle with pirates, still common enough, even in home waters. At the close of the sixteenth century the Dutch introduced many improvements in the efficiency of the rigging which the English merchantmen were slow to adopt—to the handicapping of their carrying trade. An idea of the crowding of crews can be gained from the fact that the Elizabethan and Stuart warships, which, of course, were more heavily armed for fighting, carried roughly one man to every 2 tons of displacement. Thus a warship of 100 tons would carry a crew of fifty. Before the 1580s the scale had been one man to every $1\frac{1}{2}$ tons of displacement. For ground-tackle the ships carried, according to size, from two to nine iron anchors of a pattern closely resembling the modern Admiralty pattern anchor; that is consisting of a shank with two arms at the crown forming an arc of a circle and a stock passed through the shank below the anchor ring and at right-angles to the plane of the arms. The stout cables were of tarred Baltic hemp or of finer stuff from the Mediterranean now known as Italian hemp. The cables were short and the anchors by modern standards light, so that their holding qualities were poor. There was, however, a steady improvement in ground-tackle in the sixteenth century, the length of the cables being increased to 100 or 120 fathoms; and later, in the seventeenth century, the weight of the anchors was steadily increased.[1]

The merchant ships were not the only English ships sailing the seas of north-west Europe in the first half of the sixteenth century. In addition to the fishing vessels, which we can consider as part of the merchant navy, there were the warships of the Royal Navy. In this, always excepting the special galley fleets of the Mediterranean states, the English were unique. The Royal Navy, though its roots run further back into history, was the creation of the Tudors, and essentially of Henry VIII. Whereas other states in north-west Europe relied upon hiring or requisitioning armed merchant ships for battle by sea, the Tudors relied upon a Royal Navy of ships designed specifically for war, for the defence of the realm and offence of the enemy.[2] By the creation in 1545 of the Navy Board, whose business it was to provide and administer the Royal Navy under the direction of the senior executive officer, the Lord Admiral, Henry VIII gave the Royal Navy both permanence and individuality. What is more, whereas in the fifteenth century it had been the merchant ships which had led the way in improvements in ship construction, design, and rigging—when ships of up to 1,000 tons were built—the creation of a royal fleet with royal dockyards and administrative officers to maintain it meant that the Government of the country was not merely paternally interested but was directly

[1] Tinniswood, F. T., 'Anchors and Accessories, 1340–1640', *M.M.*, Vol. 31.
[2] Oppenheim, M., *Administration of the Royal Navy*, 1509–1660 (1896), is a masterly work on the administrative and material development of the Royal Navy in the sixteenth and seventeenth centuries.

involved in ship-building and the seaman's art in general; not least in the art of conducting a ship from one port to another. From Tudor times two parallel developments are apparent in English seamanship through the direct influence of the Crown; these were improvements in ship-design and improvements in the art of navigation. Thus the establishment of the Royal Navy was a most important maritime measure, and its effects were quite out of proportion to the number of ships involved. For instance, although Henry VIII built, bought, or seized in prize numerous ships of from 100 up to 1,000 tons during his reign, at his death the royal fleet mustered only twenty-eight ships of 100 tons and upwards; again in Elizabeth's reign the fleet that defeated the Spanish Armada in 1588 contained only twenty-four royal warships of over 100 tons, the largest being of 1,000 tons. Nevertheless these few ships had a great influence. The fact is that, although bounties continued to be paid to merchants to build larger and therefore more seaworthy and potentially more powerful ships, the financial responsibility for innovation in ship-design was taken over— had had to be taken over—by the Government in the interests of the nation, not so much from slow-acting economic considerations as from the urgent problems of fighting efficiency. The merchant was quick to recognize this and was content to follow and adapt where his forbears had had to lead and experiment. But the sixteenth century was an age of transition, and we still find private men, like Sir Walter Raleigh, building a great ship of improved design, and selling it to the Government, as he did the *Ark Raleigh*, Lord Howard of Effingham's *Ark Royal* in the Armada fight. But of more direct concern to our subject is the fact that, having ships of its own, the Government was very much concerned in the problem of their preservation from the dangers of the sea. Hitherto its sailors had been obliged, like merchant seamen, to rely upon natural sea-marks; but in the sixteenth century, as we shall see, the Crown took steps to provide special sea-marks in dangerous coastal waters, and to obtain seamen competent to conduct its ships.

For long there had been Fraternities of the Sea at the more important ports. These were organizations of shipmen which appear to have been responsible, amongst other business, such as the welfare and conduct of their fellows, for the selection and supervision of pilots for their ports. From 1512 to 1514 England and France were at war. It was essentially a naval war waged with royal ships. Though the actions seem trifling enough now, it is significant that it was in 1514 that Henry VIII established the Corporation of the Trinity House of Deptford Strand 'for the advancement and benefit of navigation and commerce . . .' and for the training, licensing, and regulation of Englishmen in pilotage. Experience had shown that many foreigners had learnt the secrets of the channels to our ports and turned their knowledge to the advantage of the French.[1] Other similar corporations were set up during his reign at Kingston upon Hull and

[1] Mead, H. P., *Trinity House* (1947), p. 16.
4—A.O.N.

Newcastle upon Tyne. Apart from Portsmouth, where the first dry-dock in the world had been built in 1495, the royal dockyards were all on the Thames or on the Medway, which flows into the Thames estuary. It is therefore not surprising to learn from 'An Act concerning Sea-marks and Mariners' passed in 1565, the eighth year of Elizabeth's reign, that 'the Master, Wardens, and Assistants of the Trinity House of Deptford Strand, being a company of the chiefest and most expert masters and governors of ships', had been charged, not only 'to foresee the good increase and maintenance of ships, and of all kind of men traded and brought up by watercraft', but also with 'the conduction' of the ships of the 'navy royal'.

When Henry VIII had licensed the Corporation of Trinity House, he had done so to safeguard the royal as well as the merchant ships from loss by hazard or default, but experience showed that his measures needed strengthening. This was the purpose of the Act of 1565, for from it we find that 'By the destroying and taking away of certain steeples, woods, and other marks standing upon the main shores, adjoining to the sea coasts of this realm of England and Wales, being as beacons and marks of ancient time accustomed for seafaring men, to save and keep them and the ships in their charge from sundry dangers thereto incident: Divers ships with their goods and merchandise, in sailing from foreign ports towards this realm of England and Wales, and especially to the port and river of Thames, have by the lack of such sea-marks of late years miscarried, perished, and lost in the Sea, to the great detriment and hurt of the Common Weal, and the perishing of no small number of people.' As a consequence the Act extended the authority of Trinity House to set up and maintain, out of shipping dues it was entitled to levy, as many beacons, marks, and signs for the sea as seemed necessary on the sea-shores and heights, as well as in the approaches to ports, of England and Wales. Furthermore it prohibited, under penalty of a fine of one hundred pounds, the destruction of steeples or conspicuous trees used as recognized beacons.

The early Tudor seaman, then, besides having the familiar features of capes and bays to direct him had also the time-honoured use of church steeples and conspicuous trees and, for leading marks into estuarine channels and ports, artificial beacons of timber or stone; but it was not until Elizabethan days that he had artificial coastal beacons. In channels to ports, besides landmarks, he had buoys, their laying and maintenance, like that of the artificial beacons, being vested in the Crown through the Lord High Admiral, who could levy 'buoyage' as well as 'beaconage' to defray their cost; although generally he, or the deputy to whom he granted it, farmed out these dues. The buoys, which were of wood, were of two sorts: barrel-shaped 'tuns'; and cone-shaped 'can-buoys'. The latter had the base of the cone uppermost; the apex, as the strongest part, was used as the point of attachment for the moorings.

The first lighthouse was established in Henry VIII's reign at the entrance to Newcastle upon Tyne. It was not until the seventeenth century that lighthouses became more numerous. Their increase was hotly debated in James I's reign, the argument against them being that they facilitated a sudden invasion by an enemy.[1]

As we have seen, the English great ships were chiefly royal warships, and very few in number. All were conducted by men who had learnt their art in the mercantile school. The great ships, and this is true of all great ships until well into the eighteenth century, were none too seaworthy, and confined their cruising to the fine-weather months, roughly April to October. The merchant shipping, on the other hand, sailed all the year round. Indeed, for generations the English ships of the ancient and valuable Bordeaux wine trade had braved the autumnal storms and winter gales of the Channel and the Bay of Biscay in order to ply their trade to the best advantage by bringing in the heady wines of the new vintage demanded by palates denied finely flavoured foods in winter. Not until 1532 was the practice prohibited by legislation to put an end to the mounting toll of losses. Nevertheless, the bulk of English seamen were, and continued to be, inured to the hardships of the sea at all seasons of the year. They were essentially small shipmen, and their masters, pilots. On the whole they specialized in various carrying trades; the men of Bristol traded like those of Southampton, chiefly to the south-west with the French and Spanish Biscay ports and the Atlantic ports and islands of Portugal and Spain. The men of Southampton also specialized in the cross-Channel trade, and some, like the London men in that with the Netherlands. The men of the other East Coast ports—Harwich, Yarmouth, Kingston upon Hull, and Newcastle, to name the biggest—occupied themselves in the Baltic trade (the little there was), in that of the Netherlands, and also in the fish-carrying trade between Scandinavia, Iceland, and their home ports.

By long experience the English ship-masters knew their particular waters well, their coastline, land-marks and sea-marks. In addition they had certain aids, whose importance increased greatly, once they sailed in unfamiliar seas. Then indeed, apart from seamanship, that is to say, ship-handling skill, such aids were all-important.

If he was literate, the ship-master prized a *rutter*. This was a small pocket-book in which was recorded the magnetic compass courses between ports and capes (he often termed the ship's course 'the caping of the ship'); the distance between them, stated in kennings or distances of 20 miles (in Scottish waters 14 miles), the distance at which it was reckoned a man could discern the coastline; the direction of flow of the tidal streams; the time of high-water on days of new or full moon at important ports, headlands and channels, that is to say the establishment of the port or place; and the soundings or depth of water and nature of the sea-bed in the Soundings west of the Sleeve or English Channel, in the Sleeve itself, and in the approaches to ports.

The oldest English rutter known would seem to date from the early

---

[1] Whormby, T., *Account of Trinity House and Sea Marks*, 1746 (1861), pp. 110–11.

fifteenth century and to be based on much older lore.[1] This rutter gives the sailing directions for the circumnavigation of England and for the voyage to the Strait of Gibraltar. The first two-thirds contains the names of places on the coasts and their bearing from one another; as, 'Lizardds and Saint Mary sands of Cille est and west but beware the gulf' [Wolf Rock]; the direction of the flood and ebb, 'in the fairway between Start and Lisart the cours is est and west'; land-marks such as 'the parish steeple'; and the establishment of the ports, 'all the havens be full at a west and south-west moone betweene Start and Lisarte'. The last third of the rutter contains the soundings and nature of the sea-bed; as, 'And ye come out of Spayne . . . till ye come into Sowdyng, And yif ye have an C. fadome depe or els $\frac{xx}{iiij.x.}$ than ye shall go north till the sonde ayen in lxxij. fadome in feir grey sonde . . . between Clere and Cille.'[2]

These rutters were written originally in manuscript on vellum or scraps of paper by the pilot himself from notes he made over a pot of ale with some other ship-master in a sea-port tavern.[3] They were copied, mislaid, collected together again, and perhaps bound up to form a little leather book of ill-arranged, often conflicting information. Nevertheless the rutter was the ship-master's *vade mecum*. To this day the careful pilot compiles his own note-book. Only about half a dozen of these manuscript rutters (Italian, *portolani*; Portuguese, *roteiros*; French, *routiers*; Flemish, *lees-kaerten*) dating from before the early sixteenth century are known. But in the middle of the fifteenth century the art of printing was developed by John Gutenberg of Strassburg, and by 1480 over one hundred towns in Europe had printing presses. The first rutter to be printed in north-west Europe appears to have been *Le routier de la mer . . .*, ascribed to Pierre Garcie and printed at Rouen between 1502 and 1510. In the next century and a half it ran through over twenty editions. The oldest printed rutter known is an Italian *portolano* printed in Venice in 1490.

In 1528 'a sad ingenious and cyrcumspect Mariner of the Citie of London . . . beeing in the toune of Bourdewes bought a pretty booke Imprinted in the French Language called the Rutter of the Sea'—probably

---

[1] *Sailing Directions for the Circumnavigation of England*, Hak. Soc. Ser. 1, Vol. 79. It was first printed in 1541 by Richard Proude in *The New Rutter for the Sea for the North Partes*. It is attributed to 1408. It does not include the distance between places. The oldest surviving Mediterranean pilot is a dated MS. portolano of 1296, a copy of one of 1250–6. See Taylor, E. G. R., 'The Oldest Mediterranean Pilot', *J.I.N.*, Vol. 4, and Waters, D. W., *The Rutters of the Sea*, Yale U. P. (1968).

[2] 'And coming out of Spain [steer the courses given] until you reach the Soundings [the 100-fathom line]. Then if you find 100 fathoms depth, or 90, sail north until you sound in 72 fathoms and bring up fair grey sand between Cape Clear [cape of S.W. Ireland] and the Scilly Is.' is a free rendering of these directions.

[3] Taylor, E. G. R., *Tudor Geography*, 1485–1583 (1930), contains a valuable survey of English geographical knowledge of the period and data in rutters. Gernez, D., and Denucé, J., *Le Livre de Mer* (1936), contains a valuable description and commentary on early rutters, and in particular of MS. B. 29166 of the Bibliothèque Communale at Antwerp. See also Waters, D. W., *op. cit.* note 1, above.

the edition of 1502 'conteining many proper featee of hie ecience'. He brought the book home with him and gave it to a London book publisher, Robert Copland, for translation and publication. *The Rutter of the Sea* was the first printed rutter in English, and the sailing directions it gave were those for the Bordeaux wine trade and to Cadiz.

The rutter starts with: 'Of the tydes, that is to wit, the flood and Ebbes fro the race of Sayne [south of Ushant] into Flaunders' to which are devoted three and a half pages, and continues, devoting from one to four pages to each of the sections, with:

Courses to the race of Sain into Flaunders and how the tides toward Brittain beareth;

Routes and courses fro the race of Sayne into Flaunders;

Entrings and Harborowes of the coste of Normandy;

Floods fro Sylley and England into Flaunders;

Routes from Silley and England into Flaunders;

Entrings and Herborows all along the coste of England;

How the portes & havens of England, Britain and normandy doo lye how many leyges fro one to another;

Soundinges that ye shall finde co-ming fro Spayne Leuante, or Porting- ale to seek Ushant;

The kennings from Syllaye and England unto Flaunders;

Floods and Ebbes fro the foreland or cape of cornwailes into wales all a long by the sea coste;

and ends with the

judgments of the Ile of Auleron,

that is, with the recognized mercantile law of the sea in north-western waters.

In 1541 another section was added to the rutter: 'The Rutter of the Sea for the North Part'.[1] This was based on the English manuscript rutter of the early fifteenth century already referred to, and covered the circum- navigation of Scotland from Leith southward to the Humber, from Leith northward to Duncansby Head in Caithness, thence around the north and west coast of Scotland to the Mull of Kintyre, Mull of Galloway and the River Solway. Each section showed the direction of the tidal streams, time of flood and ebb tides, the kennings, of 14 miles distance, from cape

---

[1] The English printed rutter referred to is: The Rutter of the Sea with the Hauens Rodes, Soundings, Kennings, Windes, Floods, and Ebbes daungers and coastes of diuers regions with the lawes of the Ile of Auleron, and ye iudgments of the Sea. With a Rutter of the North added to the same. [Translated by Robert Copland from the anonymous French *Le Routier de la Mer*, probably by Pierre Garcie, and a prologue added, ?1550. First printed 1528 without the *Rutter of the North*. Colophon in the British Library. *The Rutter of the North* was compiled by Richard Proude, and printed in 1541, and based on the rutter of 1408 (anonymous). See Appendix 1. The earliest printed Dutch rutter is one of 1532].

to cape, and the havens, roads, sounds, and dangers on the route. The information it contained was more complete and better arranged than in the earlier printed part dealing with the Channel, Bordeaux, and Straits routes. This can be explained by the fact that it followed hard upon a voyage of circumnavigation of his realm made by King James V of Scotland in the summer of 1540. The voyage was made under the direction of a well-known Scottish pilot, Alexander Lindesay. The compiler of *The Rutter of the North* doubtless had access to the manuscript of Lindesay's more up-to-date rutter. However that may be, by the 1540s the English ship-master had the use of a printed rutter covering the seas around England and Scotland and the route to the Strait of Gibraltar. Unlike most other ship-masters, however, he was still generally dependent upon the written word for guidance. The French and Portuguese manuscript and French and Dutch printed rutters of this time included drawings or crude woodcuts of headlands and strips of the coast to assist in identification.

The use of manuscript rutters of northern waters continued side by side with the use of printed ones for another half century at least, while English rutters for foreign seas, except when they were embodied in printed journals or narratives of voyages, remained—with one exception—exclusively in manuscript until well into the seventeenth century.

Robert Copland listed the navigational instruments needed by a master-mariner as 'the carde, compas, rutter, dyall and other which . . . sheweth the plat . . .'. It is possible that Robert Copland referred to a manuscript rutter with charts when he listed a 'carde', for there is in the British Museum just such a sixteenth-century *Booke of the Sea Carte* (B.M. Add. 37,024). This manuscript book, besides having its contents clearly set out in titled sections with the subject-matter arranged in an orderly manner, contains sea-cards of the waters of north-west Europe. These sea-cards were not charts in the modern sense. They were little outline maps with the names of ports and a compass rose and radiating lines or rhumbs by means of which the master-mariner could fairly accurately gauge his course across Channel to his port of destination. The third book of *The Booke of the Sea Carte* contains four of these cards, namely: Scotland; the East Coast of England, Flanders, and Holland; southern England from Cardigan Bay in Wales to the Channel; and Ireland, the Irish Sea, and western England.

It has been said that the English were ignorant of the use of charts until John Cabot, who was an Italian pilot, came to England at the end of the fifteenth century. This may well be, for it was not until Henry VII's reign that Englishmen in search of trade penetrated the Mediterranean, where they might feel the need for charts. The seamen of the South and West Coast ports certainly knew of sea-cards long before this for the Venetians, who with the Catalans were the leading chart-makers until the sixteenth century, had sailed annually for centuries to the shores of England in their great Flanders galleys to fetch for the looms of Lombardy the peerless wool of England. You may certainly trace the limits, if not follow the growth, of their trade, by the gradual extension northwards of the coast-lines delineated on their charts, which, unlike the 'sea cardes', were bearing and distance charts of considerable accuracy. All semblance of accuracy, however, if further delineation is attempted in them, ends north of the Wash, and of the Scheldt in Flanders. Scotland, Denmark, Scandi-navia, and the whole of the Baltic when shown are most crudely represented until well into the sixteenth century.[1] The inference, that the northern seaman did not use a chart, is clear. The accuracy of this inference is vouched for not only by Michiel Coignet's omission of the use of the chart in his definition of the pilot's art but also by words of the first English-man to write and print a book on the practice of navigation, William Bourne. In his book, *A Regiment for the Sea*, first published in 1574, Bourne says that the ship-master should 'be a good coaster, that is to say, . . . knowe every place by the sight thereof', as Chaucer said his ship-master of Dartmouth did in the fourteenth century, and understand ocean navigation for which 'the use of the Sea-Cardes is most necessary'.[2] Furthermore, four years later, in the third impression of his book, occurs a most scathing indictment of the ancient mariner, the ignorant 'coaster', the prejudiced 'Channeller', as he calls him. 'The nature of a number of men is to dislike of all things not done by themselves', declared William Bourne somewhat bitterly, therefore

I doe hope that in these dayes, that the knowledge of the masters of shippes is very well mended; for I have knowen within this 20 yeeres, that them that wer auncient masters of shippes hath derided and mocked them that have occupied their cardes and plattes . . . saying: that they care not for their sheepes skinnes, for he could keep a better account upon a boord . . .[3]

[1] Andrews, H. C., 'Scotland in Portolan Charts'. *Scot. Geog. Mag.*, Vol. 42. (The first chart of the Baltic was a wood-cut one of 1543 by the Dutch hydrographer Cornelis Anthonisz.).

[2] A Regiment for the sea Conteyning most profitable Rules, Mathematical experiences, and perfect knowledge of Nauigation, for all Coastes and Countreys: most needful and necessary for all Seafaryng men and Trauellers, as Pilotes, *Mariners, Marchaunts &c.* Exactly deuised and made, by William Bourne. Im-printed at London, by Thomas Hacket, and are to be solde at his shop in the Royall Exchaunge, at the Signe of the Greene Dragon. [1574]. [STC 3422 The title-page of the Huntington Library copy; that of the Paris copy has 'imprinted at London for Thomas Hacket, etc'.].

[3] William Bourne's 'Preface to the Reader' in the *Regiment for the Sea*, of which the first edition was probably printed and published in London in 1574. This is from the 1577, unauthorized edition. The title reads: A Regiment for the Sea: Conteyn-ing most profitable Rules, Mathematical experiences and perfect knowledge of Nauigation, for all Coastes and Countreys: most needful and necessary for al Sea faryng men and Trauellers, as Pilotes, *Mariners, Marchaunts, etc.* Exactly deuised and made, by William Bourne. Imprinted at London, nigh vnto the three Cranes in the Vintree, by Thomas Dawson *and Thomas Gardyner, for Iohn Wight.* [1576] [STC 3423], [1577] [STC 3424].

He concludes, paraphrasing Robert Copland of half a century earlier, 'if they should come out of the Ocean Sea to seeke our Channel to come unto the River of Thames; I am of that opinion that a number of them doeth but grope as a blinde man doth . . .'.

In short the English ship-master, in common with the seamen of more northern waters and the Baltic, at this time rarely if ever used a 'sea-carde', let alone a larger chart or 'platte'; he relied for finding his way about almost exclusively on his rutter. The second book of the *Booke of the Sea Carte*, for example, gives the sailing directions for a voyage from London to Land's End (spelling modernised).

    (i)   The Courses of Tides from the Thames to the Cape of Cornwall (Land's End)
         . . . from the Cape of Cornwall to Scilly it floweth west-south-west and east-south-east . . .

    (ii) Floodes and ebbes from Thames to Dover, from thence westward to the Cape of Cornwall
         . . . At Dover the moon south full sea . . .

    (iii) Courses from the Thames to the Cape of Cornwall
         . . . The cape of Cornwall and Lizard, be east-south-east and west-north-west . . .

    (iv) Kennings from the Thames to the Cape of Cornwall
         . . . from Lizard to the Cape of Cornwall one kenning . . .

    (v)   Sounds and dangers from the Thames to the Cape
         If ye will be in the Downes cast anchor at vi or vii fathoms . . .

Besides certain tide-tables the book also includes 'The Mariners Prognostycaccion gathered out of Ptolome, Arystotelle, Plini, Virgill and other natural philosophers'. In this are recorded the signs and tokens of the sun, moon, and stars at various times and seasons; of winds, thunder, and lightning; and of rainbows and the look and the sound of the sea. Thus 'Of Winds', the writer notes: 'A sudden calm in the sea after great wind signifieth the wind to change, or then the same wind to increase and grow'—that most dreaded sign for the seaman in a storm; and 'Of the Sea' he writes, 'The rock and sands of the sea, making murmur, or sounds without, and not on shore, signifieth great storm to come. . . . The sea froth appearing in divers places, with bellowing of the water signifieth evil weather for many days after.' The emphasis is wisely on dangers to come, but, at the last, relief is promised by 'the dolphin fish swimming and leaping often-times above the water . . . in the time of a storm . . .', for that 'betokeneth calm and fair weather'.

Among other aids to the ship-master was an annual almanac containing the calendar with the phases of the moon and telling him which would be moonlight nights, and giving also an annual prognostication of more general interest. With the spread of the art of printing in Europe such works had become fairly numerous by the end of the fifteenth century, although in

England the first almanac was not printed until 1503, and then it was a crude translation of a French work. *The Kalendayr of shyppars* included not only a calendar and a description of the universe—on Ptolemaic lines— but also numerous moral precepts of a wise and homely nature; its popularity was immense, and it passed through many editions. This one apart, almanacs fell broadly speaking into two types: those intended for the astronomer, physician, scholar, and student, and those designed for use by less erudite people, or humbler folk, amongst whom we must include the ship-masters. The simpler almanacs were generally printed as broadsheets for posting up on a wall or ship's bulkhead, or as sextodecimo volumes for the pocket. The broadsheets contained the calendar and brief information showing the moonlight and dark nights, and a forecast of the weather; the pocket almanacs contained the same information as the broadsheet, but on fuller lines. The true almanac was a larger work, and consisted essentially of a table giving the chief astronomical events of the year, and the terrestrial events dependent upon them. These included the conjunctions and opposition of the sun and moon for the year, tables of the sun's declination, the positions of a few stars, the rules for using the North Star, and the rules or 'declaration' for the compilation of the calendar. The day ran from noon to noon, and the year from the vernal equinox, March 11th. Frequently the almanac covered a period of years.

It was not until 1539 that the calendar and the almanac were issued together for popular use. Quite distinct from the calendar and the almanac proper was the prognostication. Until an Act of 1541 against sorcery was repealed in Edward VI's reign, English prognostications were rare. Even when they became more numerous they were generally confined to the incidence of the weather and diseases. The authorities frowned upon the forecasting of disasters, though phenomena such as comets or eclipses naturally called for more dramatic handling. Later, from 1571, the publication of annual almanacs and prognostications was controlled by a patent which confined their issue to two London printers, Watkins and Roberts. By this time the annual or common almanac had taken the form it generally adhered to for the next century. It then comprised the ecclesiastical calendar; the canons of phlebotomy, bathing, purging, etc.; the anatomical man showing the influences of the signs of the zodiac on the body; the tables of the positions of the moon in the zodiac; the phases of the moon; and the distances by road between towns in England. By then too, the prognostication, with a separate title-page, was always annexed to the almanac. Besides forecasting the weather and happenings based on astrology, the prognostication after 1571 frequently listed the fairs held all over England, information intended for chapmen which might prove useful also for the itinerant ship-master. In the sixteenth and seventeenth centuries such annual or common almanacs were in everybody's pocket. They took the place of the modern pocket diary—indeed, even in the sixteenth century some had blank pages for entries. In the absence of modern illuminants their lunar tables were particularly useful. Many almanacs

had tide-tables, sometimes in the almanac itself, sometimes in the prognostication. These gave the 'ebbs and fluddes' for various stretches of the
English or Channel coast, and very often rules for finding the daily times
of high water. Indeed such a tide-table appeared in the earliest annual
almanac in book form printed in England. A decade later Anthony
Askham's annual almanac for 1553 contained rules for finding the time by
the stars specially compiled for mariners (though it had no tide-tables),
and this almanac incidentally was the first to follow the practice of starting
the year on 1st January.[1]

Of the instruments used by the early Tudor ship-master, probably the
most ancient was the lead and line for finding the depth of water. His forbears had needed it before ever they felt the need for determining direction. The first necessity for the seaman in the opaque waters of the northern
seas, with their varying depths caused by the rise and fall of the tide, is a
means of finding how much water he has under his ship and of detecting
the presence of hidden rocks and shoals. This he did with the lead and
line. Michiel Coignet, it will be recalled, considered it one of the two chief
instruments of the pilot, and he did so because just as the pilot could
fix his position by the contours, colour, and texture of the coast, so when
out of sight of land, or when off-shore in poor visibility, he could locate
himself, as fishermen still do, by the contours, colour, smell, taste, and
texture of the sea-bed. To the seaman whose voyage took him out of
soundings the lead and line was again an indispensable instrument. Soundings was the name he gave to the waters west of the English Channel, between Ireland and Brittany, and covering in that region what is known as
the continental shelf. The shores of the continents and larger islands of the
world do not descend in a continuous slope from the coast-line to the
ocean-bed. On the contrary, from the shore-line the sea-bed slopes, here
steeply—as off Spain and western Ireland—there gently, as to the west of
the English Channel—to a depth of about 100 fathoms, then plunges pre-
cipitously, thousands of fathoms deep—'deeper than did ever plummet
sound'—to the ocean-bed. The outer edge of the continental shelf, the line
where the continental slope thrusts abruptly up towards the surface of the
sea, is thus clearly defined by the 100-fathom line and can be found with
considerable accuracy by a deep-sea lead and line—a fact of the utmost
value to a mariner approaching the waters covering the continental shelf.
At some points, as off the west and south-west coasts of Ireland, and off all
the coast of Spain and Portugal, the edge of the continental shelf is found
only ten or twenty miles from the coast, at others it is hundreds of miles to
seaward—from the Lizard it lies distant 200 miles on the arc of the south-
west quadrant. On a voyage from England to Spain a ship passed out of
soundings when some 100 miles south-west of Ushant and entered them

---

[1] (i) The standard work on English almanacs is Bosanquet, E. F., *English
Printed Almanacks and Prognostications* (1917). (ii) 'A calendar, a calendar! look
in the almanac, find out moonshine, find out moonshine.' *A Midsummer Night's
Dream*, Act III, Sc. 1.

again only a score of miles—when within sight, by day—of the north west coast of Spain. It was a hazardous land-fall. Returning from Spain the direction made good and the progress made could be estimated only by eye during the passage across the Bay of Biscay, until soundings were struck to the south-west of Ushant, Scilly or Cape Clear. The lead and line then gave warning—the first and the most timely—of Soundings having been reached and of the dangers of shallow seas, rocky coasts, and tide races ahead; but it also gave, from the evidence of the nature of the sea-bed brought up on the lead, an indication of the ship's position in relation to the coast, and consequently, if the evidence had been interpreted aright, of the course to be steered and of the soundings to be expected in order to make a safe landfall off a chosen stretch of coast. We have seen that the earliest rutter gave the pilot such information, and in Robert Copland's the mariner approaching the English Channel from Spain is warned that, after coming into Soundings:

When ye be at lxxx fadome ye shall finde small black sande and yee shalbe at the thwart of lezarde.

When ye be at lx or lxv ye shall finde white sande, and white soft woormes And ye shall be very nigh to Lezard.

Although the earliest illustration of a lead and line is found in the frontispiece of the *Spieghel der Zeevaerdt* of Lucas Janszoon Wagenaer,[1] first published in 1584, and the earliest English descriptions of the lead and line date from the 1620s, the very fact that illustrations and descriptions fit the leads and lines used by seamen to this day points to the conclusion that those used by the English seaman of the early sixteenth century were similar. He used one of two sorts, according to the depth of water. In deep water, when he thought he was approaching the shore, he used the deep-sea or dipsie lead and line. According to Captain John Smith, who described it in his *Sea Grammar* of 1627, this consisted of a 'a long plummet, made hollow, wherein is put tallow', attached to a thin line 150 fathoms in length, marked first at 20 and then at every 10 fathoms with so many small knots in little strings fixed to each mark. Sir Henry Mainwaring in his *Seaman's Dictionary*, written between 1620 and 1623, but not printed until 1644, gave the dipsie lead a weight of 14 lb., and the length of the line as 200 fathoms. He described the 'arming' of the lead as being with 'hard white tallow', except when used on an oozy sea-bed, when white woollen cloth with a little tallow formed the arming. Both Smith and Mainwaring are agreed that the sounding lead used in shoal water, that is in depths of less than 20 fathoms, weighed as it does today, 7 lb., and was a foot long. The line was thicker than the dipsie line, and was marked

---

[1] See Pl. III.

[2] *Life and Works of Sir Henry Mainwaring*, Vol. 2. N.R.S., Vol. 56, contains the 'Seaman's Dictionary' which Mainwaring wrote between 1620 and 1623 as a guide for the Lord High Admiral, the Marquis of Buckingham; it was first published in 1644 by order of Parliament for use in the fleet.

at 2 fathoms and 3 fathoms with black leather, at 5 and 15 with white cloth, at 7 with red cloth, and at 10 with leather. The modern line differs only in that 13 fathoms is marked with blue cloth, and 17 with red, but the 20-fathom mark is two knots in a piece of string—the 20-fathom marking of the dipsie line. To use the dipsie lead the ship was hove-to, and the sounding was taken either from the pinnace or the lead was taken forward to the eyes of the ship, and the line coiled down at intervals all along the weather side of the deck to the poop. One of the crew was stationed at each coil. When the lead was hove overboard, each man as his coil ran out called to his fellow abaft him, 'Watch, there, watch', and as the line came up and down and ceased to run out the depth was taken, either so many fathoms or 'No bottom', under the eyes of the master.[1] The sounding line, being short, could be used under way. 'Soundyng ledes with lynes' were important items in the ship's stores of the royal ships.[2]

Probably the next oldest instrument the ship-master used was his compass. The mariners of the ancient world centred round the Mediterranean and Black Sea had used books of sailing directions, known as a *periplus*, 'a sailing-round' or 'port-book'. The directions they used were related to the winds, for with their simple square sail the seamen of ancient times were dependent upon a following wind for making headway. They evolved eight principal directions or 'winds', as they called them. North they identified by the Pole Star and its guards, which they saw over the mountains—*Tramontana* to the north. East and west they identified by the sun's direction at sunrise and sunset and intermediate directions by the nature or supposed source of the winds. The Greeks, who were the seamen of the Roman empire, seem to have transmitted their lore, probably through the warring and trading activities of the Byzantine empire, to the seamen of the nascent city states in Italy of the early centuries of our era. In the eighth and ninth centuries the Arabs overran much of the Mediterranean littoral popularising the lateen-sail, a form of balanced lug-sail by means of which the seaman could make headway towards the direction from which the wind was blowing. In the tenth and eleventh centuries the Norsemen overflowed from their northern coasts and penetrated the more highly civilized Mediterranean, bringing with them too a means of making good a course towards the direction from which the wind was blowing, the bowline. By means of the bowline a square sail could be trimmed around towards the wind and its luff, or leading edge, drawn tight, so that an efficient sail area was formed. By means of these two inventions, the

[1] The latter is the time-honoured method in the sailing merchant service today and there is no reason to suppose it has changed in the centuries. Journals and narratives of the early seventeenth century refer to sounding from the pinnace.

[2] *Documents and Inventories of Henry VII*, N.R.S., Vol. 8, e.g. '*The Mary Fortune* . . . Soundyng ledes with lynes. Also the seed Robert Brygandyne hath payed for ii Soundyng ledes pryce the peece xijd—ijs and for iii Soundyng lynes to the same ij of them at ixd a peece xviijd and oon at viijd—iis ijd. . . .'

lateen-sail and the bowline, the seaman was freed from the tyranny of the following wind. The consequence was that to exploit their advantages a more reliable and constant direction pointer than the sun, stars, and winds became an urgent need. So it was, in all probability, that the magnetic compass came into its own at sea. The Norsemen had divided the compass of their horizon originally into four directions or quarters, now called the cardinal points, North, East, South, and West, based no doubt upon the bearing of the sun at midday, sunrise, and sunset, and upon the Pole Star, and its guards, which was then about 8° to 10° distant from the pole. Since the directions were only general the amplitude of the sun, the amount by which the sun rises and sets north or south of true east and west, and the polar distance of Polaris did not greatly matter, and no doubt was allowed for roughly according to the season of the year and the approximate time of the day or night. The rising of the sun due east and its setting due west at the equinoxes, in March and September, was probably well known. By the fourteenth century, to judge from written notes, but the thirteenth century to judge from the rhumb (direction) lines on the oldest surviving chart, the seaman's horizon had been divided into thirty-two directions or, as he called them, 'rhumbs of the winds'. Almost everywhere the northern names for direction had been adopted—North, South, East, and West, and their various combinations to denote the twenty-eight intermediate directions—but the classical practice of referring to directions as 'winds' had continued in the Mediterranean and had been adopted by northern seamen also.

We do not know who invented the magnetic compass, nor when it first came into use at sea, in Europe. It seems to be fairly well established that it was a European invention, and most probably a Mediterranean one. Tradition associates it with the Italian port of Amalfi. One thing is certain, it was in use amongst northern and Mediterranean seamen in the twelfth century. Its use anywhere before that cannot be established. It is perhaps not without significance that the earliest records of the compass should date from within a century of the start of the first crusade (1097); that it was not until after the first-known mention of a compass (1187) that any significant force of crusaders, other than Italian ones, made their way to the East by sea (this was in 1190 when Philip Augustus and Richard Coeur de Lion initiated great sea-borne crusading expeditions from northwest Europe); and that amongst the Italian ports which by then had long-established carrying trades in the Mediterranean was Amalfi, whose ships carried, amongst other cargoes, magnetic iron ore from the mines in Elba.[1] In short, the twelfth century, which saw significant developments in ship design, may well, under the stimulus of the crusades, have also seen the magnetic compass first brought into use at sea by men of Amalfi.

It is probable that originally the compass consisted of a piece of magnetic

[1] Taylor, E. G. R., 'Early Charts and the Origin of the Compass Rose', *J.I.N.*, Vol. 4. 'The Oldest Mediterranean Pilot', *J.I.N.*, Vol. 4.

ore—a lodestone (literally 'way-stone')—placed on a piece of wood and floated in a bowl of water when the mariner wished to check the wind direction by finding the direction of north in thick weather or on dark nights. By 1187 we have the description in Alexander Neckham's *De Utensilibus* of a needle transfixing a piece of reed so that when floated in a bowl of water it indicated the four cardinal points. From his description in *De Naturis Rerum* it appears to have been used at sea only in foul weather, and then only for checking wind direction, as distinct from the ship's course. For this there were practical reasons. From the earliest times the pilot had set his course by trimming his sail to the wind, and had conned the helmsman in terms of wind direction, while the helmsman had subsequently steered so as to keep this trim of sail. With her full-cut square sail the ships of both northern and Mediterranean seamen could do little more than run before the wind. Consequently the pilot thought traditionally in terms of wind direction, a practice which even the introduction of the lateen-sail and the bowline, since each was made, it is certain, at a time when compasses were not in use, gave no cause for abandoning. The aid which the pilot felt in need of on starless nights and in thick weather was consequently one which would enable him to check the direction of the wind. The primitive lodestone and magnetic needle, floated by a reed in a bowl of water, enabled him to do just this—and no more for, being free floating, it quickly moved towards the side of the bowl and, on contact with it, became deflected from the direction of north. In a small craft in rough weather such an instrument could enable only the general direction of north to be gleaned by a snatched glance; nevertheless, this, it must be emphasized, was sufficient for the pilot's purpose of gauging the wind direction.

The essential accompaniment to the magnetic needle was a lodestone with which to magnetize it and with which to keep it magnetized, for iron loses its magnetism unless specially treated, and knowledge of this was still a mystery. The earliest mention in English records of lodestones appears to be in the inventories of 1410–12 of the *Plenty* of Hull, which had '1 sailing piece', and of the *George* for which '12 stones, called adamants, called sailstones, were bought for 6s in Flanders'.[1]

A certain amount of art was involved in sensitizing the needle. The pilot could either rub it on the lodestone before floating it or, and this was more dramatic, he could float the needle in the bowl and then magnetize it by induction. To do this he held his lodestone close to the edge of the

[1] Nicolas, N. H., *History of the Royal Navy* (1847), Vol. 2, pp. 172, 173, 180, 476, states that official records of 1338 and 1345 record the issue of 'sailing needles and dial' to royal ships, but this should be amended to read 1345-46. See Moore, A., below. It is to be noted that an inventory of a royal ship, the *Christophre* (*Xpofre*) of 1410–12 contains the following navigational instruments: iij compass, j dyoll, ij sondynglynes, j plumb. In the King's store house were also: ij saylyng nedeles ij dyoll, iij compass. Moore, A., 'Accounts and Inventories of John Starlyng', *M.M.*, Vol. 4.

bowl: as the floating needle swung towards the stone he moved the stone round the bowl. Faster and faster he swung it until he was drawing the needle round too at a good pace. When he judged the right moment had come he snatched the stone away. Bereft of its attractive influence the needle stopped circling and settled in a north-pointing direction. Such actions smacked of wizardry to the uninitiated. The pilot therefore was jealous of his art.

Besides the floating needle Alexander Neckham had also described a compass consisting of a needle rotating on a point. Thus by the close of the twelfth century the main elements of the sea-compass had been evolved. By 1218 a compass, we learn, was considered 'most necessary for such as sail the sea'.[1] By 1269, from a treatise written by a Frenchman, Pierre de Maricourt, we know that a form of compass had been developed which enabled the pilot to check the ship's course relative to magnetic north, and to take bearings. This was a dry, not a wet, compass. That is to say the compass bowl was not filled with liquid. The compass needle was mounted within the bowl on a vertical axis with a pivot at each end. The bowl was fitted with a graduated verge ring. This compass marked a further technical advance; so did a non-magnetic pin fitted at right-angles to the compass needle. By this device the moments of inertia in the two vertical planes passing through the needle at right-angles to each other were equalized. Without it the compass would have been useless in a vessel in a seaway for, under the influence of its own rolling and pitching motion the needle would have tended to turn into the plane of the ship's roll.[2] It is probable that this compass had been developed some time earlier, because in 1270, only the year after Pierre de Maricourt wrote his treatise, Louis IX of France, after six days of storm during his crusading voyage from Aiguesmortes, on the south coast of France, to Tunis, demanded to know the ship's position and was shown it on a chart to be in Cagliari Bay, Sardinia. Now such charts were drawn by plotting the compass bearings and estimated distances between places, and the oldest surviving example, which can be dated about 1275—only five years after Louis IX's experience—displays such technical excellence that it is clearly the product of a long-established skill. In short, the use of magnetic compasses designed to take magnetic bearings of objects and places from ships had been well established by the last half of the thirteenth century. An Italian ship inventory of 1294 included, indeed, 'two charts, a pair of compasses, and two lodestones'.[3] Whether by then the next step had been taken and a graduated card had been attached to the compass needle, in place of the engraved verge ring described by Pierre de Maricourt, is as yet unknown.

[1] Taylor, E. G. R., 'Early Charts and the Origin of the Compass Rose', *J.I.N.*, Vol. 4.

[2] May, W. E., 'History of the Magnetic Compass', *M.M.*, Vol. 38. May, W. E., *From Lodestone to Gyro-Compass* (1952).

[3] Taylor, E. G. R., 'Early Charts and the Origin of the Compass Rose.' *J.I.N.*, Vol 4. 'The Oldest Mediterranean Pilot', *J.I.N.* Vol. 4.

But from the excellence of the contemporary distance and bearing charts
it would seem probable that it had. The result of this development was,
of course, that it was no longer necessary to orientate the compass bowl to
the needle in order to find compass directions. The compass was now self-
indicating in all directions.

While this was a logical development, in view of the now consistent use
of charts by Mediterranean seamen, it was not easily made, for it was no
easy matter to devise a simple, strong yet sensitive instrument which,
despite the violent rolling of a vessel in a cross sea, the heavy jarring
shocks as she pounded into a head sea, and all and every alteration of course
that the master might put her through, would point steadily to north. The
solution demanded originality tempered by technical skill and balanced
by a nice sense of practical requirements. When the problem had been
solved the accuracy and frequency with which bearings could be taken
was increased, and ship-masters carried an instrument sufficiently reliable
and accurate to justify their ordering the helmsman on occasion to steer
by it instead of by the trim of the sails. This practice necessitated having
the compass permanently before the helmsman at a height and in a position
where it would be constantly visible to him by day and by night. At the
same time it had to be protected from the elements and from the ordinary
hazards of ship-board activities. As a result the binnacle or bittacle, as it
was often called, in early days, came into use. We first find binnacles
mentioned in English ship inventories of 1410–12. A binnacle—whatever
may have been its detailed form and construction in those days—was
essentially a portable wooden chest in which the steering compass was
stowed, and which could be secured to the deck before the helmsman,
care then being taken to ensure that the centre of the compass-fly lay in
the fore and aft centre-line of the vessel. The front panel of the binnacle
could be removed so that the compass, secured to a shelf within the binnacle
at a height suitable to the helmsman, could be kept constantly in view by
him. By night the compass was illuminated by a candle lanthorn placed
beside it in the binnacle, a fact which is confirmed by a German monk who
made a voyage to the Holy Land as a passenger in a three-masted galley in
1483. By these means the helmsman was able to check by day and by night
both the direction of the ship's head and the trim of his sails. In this task
he was continually supervised in Mediterranean and in all Iberian ships
by the master or his mates, using a compass in a binnacle on the poop for
the purpose.[1]

In the fifteenth century an apparent error in compasses began to be
recognized; compasses were observed to point not to the north, towards
the Pole Star, but to the east of north. By now the daily circumpolar move-

[1] Sølver, C. V., 'The Discovery of an Early Bearing-dial', *J.I.N.*, Vol. 6; Forum,
'A Norse Bearing-dial?', various authors, *J.I.N.*, Vol. 7. Naish, G. P. S., 'The
Dyoll and the Bearing-dial', *J.I.N.*, Vol. 7. May, W. E., 'The Binnacle', *M.M.*,
Vol. 40. Waters, D. W., 'Binnacles and Bittacles', *M.M.*, Vol. 41. 'Early Time and
Distance Measurement at Sea', *J.I.N.*, Vol. 8. Chaucer (c.1390) *Knight's Tale.*

Spieghel der Zeevaerdt, vande navigatie der Westersche Zee, innehoudende alle de Custe va Vranckryck Spaignen en t' principaelste deel van Engelandt, in diuersche Zee Caertē begrepe, met den gebruÿcke van dien, nu met grooter naerstichejt bÿ ēe vergadert en ghepractizeert, Door Lucas Iansz Waghenaer Piloot ofte Stuÿrman Residerende Inde vmaerde Zeestu dt Enchujsen.

Cum Priuilegio ad decennium

Reg.ÿs 5 8 3 Ma.tis
et Cancellarie Brabantie

Ioannes á Doetecum Fecit.

Ghedruct tot Leyden/ by Christoffel Plantijn/
voor Lucas Jansz Waghenaer van Enckhuysen.
Anno M. D. LXXXIIII.

III. THE LEAD AND LINE.

IV. Edward Fiennes, Lord Clinton and Saye, Lord High Admiral,
and the Sea-compass, 1562.

and lykewyse the Rose; that it decline not to one parte
oz other. And yf it be quicker then it ought to be, then
make the poynt that it goeth vpon somewhat blunter.

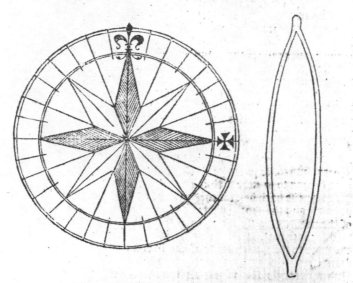

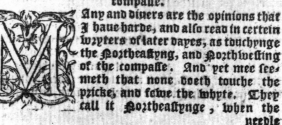

❡ The. v. Chapiter, of the effecte
oz propertie that the compasse hath to
Northeastyng, oz Northwesting
wherby is knowen the
variation of tho
compasse.

The variati on of the compasse

Any and diuers are the opinions that
I haue harde, and also read in certein
wzyters of later dayes, as touchynge
the Northeastyng, and Northwesting
of the compasse. And yet mee see-
meth that none doeth touche the
pzicke, and fewe the whyte. They
call it Northeastynge , when the
needle

V. COMPASS-FLY AND NEEDLE OF 1545.

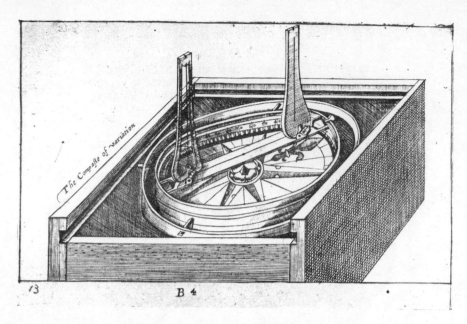

VI. The Compass of Variation, 1597.

ment of the Pole Star was known to many seamen, and was being made use of by the Portuguese pilots, but this phenomenon of variation, as the continual 'easting' of the north point of the compass was known, was a new discovery. By the Mediterranean seamen and cartographers the discovery of the discrepancy between true and compass north, even if appreciated before the late fifteenth century—which is very doubtful—was left alone. In Flanders, however, where, with the growth of trade, the manufacture of lodestones and compasses seems to have flourished from the fourteenth century, the compass-makers of the latter half of the fifteenth century, if not earlier, corrected their compasses for the variation observed in north-west Europe. This they did by so mounting the compass card or 'fly', to give it its contemporary name, on the compass needle that when the needle pointed to magnetic north the compass fly indicated approximately true north. For doing this the northern compass-makers, who all soon copied the Flemish ones, have been censured.[1]

Certainly in later years this led to a lot of confusion, and probably shipwrecks, but at the time it was not an unreasonable thing to do, for the northern ship-master, it will be recalled, did not use a chart. In the Baltic, indeed, it appears that as late as the last decades of the fifteenth century he did not even use a compass. Then he was used to steering with a rutter and a lead.[2] Free of the restrictions imposed upon Mediterranean compass-makers by a complementary and traditional art of chart-making, the Flemish compass-makers were at liberty to make innovations in the instruments they made. Perhaps they were prompted by the practice, common in north-west Europe since the middle of the fifteenth century, of

---

[1] The main authorities consulted are: Chapman, S.; Harradon, H. D.; May, W. E.; Mitchell, A. C.; Hewson, J. B. This last's *History of Navigation* (1951) does not incorporate the researches of recent years. Mitchell's researches are embodied in a fully documented critical examination of the origin of the compass which concludes: (I) That while it is possible that the Chinese were acquainted with the directive property of the magnet by A.D. 1093, they made no further use of that property for at least two hundred years thereafter. (II) That there is no evidence of the origin of any such knowledge among the Arabs, and it is improbable that they transmitted any information on the matter to Europe, their earliest mention of the compass being nearly half a century after its first mention in Europe. (III) That the compass was in use in western Europe by A.D. 1187, and taking into consideration the fact that the directive property must have been discovered much earlier, it is probable that a knowledge of that property and its application in western Europe was of independent origin and as early as, if not earlier than, that in China. Needham, J., *Science and Civilisation in China*, Vol. 1. Pt. 1, Cambridge, 1962, p. 279, proves a sea-compass in use in China by A.D. 1090.

[2] Nordenskiöld, A. E., *Periplus* (1897), p. 106, quotes a Spanish envoy's experience of sea travel in the Baltic in 1578 where he said, 'the natives never use any other chart than a small written book', i.e. a rutter. Nor was the use of the compass customary. Spekke, A., 'The Eastern Baltic Coast up to the 16th century', *Imago Mundi*, Vol. 5, cites Fra Mauro, a fifteenth-century voyager's statement 'per questo mare non se navega cum carte ni bossola ma cum scandaso'. That is, they use neither chart nor compass, only a lead for navigating.

engraving the variation upon the increasingly popular traveller's pocket sun-dials—forerunners of the modern wrist-watch. This enabled the dial to be orientated accurately and consequently the correct local time to be found. Similarly, the ship-master who used his compass-fly as a sun-dial would find the time more accurately when the fly was off-set. Whatever the source of inspiration, we find in northern waters that the compass fly was off-set in azimuth anything from half a point—$5\frac{1}{2}°$—to a whole point and a half—$17°$—to the west of the compass needle in order to compensate for the easterly variation of the compass in the particular waters in which it was intended to be used. In the Mediterranean, on the other hand, where for generations mariners had constantly used a compass in conjunction with a bearing and distance chart as well as with a rutter, variation was not allowed for by adjustment of the fly. As in the modern compass, the north point of the fly was aligned with the north point of the compass needle. Such a compass was often described in the sixteenth century as a meridional compass. At first sight the use of the meridional compass would appear to have involved the mariner of southern Europe in the problem of applying a correction for variation to every course he steered or bearing which he took when using his chart. But he knew what he was doing. He did not apply any such corrections normally, for the appropriate correction for variation was allowed for in the traditional layout of the chart which dated from the days before variation had been suspected. Consequently he had merely to read off the course on his chart which would take him to his destination, and in order to reach it, steer that course as indicated by his compass.

There are occasional crude illustrations of the mariner's or sea-compass on maps of the fifteenth century, indicating that it then consisted of a round box and a fly similar in form and layout to those in common use in the sixteenth, seventeenth, and eighteenth centuries. If not the earliest detailed illustration, certainly the earliest illustration of an English sea-compass dates from 1562.[1] The compass is shown held proudly in the left hand of Edward Fiennes, Lord Clinton and Saye, Lord High Admiral of England, who is wearing his badge of office, a golden 'call' or whistle, while the forefinger of his right hand rests on the compass box's outer edge, pointing significantly at the *fleur-de-lis* marking the north point of the fly.

It is in the third, and oldest, of the books listed by Captain John Smith on the art of navigation that the earliest description of the manner of making the mariner's common sea-compass is to be found. The similarity between this description—contained in Richard Eden's translation of 1561 of Martin Cortes's *Arte de Navegar* of 1551[2]—and the compasses

[1] See Pl. IV.

[2] Richard Eden's work is : The Arte of Nauigation Conteyning a compendious description of the Sphere with the makyng of certen Instrumentes and Rules for Nauigations: and exemplified by manye Demonstrations. Written in the Spanyshe tongue by Martin Curtes. And directed to the Emperour Charles the fyfte. Translated out of Spanyshe into Englyshe by Richard Eden, 1561. R.I. [Richard Jugge, London].

on the frontispiece of Anthony Ashley's *The Mariners Mirrour* of 1588, with an illustration in William Barlow's book *The Navigators Supply* of 1597, and an actual steering compass of the eighteenth century (in a portable binnacle) in the National Maritime Museum at Greenwich, makes it clear that all are typical of the best sea-compasses in use in England throughout the period, and that this is equally true of the compass held in the Lord High Admiral's hands in 1562. The description 'Of the makyng of the Maryners compasse for Navigation' occurs in the third chapter of the third part of Cortes's manual of navigation. We learn that on a circular piece of chart paper, four to six inches in diameter, were painted the compass points or 'winds'. The Italian seamen still often used a compass marked with the initial letters of the eight principal winds traditionally recognized in the Mediterranean, namely, T for Tramontana (north), G for Greco (north-east), Levante (east), S for Sirocco (south-east), O for Ostro (south), A for Africo (or Libeccio) (south-west), P for Ponente (west), and M for Maestro (north-west). Levante (east) was indicated not by the initial letter but by a cross. The northern compass, however, as already explained, was by now always marked with the thirty-two points still used today, and one of the first tasks of the young seaman was to learn 'to say' or, to use the modern expression, to 'box' his compass, starting from north. On all compass-flies the east point was marked with a cross, and this custom persisted into the eighteenth century. The north point was indicated by a *fleur-de-lis*, as it is to this day, a device which appears to be a formalized rendering of the thin isosceles triangle used by the fifteenth-century Italians and the Catalan eight-rayed star, imitating the stars in Ursa Minor, of which the Pole Star or Polaris is the most conspicuous.[1]

Underneath the fly was attached the compass 'wire' or needle. This was glued on with paper, and consisted of a length of iron wire, originally of the length of the circumference of the fly but bowed double and pinched together at each end until its length equalled the diameter of the fly. It thus formed an elongated hoop through the centre of which, and of the fly, a brass cone, known as the 'capital', was pushed. On this the fly could pivot. The compass box consisted of a round wooden box turned out of the solid, half the diameter of the fly in height, covered with glass, sealed in by resin, and fitted with a detachable wooden base, in the upper centre of which was fixed the brass 'pin' or pivot, for the fly.[2]

Before assembly the compass needle or 'wires' were 'fed' by being touched with 'the face of the stone', that is, with the lodestone which formed part of every pilot's outfit. The lodestone he kept in a brass filigree case, which could be locked, and hung up by a chain well clear of the compass when not required for feeding it. This had to be done fairly

[1] Winter, H., 'What is the Present Stage of Research in regard to the Development of the use of the Compass in Europe?', *Research and Progress*, Vol. 2. See Pls. V and VI.
[2] See Pls. IV and V.

frequently, for the wires, being generally of soft iron, lost their magnetism after a while. To feed his compass the pilot lifted his stone from its case, rapped it sharply, so that (as he supposed) small bearded 'icicles' appeared at its north end, 'whereon', Martin Cortes laid down, 'you shall rubbe the poynt of the iron as you wolde whette a knyfe: and so shall certen of those beards of the stone cleave and sticke faste to the iron'. This done he mounted the fly on the pin and tested it for 'quickness', blunting the end of the pin should the fly prove too lively. He then secured the base, complete with pin and fly, to the compass box. If the compass were to be used for steering or conning the ship, it was mounted in gimbals in another wooden box, either round or square, before being placed in the binnacle, in the construction of which only wooden nails were used.[1] Gimbals— the word perhaps comes from the Old French *gemel*, a twin—are two brass rings which move within each other, each perpendicularly to its plane, in such a manner that despite the movements of the ship in a seaway the compass suspended in them is kept level and the movement of the compass-fly is thus greatly reduced.[2] Cortes, who completed writing his book in 1545, appears to be one of the earliest authorities to mention gimbals. It is reasonable to suppose that gimbals were introduced with the practice of conning a ship by the compass, and consequently that they were in use in the fifteenth century. Pedro Nuñez mentioned them in 1537.

The degree of accuracy and the finish of the compass varied widely. The master mariners no doubt took good care to see that the instrument they bought was of the finest materials and craftsmanship, but the coasting pilot's compass, if it was not his own rough and ready manufacture, was often crude enough. Writing in 1597, William Barlow, in *The Navigators Supply*,[3] specifically warns mariners against the 'errors that dayly are committed in the making and framing' of the common sea-compass 'such as are in common use, and are sale-ware for Masters and Pilots'. The errors he describes must make a seaman's flesh creep to read: the fly unequally divided; the wires of the fly imperfectly joined, eccentrically mounted, rusty, roughly cut, and, to level up the fly, daubed with wax; the capital set on the fly eccentrically, likewise the pin in the base on which it pivoted; the glass cover cracked or gnarled, ill-cut and, worse, set into the cover with excess of resin; the gimbals so imperfectly made 'that you should offer a Tinker discredit to compare his works with this'; the riveting of the gimbals done with iron; iron nails holding gimbals in position; and iron nails used in the making of the very binnacle. In spite of these strictures we find him still writing in 1616 that amongst Englishmen and others

[1] *Documents and Inventories of Henry VII*, N.R.S., Vol. 8. *The Marie of the Tours* (1485). 'Compass iij, Rennyng Glasses j, Soundyng leeds j, Bitakles j.'

[2] See Pl. VI.

[3] Barlow, W., *The Navigators Supply* (1597). The full title will be found on p. 216.

An excellent example of a crudely made sea-compass is in the National Maritime Museum, Greenwich. It is a Portuguese fisherman's of the turn of this century.

'the compass needle ... is ... so hungerly and absurdly contrived, as nothing more', so that we may suspect that in the early part of the sixteenth century many compasses were no better.[1] We know that in twelfth-century ships the compass was illuminated at night. From the *Sea Grammar* we know that in Captain Smith's time for night use a special 'dark compass' was provided. On the fly of this type the points were painted in black and white only, and not in the usual bright, but at night indistinct, colours. That wooden pins were used in the construction of the best binnacles of the sixteenth and seventeenth centuries shows that deviation—the compass error induced by the presence of iron—though not named was appreciated. Indeed Captain Smith says treenails were used 'because iron nailes would attract the Compasse'; Cortes implies this.

Whether before the 1580s a lubber's line was marked on the compass box to indicate to the helmsman the position of the ship's head in relation to the fly is not clear. Cortes does not mention it. The earliest mention of such a mark on the compass bowl appears to be that in the Spaniard Zamorano's navigation manual of 1581, a later edition of which was translated into English and published in 1610.[2] Until it was introduced—and it was the increased size of ships that made it necessary—the helmsman used the masts or stem for a guide. From the accounts and inventories of Henry VII's royal ships we learn that the 'Kynge's ships' at the close of the fifteenth century carried, according to their size, from two to four compasses as part of their equipment, and it would appear that this was the usual establishment throughout the sixteenth and early seventeenth centuries.[3]

[1] William Barlow's *Magneticall Advertisements*, London, 1616.

[2] Edward Wright's *Certaine Errors in Navigation* (2nd ed.), 1610, contains a translation of a Spanish navigation manual of 1588 describing the use of the lubber's line at night.

It is interesting to find that the early form of the lubber's line was a point.

Edward Wright got a friend to translate *Compendio del arte de navegar*, dei Licendiado Rodrigo Çamorano. Impresso en Seville, Año 1588. It is almost identical with the first edition of 1581—in the 1588 edition a compass rose is substituted for a circular diagram showing thirty-two radial lines representing the rhumbs of the winds—*Compendio de la arte de navegar*, de Rodrigo Çamorano, en Seville, Año 1581. (The date in the colophon is 1582.)

In Chapter 17 this reads in the translation: 'The Sea Compasse is . . . a round box of wood . . . within two hoopes of latin . . . fastened within a square box, or a round . . . placed . . . in the midst of the pup of the ship where the bittacle standeth in a right line, which passeth from the boltsprit by the midst of the mainemast to the puppe, it serueth continually to gouerne the ship by mouing of the rudder, till the winde or the line of your compasse, towards which we desire to shape our course, stand directly towards the prow or boltsprit of the ship. They vse also for the night to marke a point within the inner part of the inner box, which in respect of the capitell of the compasse [the pivotal point of the fly] may stand directly towards the prow of the ship: And alwaies in guiding the shippe, you must take heed that the said point be continually ioyned with the winde of the rose towards which you intend your course.'

[3] *Documents and Inventories of Henry VII*, N.R.S., Vol. 8, p. 50 gives: '*The Marie of the Tours* (1485), at Hamble, Compasses iij'.

Whatever its faults, and they were often many, in the early sixteenth
century the sea-compass was, with the lead, unquestionably the English
ship-master's most vital instrument. This is not to say that he no longer
used the stars as guides. As in earlier times, he used the Pole Star, the
stella maris or *Tramontana*, easy to find by its terminal position in the tail
of the Little Bear, for finding the north. But if it was still for long the
cynosure of the lodeman's eyes on many a black and stormy night, the
lodestone could justly claim:

> I guide the Pilots course,
> his helpyng hande am I.
> The Mariner delights in me,
> So doth the Marchaunt man.[1]

The ship-master used the compass not only as a direction indicator
but also as a rough time-piece. 'It hath beene an ancient custom among
Mariners to devide the Compasse into 24 equall partes or howers, by which
they have used to distinguish time', explained John Davis, at the end of
the sixteenth century, 'Supposing an East Sunne to be 6 of the clocke,
a South-east Sunne 9 of the clocke, and a South Sunne 12 of the Clocke,
etc.,' and he gives in his *Seamans Secrets* a diagram of a compass rose
so marked.[2] This practice arose from the lack of mechanical time-keepers
and from the impracticability of using sun-dials on board ship. Some
method of time-finding was necessary in order to determine the state of
the tide. The Mediterranean seaman was little affected by tides. But on the
Atlantic coasts, and much more on the northern coasts, the rise and fall
of the tides and the changes in direction of the flowing of the tidal streams
were important considerations for the ship-master. He was particularly
concerned with knowing the times of high- and low-water at each port of
call, the depth of water at those ports at those times, and the direction of
flow of the tidal streams likely to be experienced between them. Few
ports had public clocks. Like the smaller house-clocks introduced into the
houses of the wealthy early in the sixteenth century and the little watches
—little more than rich men's novelties—public clocks erred by anything
up to an hour in the day. All had to be regulated by sun-dials, and because
of their errors had only an hour hand. Over any length of time sand-glasses

---

[1] Norman, R. *The Newe Attractive* (1581). The full title will be found on p. 153.
[2] The Seamans Secrets,

Deuided into 2. partes, wherein is taught the *three Kindes of Sayling, Horizontall,
Paradoxall, and sayling vpon* a great Circle: also an Horizontall Tyde Table for
the easie finding *of the ebbing and flowing of the Tydes, with a Regiment newly calcu-*
lated for the finding of the Declination of the Sunne, and ma*ny other most necessary
rules and Instruments, not heeretofore set foorth by any.*

Newly published by *Iohn Dauis* of *Sandrudge,* neere *Dartmouth,* in the County of
Deuon. Gent.

Imprinted at London by Thomas Dawson, dwelling at the three Cranes in the
Vinetree, *and are these* [sic] *to be solde.* 1595.

See also Appendix No. 3. See also Chaucer, "The Merchant's Second Tale".

were equally unreliable.[1] This rise and fall of the tides had been associated with the motions of the moon for many centuries. The earliest surviving tide-table, compiled by the monks of St. Albans in the thirteenth century, gives the times of high-water at London Bridge on each day of the moon's age, but without a sun-dial this was useless for seamen. They accordingly hit upon the practice of recording the times of high-water according to the age and compass bearing of the moon. For simplicity and ease of memory they noted the times of high-water at the various ports on the days of full and new moon—at 'full and change'—in terms of the compass bearing of the moon at the moment of high-water. This, since the highest high-waters or spring tides were found to occur at about full and change, became the establishment of the port. Thus the establishment of Dieppe, for example, was expressed as 'Dieppe is North-North-West and South-South-East', that is 'High-water occurs at Dieppe on days of full and new moon when the moon bears North-North-West or South-South-East' (10.30 p.m. and 10.30 a.m.); and high-water occurred on days of full and change at ports on the English coast 'betweene Start and Lisarte (Lizard)', according to the oldest English rutter, it will be recalled, 'at a west and south-west moone' (4.30 p.m. and a.m.); and 'at Dover', ran the *Booke of the Sea Carte*, 'the moon south—full Sea' (noon and midnight). If he arrived off a port whose establishment he knew, on a day other than that of full or change, the seaman had to calculate the time of high-water. This was because owing to the different motions of the sun and moon successive high tides normally occur at intervals of about 12 hours and 24 minutes. Thus in the 24-hour solar day there is a daily retardation in the times of high-water of 48 minutes or $\frac{4}{5}$ hour. In a lunar month of 30 days (more nearly $29\frac{1}{2}$ days) there is thus a complete cycle of tides. The daily retardation can thus be expressed as $\frac{24}{30}$ or $\frac{4}{5}$ of an hour. This was the retardation recorded in the St. Albans tide-table, and in Portuguese tide-tables. But this was not a convenient figure for the northern seaman, who had frequently to compute the tide and to do so with the aid of the 32 points of his compass. He therefore often adopted a daily retardation of $\frac{24}{32} = \frac{3}{4}$ hour or 45 minutes. By this means he was able to calculate quite accurately enough for practical purposes the daily change in the time of high-water by the compass bearing of the moon —the chief arbiter of the tides—and thus the time of high-water. Accordingly he adhered to the practice of marking his fly in hours, as explained by John Davis, making each point worth 45 minutes of time. When he knew the establishment of a port all he had to do to find the time of high-water on a particular day was to find from his almanac the age of the moon and add the daily retardation—one point for every day of the moon's age. Suppose that high-water at a port coincided with the moon's meridian passage at full or change, then the establishment of the port was North and South, that is, noon and midnight. As each point was worth $\frac{3}{4}$ hour, the two daily high-waters were deemed to occur at intervals of about 12 hours apart, 16 points.

[1] Findlay, J. R., 'Obsolete Methods of Reckoning Time', *Scot. Geog. Mag.*, Vol. 43.

As each day the cycle of high tide retarded one point—45 minutes—according to the compass clock, when the moon was eight days old high-water occurred at West and East, that is to say, at six in the morning and six in the afternoon. However, by using a daily retardation of 45 minutes instead of the more accurate 48 minutes, at the end of fifteen days the compass clock was one point out. This error was generally remedied by starting on the same point on the sixteenth day.[1] When the daily retardation of 48 minutes was used each day of the moon's age was taken as equal to a retardation of one compass point and three minutes.

Some idea of the accuracy of the establishments and of this rule is afforded by comparing the establishment of Dover with a modern tide-table. Dover's establishment was given as North and South—high-water at full and change at midnight and noon. On 9 March 1940 the moon was 29·7 days old and high-water occurred at Dover at 11.47 p.m. On the 10th, when it was just under one day old, high-water at Dover occurred at 12.05 p.m. On 18 March, when the moon was eight days old, high-water occurred at 5.47 p.m. According to the rutters and the rule for calculating the time of high-water by the compass rhumbs and the moon's age, it was at 6 p.m.[2]

The establishment of the various ports was given in the ship-master's rutter in the course of the sailing directions, generally for high-water, though sometimes the bearing of low-water was given instead. The haphazard arrangement was far from convenient for a ship-master sailing on a route with which he was not very familiar. In the first half of the sixteenth century a Breton of Conquet, G., probably Guillaume, Brouscon, who issued simple almanacs for farmers, hit upon the idea of issuing tide-tables for the often more or less illiterate seamen, which enabled any port's establishment to be picked out at a glance. For his tide-tables he drew rough outline charts of the coasts between Biscay, the Channel, and Irish Sea, wrote in the names of the ports on the coastline, drew a compass rose on the sea area, and linked the various ports by weaving lines to the compass point of their establishment. In addition he included eight circular diagrams, one for each of the cardinal points in half the compass. In the centre of each diagram he drew an eight-point compass rose orientated so that the point or rhumb of establishment was at the bottom.[3] Around the compass rose he drew four concentric rings divided into 29 equal parts corresponding to the 29 lunar days. The outer circle indicated the moon's

[1] Ward, F. B., *Time Measurement* (1947). A valuable paper on medieval tide-tables and tidal data up to the nineteenth century is contained in Gernez, D., 'Les Indications relatives aux Marées dans les anciens livres de Mer', *Archives Internationales d'Histoire des Sciences*, No. 7, 1949, pp. 571–91. See also Appendix No. 3.

[2] The phases of the moon for March 1940 are from Brown's *Nautical Almanac*, Glasgow (1940), and the times of high-water at Dover from *The Admiralty Tide Tables, Part I, 1940, Section A*. London (1939).

[3] See Pls. VII and VIII.

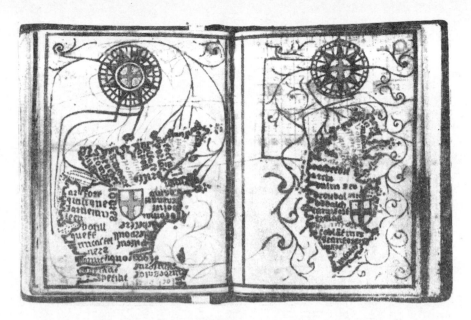

VII. Establishment of English and Irish Ports, *c.* 1548.

VIII. Circular Tide-tables for Ports with Establishment of South-south-east and South. High Water on Days of Full and Change at 10.30 and 12.00. Brouscon's Tide-tables and Almanac of *c.* 1548.

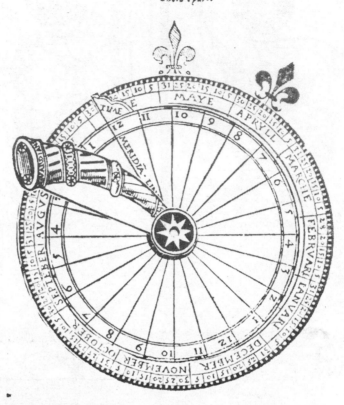

To find the houre with the instru- ment. The instrument thus ended and brought to perfection, when you desyre to knowe the houre, you shall turne the inder of the lesse rundell (in the whiche is wrytten tyme) to that part of the great rundell where is marked the daye in the whiche you desyre to knowe the houre: And directynge your face towarde the North, you shall make the head towarde the heyght of heauen, at the.19. of Apryll.

IX. A Nocturnal of 1545.

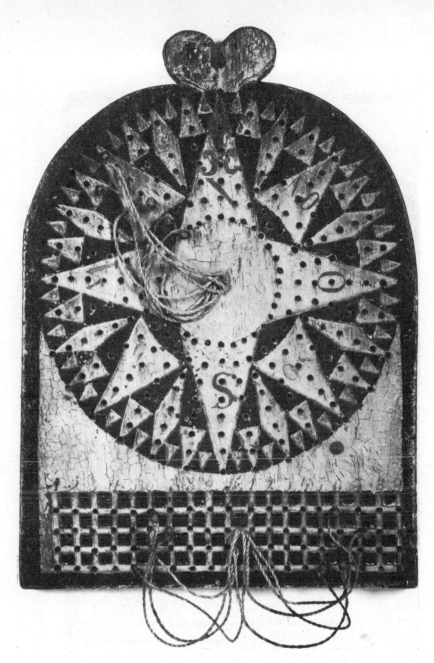

X. A Traverse Board.

XI. The Rule of the North Star, and Distance to Raise or Lay 1° of Latitude and the Almanac for January and February, in Brouscon's Tide-tables and Almanac of c. 1545.

age, and its divisions were numbered clockwise, from the bottom, from 1 round to 29 (1 was also numbered 30). The circle next to, and inside, that of the moon's age contained eight symbols, four representing the phases of the moon, and four the states of the tide—springs or neaps. The next inner circle contained the time, in hours and quarters of the hour, of high-water on each day. The innermost circle contained the times of low-water. By counting the lunar month as consisting of 29 days the cumulative error caused by the use of 45-minute differences of time instead of 48 was neatly eliminated. A calendar of the age of the moon accompanied the tide-tables, from which, knowing which one was appropriate for the establishment of the port, and knowing the age of the moon, it was simplicity itself to find the time of high- or of low-water.

Sometimes the illiterate seaman was aided in the elucidation of such tide-tables by the symbolic representation of place names. Such a printed English tide-table of 1569 survives and, indeed, had been included in an almanac.[1]

An interesting feature of Brouscon's tidal diagrams is that he showed the spring tides, that is the highest and lowest tides that occur twice each lunar month when the moon is full and new, as occurring two days after new and full moon. Comparison with modern tide-tables shows this to be correct. Brouscon's tide-tables, because of their simplicity and ease of working, were extremely popular, and at least one Englishman, John Marshall, copied them, adding an explanation of their use. A transcript of his, dedicated to the Earl of Arundel, is in the British Museum.[2]

It is to be observed that the depth of water shown in the rutters for various places rarely discriminated between the depth of water at spring tides and at other tides. For instance, when the moon is in its first and third quarters the rise and fall the range of the tide is smaller than at spring tides. The difficulty of discriminating between the different ranges of tide was caused by the lack of a common zero or basic depth of water to which the tidal range could be related. The establishment of such a level was too difficult for the times to be general, although a simple example of such differences occurs in the tide-tables of an almanac of 1569.[3] On the other hand, the effect of wind on the time of high-water was often noted for certain places. For instance, in Robert Copland's printed rutter high-water at spring tides in the Somme was noted as occurring at 'moone in the south', that is at noon or midnight, but 'with nep tides, and northe winde the moone in the south-south-east ful see', that is with neap tides a north wind caused high-water to occur an hour and a half earlier.

[1] *A verie plaine and perfecte table, etc.*, 1569. (B.M. Bagford Fragments. Harl. 593719). It is from a copy of Philip Moore's *Almanack*, see pp. 128-29.

[2] See Appendix No. 3.

[3] Hubrigh, Joachim, *An Almanack and Prognostication for the yere of our Lord God*, 1569.

What no rutter included was the strength of the tidal stream, and we may mention here that such information, though English navigators had started to collect it early in the seventeenth century, only began to be included in sailing directions in the latter part of the eighteenth century. On the other hand from the earliest times it had been recognized that the flood stream did not cease to flow off-shore at the time that it did inshore, that is at the time of high-water inshore. For example, in the English Channel the flood-stream which flows up-Channel towards the Dover Strait is extremely complex. It continues to flow in mid-Channel when inshore the tidal stream has already turned, the ebb set in. Similarly the ebb continues to flow down-Channel in the offing when inshore the flood has already set in. In the upper part of the Channel near the Dover Strait the flood continues to flow some three hours after high-water, and the ebb for three hours after low-water. For the ship-master crossing the Channel or, instead of caping, sailing in mid-Channel, this difference, which was greatest in the Straits, was obviously of importance. The phenomenon was known, and explained, by the expression that the tides in the offing flowed 'one under other' for a period measured in fractions of a tide. Thus if the flood in the offing flowed for three hours longer than it did inshore, it was said to flow tide and half tide; tide, half and half-quarter meant it flowed for five points —$3\frac{3}{4}$ hours longer: 'by longer is not meant more hours', explained Main-waring, whose explanation appears to be the earliest, 'but thus: if it be high water at the shore at twelve o'clock, it shall not be high water in the offing till it be three o'clock (which is the compass and time for the running of half a tide).' The further explanation was that, while the flood was flowing thus in the fairway, the ebb was flowing beneath it, close to the ground.

Tidal knowledge, then, was rough by modern standards, but for the times generally good enough, though it was not uncommon for ships to run aground 'from mistaking of the tide', even in well-known ports. Lack of knowledge of the strength of tidal streams was a frequent source of error, but it was one which could only be avoided by long experience of ship-handling in the waters concerned.

Although the mariner could use his compass in sunny weather as a clock or crude sun-dial, its horizontal position rendered it extremely inaccurate in these northern latitudes. Only at the times of the equinoxes, in March and September, does the sun rise due east at six o'clock, and set due west at six in the evening. In midsummer, for instance, 'for us in England (the Sunne having his greatest North declination) it is somewhat past 7 of the clocke at an East Sunne, and at a South-east Sunne it is past 10 of the clocke', to quote John Davis's explanation in his *Seamans Secrets*. In midwinter the sun rises at eight, south of east, and sets at four, south of west. Except therefore at the equinoxes, in spring and autumn, the mari-ner's compass was an extremely unreliable time indicator. At night, until the latter part of the sixteenth century, the English seaman was not much better off. Although he could tell the time by the stars he had almost

certainly to do so without the aid of the instrument—the nocturnal—
which the more sophisticated southern seaman used.[1] The Little Bear was a
favourite time indicator. Nightly it swung anti-clockwise around 'the axis
of the world', pivoting about Polaris, the Pole Star, the last star in its long
curved tail. At the head of its body the bright stars β (Kochab) and γ
served as pointers. By the position of the 'Guards' (in practice, of Kochab)
the time could be estimated. Making a wider sweep around the heavens, yet
never dipping completely from sight, was the constellation of the Great
Bear, the 'Plough' or 'Great Dipper', with its two pointers, the bright stars
Dubhe and Merak, which could be used to as good effect as those of the
'Little Dipper', particularly if Polaris and the Little Dipper were obscured.
To an observer the sun appears not only to take part in the general rotation
of the stellar system but also to have a slower motion of its own through
the stellar system, doing a complete orbit in a year. Each day it seems to
slip back a little, slantwise across the celestial sphere. Life being regulated
by solar time, the same stars rise a little earlier on each successive night.
In other words the sidereal day, the day measured by reference to the stars,
is three minutes and fifty-six seconds shorter than the (mean) solar day.
This complicates time-finding by the stars, for to an observer watching
the skies each night the Guards appear in a slightly different position at
the same solar hour, having slipped back slightly in their circuit. For
instance, early in March the Guards of the Great Dipper are in line and
high above the Pole Star at midnight. In mid-June they are due west
of it at midnight, early in September in line below it at that hour, and three
months later due east. Thus to an observer regarding them at the same
solar hour each night they appear in the course of a year to move anti-
clockwise right around the pole, or as time-keepers to lose an hour every
fifteen days. Where in March they indicated midnight, a month later, in
April, their same position will indicate ten o'clock, in May eight o'clock,
in June if they are visible, six, and so on. No doubt the keen ship-master
of early Tudor days memorized the rules giving the positions of the Guards
at midnight during the year, and could judge the time within an hour at
most seasons, or from the middle of the century referred to an almanac,
such as Anthony Askham's, containing rules for finding the time.[2] Both
methods were rough and ready, though good enough in general, for the
ship-master rarely had need to measure time accurately in hours and
minutes for purposes of calculation. Mostly he caped his way about the
seas: not always, however; it was then that he had need of a time-keeper,
and he used a sand-glass, either an hour or a half-hour glass, to enable him
to keep a check on the distance sailed. He did not use it for measuring his
speed—this he judged by eye—but having done so he could, by aid of the
sand-glass, reckon how far he had run, or, more usually, how soon he
reckoned to make his landfall. He started his hour-glass or 'rynnyng

[1] See Pl. IX. He could and sometimes did use his compass as a moon-dial.
[2] *Askham, A., An Almanacke . . . Uery pleasaunt for mariners and sea men, etc.*
(1553).

glass' at noon when the sun bore due south and appeared highest in the heavens.[1] Once again, this was only a rough check, for the sun appears to hang in the heavens at its highest point, and its change of bearing is not rapid to the unaided eye, particularly when its northerly declination is great, as in summer.

The ship-master also needed a sand-glass (Robert Copland's 'dyall', a corruption of the Latin *diurnalis* = relating to a day) for gauging the passage of the watches for the relief of the hands and the running of the ship's routine. For this purpose he kept an hour-glass or, as was customary by the seventeenth century a half-hour glass, hung in the binnacle under the eye of the helmsman, who turned the glass each time the sand ran out and marked the passage of the time by ringing the 'Watche belle' at each half-hour, sounding one stroke for every half-hour that had passed of the four-hour watch.[2]

Besides needing the running-glass for keeping a record of the distance run, the ship-master needed it for keeping a record of the courses steered in order to estimate the course 'made good' during the watch. Although, until the latter part of the sixteenth century, the English ship-master rarely used any form of chart, indeed despised the use of any such aid, we know from William Bourne that in the 1550s the 'auncient masters of shippes' reckoned that they 'could keep a better account upon a boord' of the way they had sailed. Robert Copland, writing in 1528, did not mention 'the board' as a necessary instrument, probably because it was only necessary when not caping. In the Bordeaux wine trade, of which he was thinking in particular when he wrote, the masters did mostly cape. When out of sight of land, however, for any appreciable time, as on a voyage to Portugal (to follow the coast of France and northern Spain all the way would have been uneconomic even in those days), or on the return voyage when the persistently northerly winds experienced off the coast of Portugal often forced him to work his way homeward with a long sweep out into the Atlantic, the ship-master had to keep a reckoning. He kept a 'dead reckoning'. That is, he estimated and recorded the way his ship had gone, taking into consideration not only her mean speed and course but also the effect of wind and tide, of waves and of the waywardness of his ship. He kept a record of the course steered on a 'traverse board', William Bourne's 'boord'. 'Upon the Binnacle is also the Travas', explained Captain Smith in his *Sea Grammar*, 'which is a little round boord full of holes upon lines like the Compasse, upon which, by the removing of a little sticke, they keepe an account, how many glasses (which are but halfe hours) they steare upon every point.'

Mainwaring in his *Seaman's Dictionary* of the 1620s explains further

---

[1] *Documents and Inventories of Henry VII*, N.R.S., Vol. 8, p. 323, gives *The Mary Fortune* . . . ij *Compaseys and a Rynnyng glasse* . . .

[2] *Ibid.*, pp. 258–261. *The Regent* . . . *Watche belles* ij . . . *Soundyng ledes* xiiij lb j . . . *Sowndyng Lynes feble* ij.

that it 'is for him at the helm to keep (as it were) a score . . . to save the Master a labour, who cannot with so much curiosity watch every wind and course so exactly as he at helm, especially when we go by a wind, that is sail with a following wind, and the wind veers and hauls'.

In the traverse board illustrated, rows of holes at the base enabled the estimated—or measured—speed to be recorded each half-hour by the insertion of a peg in the appropriate hole, but these were almost certainly not a feature of traverse boards before the introduction of the knotted log line probably about 1600.[1] Even so, finding the speed was not the task of the helmsman, who was partly between decks where he could see best how the sails drew. By Captain Smith's death it would appear, however, that the most capable navigators did use such an addition to the traverse board for logging their speed. It will be noticed that the thirty-two compass points each have eight holes, one for each half-hour of the watch. Every two hours or at the end of the watch the master reckoned, by sighting the pegs, the mean course steered, and noted it, together, if he were well skilled, with the distance he reckoned the ship had run, in chalk on a board or slate. He then cleared the traverse board for the next watch. That masters began increasingly to use a traverse board in the sixteenth century is indicated by the absence, after the middle of the century, of references to distances in kennings and the regular use from that time of leagues as measures of distance. A kenning could not be related conveniently to the ship's speed; a league could. A league in northern waters was 3 miles, and this was something that could be gauged, for the ships commonly sailed 3 to 4 miles in the hour.[2] If the master were particularly well advanced in his art, he probably possessed a 'martcloio' copied from some Italian, French, or Iberian pilot. Italian and Catalan pilots had been using such traverse tables, drawn on charts, since the thirteenth century. Andrea Bianco, a famous Italian cartographer and a captain of a Venetian galley in London, in 1448, has left one on one of his charts.[3] When obliged by the unfavourable direction of the wind to tack frequently, the pilot could calculate his dead reckoning much more accurately with the aid of this table. It enabled him to calculate the distance made good along the course necessary to bring him to his intended landfall. But English pilots who practised these refinements of navigation were rare in Tudor England before Elizabeth's day. If any used a traverse table, it was more probably the later Portuguese and Spanish 'Rule to Raise or Lay a Degree

---

[1] See Pl. X.

[2] Hues, R., *Tractatus de Globis et eorum usu*, London, 1594 (translation in, Hak. Soc., Ser. 1, Vol. 79), refers to vessels in the latter part of the sixteenth century on voyages to the Cape of Good Hope sailing a degree a day—60 miles in 24 hours, and this is confirmed by plotting the tracks of ships of the period as recorded in their journals.

[3] Taylor, E. G. R., 'Five Centuries of Dead Reckoning', *J.I.N.*, Vol. 3. Franco, S. G., *Historia del Arte y Ciencia de Navegar* (1947) Vol. II, p. 95.

of Latitude', which gave the distance that had to be sailed on a given course in order to raise or lay a degree of latitude.[1]

[1] 'The rule to Raise or Lay a Degree' was the formula:

$$\text{distance} = \frac{\text{difference of latitude}}{\text{cosine (course)}}$$

Given $17\frac{1}{2}$ leagues $= 1°$, then to raise or lay one degree of latitude on the following courses the distance shown opposite them had to be sailed:

Courses	Distance
North and South	$17\frac{1}{2}$ leagues
1st point 11° 15′	$17\frac{5}{6}$,,
2nd point 22° 30′	19 ,,
3rd point 33° 45′	21 ,,
4th point 45°	$24\frac{3}{4}$,,
5th point 56° 15′	$31\frac{1}{4}$,,
6th point 67° 30′	$45\frac{3}{4}$,,
7th point 78° 45′	$89\frac{2}{3}$,,

The early rules were often in error as much as $2\frac{1}{3}$ leagues on some points. See Pl. XI.

Chapter Two

THE DEVELOPMENT OF THE ART
OF NAVIGATION

*' . . . here do I not saye that Nauigation is not a thynge of antiquitie. . . .
But I saye that I am the first that have brought the arte of Nauigation into
a briefe compendiousness, geuing infaylable principles and euident demonstrations, descrybying the practyse and speculation of the same, geuying
also true rules to Maryners, and shewying wayes to Pilotes, by teaching
them the making and use of instruments, to knowe and take the altitude
of the sunne, to knowe the tydes or ebbyng and flowying of the sea, howe
to order theyr cardes and cōpasses for Nauigations, geuing them instructions
of the course of the Sunne and motions of the Moone; teaching them furthermore the makyng of Dyalles both for the day and for the night, so certen,
that in all places, they shall shewe the true houres without defaute. And
haue likewise declared the secrete propertie of the lode stone, with the maner
and causes of the Northeastinge and Norwesting (commonly called the variatiō of the compasse) with also instrumentes therunto belonginge.'*
Martin Cortes's Epistle Dedicatory to Charles V. (*The Arte of Nauigation . . . by Martin Curtes. Translated out of Spanyshe into Englyshe
by Richard Eden,* 1561.)

THE art of navigation was developed out of the art of pilotage to meet
the needs of the oceanic explorers and seamen who wished to find
their position when out of sight of land, and to ascertain the location
of new lands when they first discovered them or attempted to return to
them. The Italians, situated centrally in the Mediterranean, had for centuries been the link between East and West. Under the impetus of the
crusades they had built up great commercial empires based upon the carriage of goods by water between Italy and the Black Sea and Levantine ports
in the east, and between Italy and the Lowlands of Flanders and the Fens
of England in the north-west. Apart from force of arms the power and
wealth of the Italian Republics, of Genoa and Venice in particular, depended upon the skill of their shipwrights, seamen, and pilots. In the
thirteenth century a Genoese expedition had pushed south down the coast of
West Africa and rediscovered the Canaries. Early in the fourteenth century
the Portuguese had enlisted the services of Genoese pilots to create a navy
and explore to the southward. The Azores, 700 miles to the westward of
Lisbon, had been newly discovered. The Canaries were colonized in 1402,
the Azores thirty years later. Under the inspiration of Prince Henry the
Navigator (1394–1460) the push to the southward was continued in an
endeavour to turn the flanks of the Moslem 'infidels', and so open up new
marts. By 1471 the equator was crossed, and seventeen years later the
Cape of Good Hope rounded, and the southern route to the Indies revealed.

From 1497 when Vasco da Gama made the first voyage to India by this route the Portuguese traded regularly with the trading posts they rapidly established in the Indian Ocean and East Indies.

Although the ability of man to navigate, 'to conduct a ship' over the waters of his known world, has determined the extent of his trade, it has been the 'sufficiency' of his ship that has determined its volume, and that has made long sea voyages economically possible. The skill of the ship-builder and the wares of the ship-chandler have been vital ingredients in the development of the art of navigation. The Italians, as might be ex-pected from their long history of successful maritime commerce, were the master-shipwrights of the western world in the fifteenth and early sixteenth centuries. Indeed the stage of development already reached by western shipbuilders had much of their inspiration and experience behind it. Even in the fifteenth century the length of the oceanic voyages down the coast of Africa made bulk an essential feature of the ships that were to perform them economically. The size was necessary to enable stowage room to be sufficient for the carriage of cargoes large enough to be profitable. The long Atlantic coastline of Africa afforded few safe watering places and few places where supplies could be got for the crews; the ships, accordingly, had to be self-sufficient in food and water. As the running gear was ineffi-cient, and piracy prevalent, large crews had to be carried, and conse-quently large quantities of stores. The science of food preservation was very imperfectly understood. The best containers were found to be casks. Even so, unscrupulous suppliers or incompetent storage meant that much of the food became putrescent before it could be eaten; wine went sour and water stagnant. Dietetics were likewise not understood. In the short voyages in European waters men fed on ships' stores for only a few days, then ate on shore fresh food and fruit. At sea fresh food and fruit perished before an oceanic passage had been half completed. Scurvy set in, and the crews sickened and died. On shore there was little or no regard for hygiene, and in the summer disease stalked the narrow streets. At sea uncleanliness meant certain death on a long voyage. All this had to be learnt painfully by bitter experience, and taught by the experienced to ignorant and heedless men. Discipline had to be strict. These are aspects of the art of navigation often overlooked, but the master-pilot who over-looked them, no matter how great his skill as a pilot, sooner or later came to grief. As William Bourne put it,[1] 'the maister of shippes in Nauigation . . . ought to be such a one as can well governe himselfe, for else it is not possible for him to govern his company well . . .', and as Captain John Smith further advised,[2] 'he that desires command at Sea, ought well to consider the condition of his ship, victuall, and company . . . for there is no dallying nor excuses with stormes, gusts, overgroune Seas, and lee-shores, and when their victuall is putrified it endangers all. . . . Many suppose any thing is good enough to serve men at sea. . . . A Commander

[1] Bourne, William, *A Regiment for the Sea* (1577).
[2] Captain John Smith, *A Sea Grammar* (1627).

at sea should do well to thinke the contrary, and provide for himselfe and company in like manner.' The wise one did. Not least amongst the reasons why the English under the early Tudors were ignorant of oceanic navigation was that they not only lacked the skill with which to build 'sufficient' ships, but were ignorant too of the hygiene, discipline, and logistics necessary for successful oceanic voyaging.

The pioneer explorers of the fourteenth and fifteenth centuries had been essentially pilots—masters of the art of pilotage—finding their way at sea primarily by observation of terrestrial objects while in sight of land, and by observation of the ship's course as indicated by the compass for the short periods that they were out of sight of land. But as their voyages lengthened, and when winds were unfavourable, they had had to practise the art of calculation, using the simple traverse table already described, in order to ascertain their mean course. They had also observed as they progressed southwards the Pole Star dropping lower and lower in the northern horizon astern. On such voyages its altitude had served as a rough guide to position. Almost insensibly astronomy and cosmography had been called in to their aid. That the earth was a sphere was common knowledge to the Christian scholars in the middle ages who calculated the Church's calendar, and to the Jewish cosmographers who advised the Mediterranean seamen. Early in the thirteenth century a text-book on the doctrine of the sphere, *Sphaera Mundi*, had been written by an Englishman, John Holywood (Sacrobosco). It was in print in 1478, and a Portuguese translation was used by the Portuguese explorers. The possibility of the circumnavigation of the earth had been explained in the fourteenth century by Sir John Mandeville in his *Travels*, but, as he wrote, ' . . . for that it asketh so long tyme and also there are so many perils to passe . . . few men assay to go so, and yet', he added, 'it might be done'. The classical explanation of the cosmos known as the Ptolemaic was common doctrine to the learned schoolman and pilot.[1] It supposed the earth to be fixed to the centre of the world, and that all the celestial bodies moved around it in their daily and yearly revolutions. The world consisted of elementary and celestial parts. The elementary part consisted of four elements, earth and water which made up the sphere or earth on which man dwelt, air which encompassed the earth, and fire which filled the space between air and the sphere of the moon. These four elements were subject to continual change one into another. Enclosing them were eleven concentric spheres, each one solid yet transparent. In order, outwards, these spheres were those of the seven planets: the Moon, Mercury, Venus, the Sun, Mars, Jupiter, and Saturn. The eighth sphere was the firmament, and in this sphere were embedded the fixed stars. The ninth sphere was the crystalline Heaven or Second Mover; the tenth was the *Primum Mobile* or First Mover; the eleventh, added by the schoolmen, 'the Imperial Heaven, where God and His

---

[1] Almost every navigational work of the sixteenth and seventeenth centuries contains a description of the Ptolemaic system. It remained standard into the eighteenth century.

Angels were said to dwell'. This, like the earth, was immovable. The First Mover revolved from east to west in twenty-four hours, and by the violence of its motion carried all the other spheres, except that of the Imperial Heaven, around with it. Its axis formed the poles. Now, at the equinoxes the sun is on the celestial equator, the line on the celestial sphere equidistant from the poles. But the point on the celestial equator of this equinoctial rising marked by the fixed stars undergoes a slow change, known as the precession of the equinoxes, which returns on itself every 26,000 years—reckoned in those times to be 36,000 or 49,000 years. This motion was explained by the crystalline sphere having, in addition to its diurnal east-to-west motion, a slow west-to-east motion, which it transmitted to the firmament carrying the stars. Hence the crystalline sphere was also known as the Second Mover. Each of the seven spheres of the planets also had, in addition to the east-to-west motion imposed by the First Mover, a contrary west-to-east motion. This, which was their own and made around their own orbit, accounted for their wandering in the heavens. The orbital period of the moon was a month, of the sun a year, that of Saturn as long as thirty years. That is, thirty years elapsed before he returned to the same position relative to the fixed stars. The orbit of each of these wandering bodies was inclined to the plane of the celestial equator, and as each one circled in its course it 'declined' northward and southward among the fixed stars. The most important orbit, that of the sun, was called the ecliptic, since only on it did eclipses take place. Its inclination was about $23\frac{1}{2}°$. The five wandering stars, the planets, like the moon, had been observed to confine their motions within a belt 12° wide, 6° wide on either side of the ecliptic. This celestial girdle was known as the zodiac. The zodiac was divided into twelve signs, or sections, each 30° long. Six of them, Aries, Taurus, Gemini, Cancer, Leo, and Virgo, were northern signs, and measured northern declination; the other six, Libra, Scorpio, Sagittarius, Capricornus, Aquarius, and Pisces, the southern signs, measured southern declination. They took their names from the various constellations against which the sun had been seen to rise in its annual westward movement through the heavens along the ecliptic when the zodiac was first devised. At the spring or vernal equinox the sun had risen in line with Aries. Accordingly the first point of Aries had been taken as the datum point of the ecliptic. Owing to the precession of the equinoxes, the sun no longer rose at the vernal equinox in line with Aries. However, the point of its rising was still called 'the first point of the constellation of Aries', and the position of the sun in the heavens, its declination each day of the year, was given according to its position in the zodiac. It was recognized by scholars that the four seasons and the variation of the length of the natural day in different parts of the earth were caused by the sun's declination. They also understood the causes of eclipses.[1] By the early fif-

---

[1] Taylor, E. G. R., *Ideas on the Shape, Size and Movements of the Earth* (1943) is a valuable brief treatise on the subject from classical times to the eighteenth century. See Pl. XII.

teenth century the division of the world into parallels of latitude north and south of the equator was already marked on some maps. Meridians of longitude, lines passed through the poles to indicate position east and west on the surface of the globe, were also sometimes drawn. This was in maps as distinct from charts. Ptolemy's *Geography,* brought to Italy from Byzantium, translated into Latin by Manuel Chrysoloras and Jacobus Angelus in 1406, with maps by Francesco Lappacino, was the source of these innovations.

Parallels of latitude indicate angular distance on the earth's surface north and south of the equator, measured from the earth's centre. Meridians of longitude indicate angular distance east or west of a selected prime meridian on the earth's surface, also measured from the earth's centre. The art of the navigator consists in determining as precisely as possible with the scientific instruments and information at his disposal the angular position of his ship north or south of the equator and east or west of his prime meridian. By means of this art, whether he be within sight of land or not he can be reasonably sure of his position on the earth's surface. The problems that the voyages of discovery of the fifteenth century gave rise to involved those of developing instruments for measuring the movements of celestial objects and recording

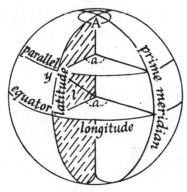

Fig. I

THE ANGULAR RELATIONSHIP OF LATITUDE AND LONGITUDE TO THE GLOBE

them, of devising simpler instruments and data suitable for use at sea, and mathematical systems of calculation whereby seamen could observe the position of celestial objects, and then calculate their ship's angular position on the globe.[1]

The great scientific achievement of the Portuguese pioneers was that they brought together and systematized navigational lore; and it was upon this approach to a scientific system of navigation that their discoveries depended. The problem facing them in their southward advance down the African coast was how to determine their position more accurately than by dead reckoning. At first they used the Pole Star. But the Pole Star did not indicate the true elevation of the pole. In the late fifteenth century it was about 3½° away from the pole, revolving about it in twenty-four hours. Today, owing to the precession of the equinoxes, it is barely 1° distant from the pole.[2] If the navigator was to determine his latitude by the Pole Star, he had to make a correction according to whether it was above, below, or to one side of the celestial pole.[3] He determined the height of the pole by observing the position of the Guards of the Little Bear as they swung around the Pole Star. A system for determining the correction to be supplied to an

[1] See Fig. 1.   [2] See Fig. 2.   [3] See Fig. 3.

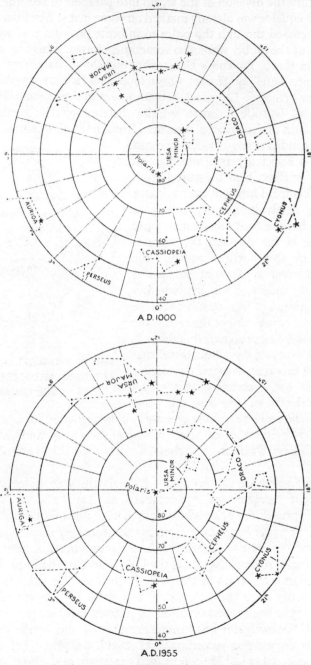

Fig. 2

THE PRECESSION OF THE EQUINOXES

Observe the polar distance of Polaris in A.D. 1000 (about 7°) and in 1955 (about 1°). In 1500 Polaris had a polar distance of about 3¼°.

The Guards of Ursa Minor and Ursa Major are conspicuous.

observation of the Pole Star, known as 'The Regiment of the North Star', was devised, and from the latter half of the fifteenth century formed part of the navigator's fund of knowledge. The earliest written directions surviving are in the *Regimento do estrolabio e do quadrante*, dated 1509? (first edition 1495 ?). 'When the guards are on the West Arm the North Star stands above the Pole one degree and a half', is one of the rules.[1] If the navigator had just taken the altitude of the Pole Star, he would accordingly subtract 1½° from his observed altitude in order to find his latitude.

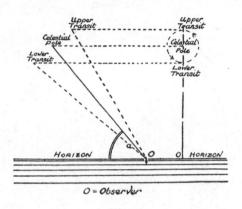

Fig. 3

THE THEORY OF THE RULE OF THE NORTH STAR

It would appear that a simple instrument to show the rules mechanically was in use in the fifteenth century, though the earliest detailed description of one in print appears to be contained in Martin Cortes's *Arte de Navegar*, written in 1545, published in 1551. This (retaining the nomenclature of the earlier instrument which had contained a human figure as a pointer) consisted of a disc or volvelle marked with the four cardinal points termed also 'The Head', 'The Foot', 'The Right Arm', and 'The Left Arm', with an inner circle drawn on it marked with the degrees of correction to be applied to the Pole Star to find the true pole.[2] The navigator rotated a pointer in the form of a trumpet, marked with the seven stars in the constellation of Ursa Minor, until it coincided with the position of Ursa Minor, holding the instrument up meanwhile and sighting the Pole Star through a hole in the centre. Martin Cortes's particular pattern was a singularly good one, as it clearly showed the rotation of Ursa Minor, including the Pole Star, around the true pole. Unfortunately he used the astronomer Werner's erroneous (1541) Polar Distance of 4° 9′ instead of the

[1] Brown, L. A., *The Story of Maps* (1949) is a somewhat erratic work on the development of cartography. It has helpful material on navigational matters such as 'The Rule of the North Star' quoted. It has a valuable bibliography. See also *The Book of Francisco Rodrigues*, Hak. Soc. Ser. 2, Vol. 90, where an early Portuguese navigation manual is reprinted and translated.

[2] See Fig. 4.

seamen's more accurate 3° 30′ of that time, which, however, he included in the text, so that he unwittingly condemned his navigators to faulty observations.

Altitudes had been taken at sea in the fifteenth century by means of the quadrant, and the astrolabe. Of these the quadrant was the first to be adapted for use by seamen.[1] As used by the astronomers who advised the pilots sent out by Prince Henry the Navigator from 1415, it consisted of a

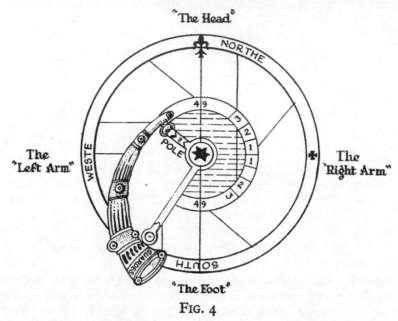

FIG. 4

DRAWING OF INSTRUMENT FOR FINDING THE RULE OF THE NORTH
STAR

From the diagram in Cortes's *The Arte of Navigation* (1561), the first English edition of his manual, which was first published in Spain in 1551.

The instrument was held out at arm's length towards the north with 'The Head' upwards. The 'Horn' was then rotated until its position relative to the Pole Star, as indicated by the main 'guard', *Kochab*, was similar to that of the stars in *Ursa Minor*. The correction in degrees was then indicated by the mouthpiece of 'The Movable Horn'. This showed that the Pole Star was 3° above the Pole and north-west of it.
    Cortes used an erroneous Polar Distance of 4° 9′ in the diagram, but gave the usual one of 3½° in the text. In fact by 1545 Polaris was less than 3° from the Pole.

quadrant of a circle, in wood or brass, graduated on the arc from 0° to 90° and fitted with two sighting vanes along one edge and a plumb-bob suspended from the apex. The altitude of the heavenly body (at first the Pole Star) seen through the sighting vanes was indicated on the arcuate scale by the plumb-line. It was not a practical instrument for shipboard use, but in the mid-fifteenth century, when the voyages were being made

[1] See Pl. III. Earliest known use of quadrant by mariner, 1460, of astrolabe, 1481.

down the African coast, this did not matter, for it was quite practicable for the pilot to go on shore to take his observation. The quadrant had the great advantages of simplicity of manufacture, a large scale, and the possibility of being used in the simple manner suited to the pilots' limited mathematical knowledge. The pilot was as yet accustomed to using only bearing and distance charts, which had no latitude scales. At first, therefore, he was taught to use his quadrant as a means of measuring his linear distance south (or north) of his port of departure, generally Lisbon. He was taught to observe the altitude of the Pole Star at his port of departure when the Guards were in a given position and to mark this elevation on the quadrant scale, as indicated by the plumb-line. Subsequently during the voyage he observed the Pole Star when the Guards were in the same position and marked on the scale where the plumb-line now cut it. He was taught that every degree division represented $16\frac{2}{3}$ leagues of 3 miles to a league. He was thus able to check by observation the distance sailed south (or north) of his datum port—if there were three divisions between the datum mark and that of his latest observation, he was 50 leagues south (or north) of his datum port. When in the middle of the century the Azores and Madeira were colonized it became the practice to mark the quadrant with the altitude of the Pole Star (with the Guards in a given position) at various points on the coast or at the islands, and the pilots then sailed down the coast to the 'altitude' and, if they were seeking one of the islands, having reached it, ran down this altitude to the westward to reach their landfall. As their mathematical ability increased, a latitude scale was added to their charts and they were taught how to convert their altitude observation by means of the rule of the North Star into observed latitude.[1] But, as already remarked, the quadrant was not an instrument suitable for shipboard use, and with the growth of oceanic voyaging the need for suitable shipboard instruments became urgent. As pilots were now accustomed to working in degrees of altitude and latitude it seemed that they might now be able to make use of instruments such as the cross-staff and the astrolabe, both of which instruments, not requiring a plumb-bob, could be used at sea. They were, however, much more complicated than the navigator needed, being graduated to serve the astronomer and astrologer in making their observations.

In 1484 King John II of Portugal formed a commission to tackle the urgent problem of position-finding by navigators at sea and in the southern hemisphere, where they no longer had the use of the Pole Star. The result of their work, tested off Guinea in 1485, was simplified solar tables, derived from those (1473-78) of the Jewish astronomer Zacuto of Salamanca, enabling the daily declination of the sun to be calculated. 'The Regiment of the Sun' enabled the navigator to use the sun as a means of latitude determination.

[1] For the early use of the quadrant by pilots and the evolution of the Rule of the North Star, see Taylor, E. G. R., 'The Navigating Manual of Columbus', *J.I.N.*, Vol. 5.

He could thus find his angular position south of the equator as well as north of it astronomically.

Like the early Pole Star observations, the first solar ones had been used by pilots for checking their linear distance north or south of a port of departure. Declination had been ignored. A noon observation had been made, at say Lisbon, on the day of departure, and on several following days during the voyage. The angular differences observed had been converted into leagues and used as the measure of the northing and southing made good. But this method, pilots had been warned, was confined to the first few days' sailing from the 'datum' port. After that the cumulative effect of the daily change in declination rendered such observations useless. The next development had been the tabulation of the sun's noon altitude on each day of the year at Lisbon, and other 'datum' ports. By this means a pilot, on observing the altitude of the sun at noon, could compare it with that at the nearest convenient datum port, determine the angular difference, convert this into leagues and so find his linear distance north, or south, of the selected datum port. He had thus still been spared the problem of allowing for solar declination—but at the price of being able to use his solar observations only as a check on the distance run north or south from the last known position, and then only provided that his track from that was roughly north or south. Clearly, as soon as he began to round the curve of the Guinea coast, and while he was sailing along the thousand miles of coastline running east and west in the Gulf of Guinea, his solar observations, if converted into leagues, were grossly misleading. The same applied to any voyages that might be made to the westward. The crossing of the equator in 1471 made the preparation and use of solar declination tables imperative if Africa was ever to be rounded and the sea route to the East found out. So the tables were prepared and the pilots were taught to apply declination to their solar meridian altitude observations. By this means they were able for the first time to find their latitude in any part of the world.

When finding the latitude by Polaris the navigator had learnt to apply the rule of the North Star in such a way that he eliminated the effect of the rotation of Polaris around the celestial pole and thus found the true elevation of the pole above the horizon. The angular distance between the pole and the horizon was, he learnt, the same as the angular distance between his place of observation and the equator, measured from the centre of the earth —in a word, his latitude. This is because, owing to the vast distances of Polaris (and of all stars) from the earth, and because of the relatively minute size of the earth, the angle made by Polaris and an observer's horizon on the earth's surface is, for all practical purposes, the same as the angle made by Polaris with the rational horizon passing through the earth's centre. This is the same as the angle, at the earth's centre, between the observer's zenith and the equator, which is the angle of his latitude. Thus, suppose the altitude of the celestial pole be found to be 48°, then the celestial pole makes an angle of 48° with the rational horizon at the earth's centre. Now the zenith is, by definition, 90° overhead from the horizon. Therefore the distance between the celestial pole and the zenith, the zenith distance, is 90° − 48° = 42°. But the celestial equator is also, by definition, 90° distant from the celestial pole. Consequently the zenith must be 48° distant from the celestial equator. As the zenith is vertically above the observer's position on the earth's surface, the observer must be in latitude 48°, that is 48° from the equator. In short, the angle between the

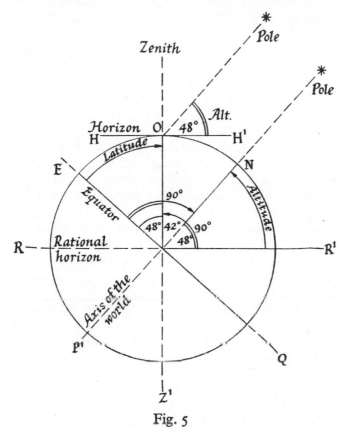

Fig. 5

THE THEORY OF THE DETERMINATION OF LATITUDE BY
OBSERVATION OF THE POLE STAR

Altitude of the Pole Star, corrected by the Rule of the North
Star, 48°, therefore latitude of observer is 48° N.

celestial pole and an observer's horizon is the same as the angle between the celestial equator and the observer's zenith, consequently it is equal to his latitude.[1]

To find the latitude by the sun the navigator was taught to find the altitude of the sun by observation of its meridian passage, when its height above the horizon is greatest, and to write this down. He was then taught

[1] See Fig. 5.

how to look out the sun's declination for that day in his 'Regiment of the Sun', and to write that down beneath the entry of the sun's observed meridian altitude. He had now to consult certain written rules instructing him how to convert these astronomical data into his angular position north or south of the equator. The rules depended upon whether he was north or south of the equator, whether the sun's declination was north or south of the celestial equator, and whether it was greater or less than the latitude when both had the same name.[1] The rules were framed so as to determine first the altitude of the celestial equator above the observer's horizon. Having found this he was taught that the result subtracted from 90° gave him his latitude. Thus, for example, if the navigator were well north of the equator, observed the sun's meridian altitude to be 62°, and found its declination to be 20° N, his rules instructed him to subtract the sun's declination from its altitude in order to find the elevation of the celestial equator—in this example he would find it to be 42°—and then to subtract this angle from 90° in order to obtain his latitude—in this example 48° N.[2] Had the navigator taken a similar observation six months later, on looking out his declination he would have found it to be 20° S and he would have had to apply a different rule. In being taught to reduce the sun's observed altitude into terms of the celestial equator's altitude and then to subtract this from 90°, the navigator was really being made to measure the angle between the celestial equator and his zenith, which, as we have seen in discussing the Pole Star sight, was the measure of his latitude. It would therefore have been simpler if the navigator's instruments—quadrant, astrolabe, or cross-staff—had been graduated with 0° at the zenith and 90° on the horizon instead of, or, since he might need them for star sights, in addition to, being graduated from 0° on the horizon to 90° at the zenith. By this means, as a result of observing the sun's meridian altitude he could have read off the sun's observed *zenith distance* on the scale on his instrument. The rules of how to apply declination would then have been worded so that latitude was obtained simply by adding or subtracting the declination from the zenith distance.[3] In general the more roundabout method was employed. The explanation for this would seem to lie partly in the fact that the instruments of observation had originally been designed primarily for measuring the altitude of celestial bodies and therefore, on adaption to nautical use, re-

[1] These rules were often expressed in very involved terms, and included observation of the direction of the observer's shadow. They can nowadays be expressed by the simple formula, $l = d - Zm$, where the latitude, l, is expressed as a function of the sun's declination, d, and of the meridional zenith distance, Zm, northern declination and latitude being considered as positive ($+ ve$), southern as negative ($- ve$), and Zm as positive or negative according to whether the observation was made towards the north or south.

[2] See Fig. 6.

[3] By the opening of the sixteenth century some Portuguese navigators were observing zenith distance instead of altitude, and were using appropriately engraved instruments, but the Spaniards, from whom the English learnt so much, do not appear to have done so until much later.

tained this scale; partly in the adaption to nautical use of thirteenth-century
Spanish rules originally designed for the determination of latitude by
measuring altitude; and partly in nautical tradition, continuance of the
practice of observing the sun's altitude for position-finding although it was

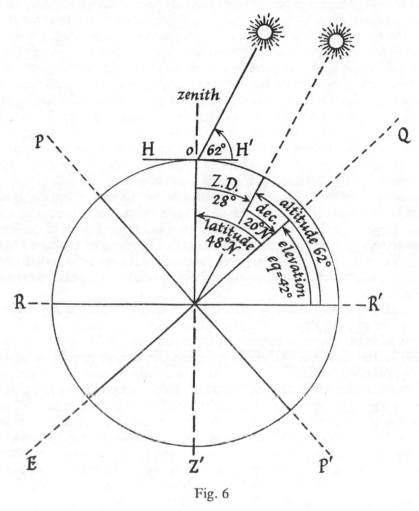

Fig. 6

THE THEORY OF DETERMINATION OF LATITUDE BY OBSERVATION OF THE
MERIDIAN ALTITUDE OF THE SUN

Sun's altitude	62° S.
Sun's declination	20° N.
Altitude of the equinoctial	42° N.
Latitude of the observer	48° N.

now angular distance from the equator and not linear distance from a
'datum' port that was required. The existing astronomical tables expressed
the sun's annual (apparent) motion around the earth in terms of its angular
movement, through each of the twelve signs of the zodiac, along the ecliptic.

What the navigator wanted was a record—a prediction—of the sun's angular position north or south of the equator. Sometimes he was given tables to enable him to convert the sun's recorded diagonal movement—relative to the celestial equator—along the ecliptic into its vertical movement north or south of the celestial equator.[1] Sometimes the conversion was done for him, the results being tabulated for noon for each day of the year.[2] In either case the most obvious thing to do with the declination when found, since the result was expressed in terms of the sun's position north or south of the celestial equator, was to treat it as a correction of the sun's altitude for finding the celestial equator's altitude. That it could serve equally well as, and be tabulated as, a correction of the sun's zenith distance for finding the celestial equator's zenith distance was not generally recognized. The result was that the method of finding latitude from the sun's meridian altitude was usually more laborious than was strictly necessary. Moreover the rules formulated were not always expressed as clearly as they might have been. In fact, by the sixteenth century the seaman who could call himself a navigator because he could find his latitude by the rule of the Pole Star could no longer do so unless he could apply with equal confidence and accuracy the much more extensive and complicated Regiment of the Sun. Indeed in order to justify the appellation of navigator he had to have a firm grasp of the theory of astronomical observations for position-finding and, in order to be able to put it to practical use, to be something of a mathematician.

Unlike the Pole Star's Regiment, which scarcely changed appreciably in a century, the Regiment of the Sun remained reasonably accurate for only about twenty years. It had then to be recalculated. In addition to this, due to the fact that the earth completes its annual motion in about $365\frac{1}{4}$ days and not exactly in 365, the sun's daily position in the ecliptic changes during every cycle of four years: by the sixteenth century, therefore, the best navigators used almanacs with four declination tables. These gave the sun's declination in leap years and in the first, second, and third years after leap years. Other navigators were content with the simpler single-table type of almanac possibly calculated for the leap year March 1475 to February 1476. As the order of accuracy of the four-year tables was to within 5' to 10', even this single table was in practice far more accurate than was necessary. The navigator observed without the aid of optical instruments. Telescopes were not developed until 1608, and optical sights later. Open-sight observations at this time by even the most skilled navigator were rarely more accurate than to within half a degree (30').

The Portuguese *Regimento do estrolabio e do quadrante* of 1509, already noticed, was a sort of nautical almanac. But besides containing the rule of the North Star, the Regiment of the Sun, a calendar, and declination table for a leap year, it included a traverse table for raising and laying a degree of latitude, and Sacrobosco's explanation of the universe—*De*

[1] See Pls. XIII, XIV and XV.   [2] See Pl. XVI.

Sphaera Mundi. It was both the first of the printed nautical almanacs and the first of the printed manuals of navigation.

The Arabs had for long used the *kamal* at sea. The primitive one consisted of nine rectangular boards of different sizes threaded on a length of cord through a hole in the centre. One or other of the boards was held out towards the star to be observed, the end of the cord being gripped between the teeth or in the hand and held close to the eye. The board chosen was that which allowed of the horizon being just seen under the

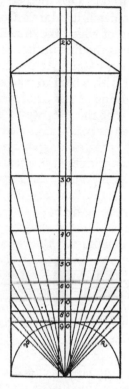

FIG. 7

METHOD OF GRADUATING THE MARINER'S CROSS-STAFF
(After the drawing in Cortes's *The Arte of Navigation* (1561))
The cross-staff was adapted for the use of seamen at the
beginning of the sixteenth century.

lower edge and the star on the upper. Thus according to the board used, the altitude of the star was known. Later versions consisted of a rectangular board, its length being twice its breadth, threaded on a cord with seven knots along its length. Thus with one *kamal* fourteen different altitudes could be observed. This simple instrument was first made known to European navigators by the Arabian pilot whom Vasco da Gama employed to cross the Indian Ocean in 1498. It may have inspired the adaptation of the complexly graduated astronomer's cross-staff for nautical use in the early sixteenth century. The mariner's cross-staff consisted of a straight staff, four-square, graduated on one side in degrees and minutes. It was commonly made of pear or boxwood. A wooden cross-piece made so as to slide evenly along the staff formed the other part of the instrument, which was usually about 3 feet long and about $\frac{3}{4}$ inch in cross-section; greater length caused increased handling difficulties in a breeze. Except that one end was held to the eye, the cross-staff was used like the *kamal*, the cross taking the place of the board, but it had the advantage of having the staff graduated from about 20° to 90°. One method of graduation and of construction can be followed in detail in Martin Cortes's book on navigation, from the English translation of which the drawing showing the method of graduation is copied.[1] He was the first author to publish, for the guidance of seamen, how to make a cross-staff. At the best of times the cross-staff was not an easy instrument with which to take accurate observations. The successful simultaneous sighting of star or of sun's centre and the horizon, done by the rapid blinking of the eye, was a difficult knack to acquire. Add to this the error, known as parallax, caused by the observer not holding the eye end of the staff at the exact spot against his cheek-bone which ensured that its end coincided with the eye's centre, the difficulty of keeping the cross in the plane of the meridian, the vertical plane, throughout the observations; add on to that the fact that the shooting of the sun at its meridian altitude was a quite lengthy business entailing the retention of an arm-aching posture and eye-blinding attitude for minutes on end, and something of the skill and long practice that were necessary can be appreciated.[2] The exact time of the sun's meridian passage being unknown, the navigator had to shoot it for some minutes beforehand. As soon as he found that to keep the sun's centre and the horizon just in view he was sliding the cross no longer towards his eye but away from it, he knew the sun had passed its maximum altitude. To gauge this instant was no easier than to retain a steady posture on a heaving deck. As originally developed the cross-staff had definite limitations. It could not be used to sight the sun below 20° of altitude because its graduations ended there, nor in practice above 60° of altitude, although it was graduated up to 90°. The cause was two-fold. In the first place the observer's scan of eye was limited physically to a maximum arc of 60°; in the second place, even if he could shoot the sun above 60°, the graduations on the staff became so small that the slightest error in observation made a difference of degrees to the observed altitudes. Also, it must be remembered, in latitude 40° N, approximately the latitude of Lisbon and the Azores, the sun is already transiting 50° above the southern horizon in the middle of March—the equinoxes. This altitude increases, at first rapidly, with the advancing year. At midsummer the sun transits $73\frac{1}{2}$° above the horizon. Not until September does it reach the 60°s again; not until the equinox—23 September—does it transit once again 50° above the horizon. Thereafter, in the winter

[1] See Fig. 7. The earliest reference to a nautical cross-staff is *c.* 1514.
[2] See Pl. XVII.

months, it transits lower and lower over the horizon until, at midwinter, it makes its lowest meridian passage at an altitude of 46½°. Thus in latitudes below about 35° N (below 35° S, in the winter months) the cross-staff could not be used for solar sights. A navigator in more northern waters could use it in the summer months, however, though not in the winter months, as the following table shows:[1]

	Latitude	Sun's Declination	Sun's Meridian Passage Altitude
Vernal Equinox 21 March	⎰20° N		70° S
	⎱50° N	0°	40° S
Summer Solstice 21 June	⎰20° N		86½° N
	⎱50° N	23½° N	63½° S
Autumnal Equinox 23 September	⎰20° N	0°	70° S
	⎱50° N		40° S
Winter Solstice 21 December	⎰20° N		46½° S
	⎱50° N	23½° S	16½° S

In latitude 60° N the sun's altitude becomes respectively 30°, 53½°, 30°, and 6½°.

Between roughly 20° N and 20° S, the cross-staff could be used at no season of the year—even at midwinter the sun's altitude was too great.

The medieval astrolabe was an instrument of exquisite workmanship which enabled the astronomer not only to observe the altitudes of heavenly bodies but also to plot their positions and follow their motions in the sky on a planisphere. Essentially it consisted of a brass disc engraved with a stereographic projection of the celestial sphere covered by a net-like plan of the heavens, graduated in degrees around its perimeter, fitted with a suspension ring at its top edge and a rotatable sight bar or alidade at its centre.[2] Stripped of all its astronomical accretions it became a sea-astrolabe. The earliest ones appear to have been of wood, or discs of brass, but an improved cast brass model was later developed. It was a thick, heavy openwork ring of solid brass, to resist corrosion, reduce wind-resistance, and yet gain stability, suspended from a ring, graduated in one quadrant from 0° to 90°, and fitted with an alidade consisting of a bar with two sighting vanes, not so widely spaced as to make sighting difficult, each having a small and

[1] On observations made during Frobisher's second voyage to the north-west (1577) we read:

here the North Starre is so much elevated above the Horizon that with the staffe it is hardly to be well observed and the degrees in the Astrolabe are too small to observe minutes. Therefore wee alwaies used the staff and the sunne as fittest instruments for this use.

Hakluyt's *Principal Navigations*, Hak. Soc., Extra Ser., Vol. 7, p. 317.

[2] See Pls. XVII and XVIII.

large sighting hole. To reduce wind resistance further, the size of the astro-labe was kept down to 5 or 6 inches in diameter, even though this had the disadvantage of reducing the size of the graduation and so the accuracy of observations. English navigators, when later they took to the use of the astrolabe, preferred larger ones, 6 or 7 inches in diameter, and with wider-spaced sighting vanes. By then the astrolabe generally had two quadrants divided into 90°, so that the navigator could avoid instrument errors caused by faulty graduation or suspension. By taking sights in succession, using each quadrant, he could check his instrument for error.[1]

Once again we are indebted to Martin Cortes for the earliest description of the method of making, graduating, and using the astrolabe. For taking a sight it was suspended not by the thumb but 'by a threade or lyne' held in the hand. The navigator used a pair of sighting holes 'as bigge as may conteyne a great pinne' for shooting a star, and another 'so subtile and small as a fyne sowyng needle' for shooting the sun.[2]

As indicated by the now numerous almanacs in print, the navigator was no longer confined to the use of the Pole Star at night. The stars, as they steadily rise and set across the night sky, rotate around the pole. Those conspicuous ones whose distance from the pole had been tabulated could be observed at their meridian transits, either north or south, above or below the pole, exactly as was the Pole Star, Polaris. The reason why Polaris was preferred was that it could be observed not only at the time of its meridian transits but, thanks to the rule of the Pole Star, at any time; because it was easy to pick out and easy to identify; because, just like shooting the sun, the meridian transit of stars more distant from the pole meant judging the moment of transit not by the relative positions of Guards but by the change in altitude; because the best time for taking star sights with a cross-staff is at sunset and dawn when the stars are still bright in the heavens and the skyline sharp and clear against the diffused light of the sun, and Polaris was the only star which would probably then be observable: the others might transit hours earlier or later when the hori-zon was indistinguishable from the night sky; and because the position of Polaris had been pretty accurately observed, the positions of other stars not always so accurately. However, the navigator in low northern and in southern latitudes had no choice. His favourite star was in the Southern Cross, first seen in 1455, for which a 'Rule', on the lines of that of the Pole Star, had been evolved, using the Southern Cross itself as a 'guard', by Pero Añes about 1505. The rule was that when the head and foot of the Crozier, as the Southern Cross was often called, were in line with a plumb-line held out before the navigator, the Cock's Foot was 30° above the south pole. Therefore, having taken the altitude or height of the Cock's Foot above the horizon, he subtracted 30° from the altitude, the

---

[1] See Pl. III.   A sketch of 1517 of a cast sea-astrolabe is the earliest known. See: L de Albuquerque, Projecção da Náutica Quinhenista Portuguesa na Europa, Lisboa, 1972, 185, Vol. 11.

[2] See Pls. XVIII and XIX.

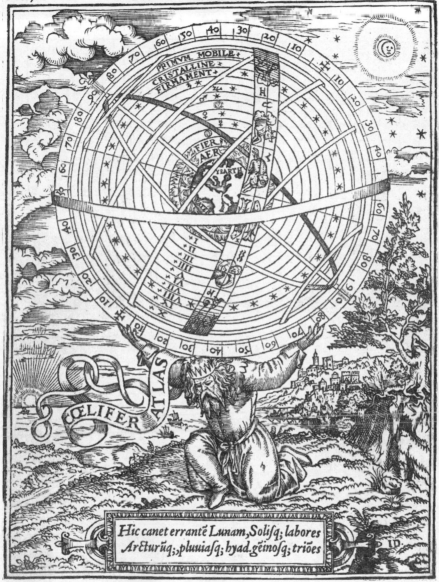

XII. The Ptolemaic World System.

The Table of the Equations of the Sunne.

The yeere of our lord to be abbreuiated	The equation	The yeere of our lord to be added	The equation	The yeere	The equation	The yeere	The equation
1545	I 0	1581	I 1	1617	I 16	1653	I 48
1546	45	1582	I 1	1618	45	1654	I 33
1547	30	1583	46	1619	I 2	1655	I 18
1548	15	1584	32	1620	47	1656	I 3
1549	I 2	1585	18	1621	33	1657	I 49
1550	47	1586	3	1622	18	1658	I 34
1551	32	1587	48	1623	48	1659	I 19
1552	18	1588	33	1624	49	1660	I 4
1553	4	1589	19	1625	35	1661	I 51
1554	49	1590	4	1626	20	1662	I 36
1555	34	1591	49	1627	5	1663	I 21
1556	19	1592	35	1628	51	1664	I 7
1557	5	1593	21	1629	37	1665	I 53
1558	50	1594	6	1630	22	1666	I 38
1559	35	1595	51	1631	7	1667	I 23
1560	21	1596	36	1632	53	1668	I 9
1561	7	1597	23	1633	38	1669	I 55
1562	52	1598	8	1634	23	1670	I 40
1563	37	1599	53	1635	8	1671	I 25
1564	23	1600	39	1636	54	1672	I 10
1565	9	1601	25	1637	40	1673	I 56
1566	54	1602	10	1638	25	1674	I 41
1567	39	1603	55	1639	10	1675	I 26
1568	25	1604	40	1640	56	1676	I 12
1569	11	1605	26	1641	42	1677	I 58
1570	56	1606	11	1642	27	1678	I 43
1571	41	1607	56	1643	12	1679	I 28
1572	26	1608	42	1644	58	1680	I 13
1573	12	1609	28	1645	44	1681	I 0
1574	47	1610	11	1646	39	1682	I 45
1575	43	1611	42	1647	14	1683	I 3
1576	28	1612	28	1648	0	1684	I 15
1577	14	1613	12	1649	46	1685	2 2
1578	59	1614	59	1650	31	1686	I 4
1579	44	1615	45	1651	15	1687	I 3
1580	30	1616	30	1652	I 1	1688	I 18

The 2. part.

Of the Sunne.

Mo. neths. Daies	June. Cancer.		August. Leo.		September. Virgo.		October. Libra.		November. Scorpio.		December. Sagitta.	
1	18	26	18	2	18	4	17	39	18	49	19	24
2	19	23	19	0	19	2	18	39	19	50	20	26
3	20	20	19	58	20	0	19	58	20	51	21	27
4	21	17	20	55	20	58	20	38	21	52	22	29
5	22	14	21	53	21	57	21	38	22	53	23	30
6	23	11	22	51	22	56	22	38	23	54	24	31
7	24	8	23	48	23	55	23	38	24	55	25	33
8	25	5	24	45	24	54	24	38	25	56	26	34
9	26	2	25	44	25	54	25	39	26	57	27	36
10	27	57	26	42	26	53	26	39	27	58	28	37
11	27	55	27	40	27	51	28	39	28	59	29	38
12	28	57	28	38	28	51	28	39	0 47		0	39
13	29	51	29	36	29	50	29	39	1		0	40
14	0 48		0 34		0 49		0 39		1	1	42	
15	1	46	1	30	1	48	2	40	2	3	43	
16	2	43	2	30	2	47	3	40	3	4	45	
17	3	40	3	28	3	46	4	41	4	6	46	
18	4	38	4	26	4	45	5	41	6	8	48	
19	5	35	5	24	5	44	6	42	7	9	49	
20	6	32	6	22	6	44	7	42	8	7	51	
21	7	30	7	21	7	44	8	43	9	8	52	
22	8	27	8	19	8	43	10	11	10	11	54	
23	9	25	9	17	9	42	10	44	11	11	55	
24	10	22	10	16	10	42	11	45	14	11	57	
25	11	20	11	14	11	41	12	45	15	13	58	
26	12	17	12	13	13	41	13	46	16	15	59	
27	13	15	13	11	13	41	14	47	19	16	1	
28	14	12	14	10	14	40	16	47	20	17	3	
29	15	10	15	8	15	40	16	48	22	18	5	
30	16	7	16	7	16	39	17	49	23	19	6	
31		17	5	17			17	49		20	10	7

XIII and XIV. DECLINATION TABLES, 1545-1688.

Plate XIII gives the first table for calculating the true place of the sun in the Zodiac. The table for the months July (misprinted June) to December is shown. Plate XIV gives the Table of the Equation of the Sun. Whereas Medina in his manual of 1545 gave the sun's declination in terms of its distance at noon north or south of the equinoctial (see Plate XVI), Cortes retained the customary astronomical method by which it was expressed in terms of the degrees of the signs of the Zodiac – the true place of the sun in the Zodiac. This method necessitated conversion into declination. The method was as follows: in the first table, 'The Table of the true place [of the sunne]' (Plate XIII), the month was looked out at the head of the table, the day of the month on the column on the left; then against the day, under the month was given the sun's position in degrees and minutes of the sign of the Zodiac shown under the month heading; to the degrees and minutes thus found was added 'The Equation of the Sun' for the year; this was found in the next table, 'the Table of the Equations of the Sunne' (Plate XIV); the sum of the two sets of figures was the true place of the sun in the Zodiac, except that in common or non-leap-years, from the end of February to the end of December 1° had to be subtracted from the sun in order to get the true place. The true place of the sun having been found, the declination was obtained from the third table (Plate XV). This contained at the head the Signs of the Zodiac in which the sun's declination increased; on the left the degrees of the Signs from 0 to 30, downwards; at the foot the Signs in which the declination decreased and on the right the degrees of the signs from 0 to 30, upwards. If the true place of the sun had been found in minutes as well as degrees the declination had to be obtained by interpolation.

Sig- nes.	♈ ♎		♉ ♏		♊ ♐		Sig- nes.
G	G	M	G	M	G	M	
0	0		11	30	20	12	30
1	0	24	11	51	20	25	29
2	0	48	12	12	20	37	28
3	1	12	12	33	20	49	27
4	1	36	12	53	21	0	26
5	2	0	13	13	21	11	25
6	2	23	13	33	21	22	24
7	2	47	13	53	21	32	23
8	3	11	14	13	21	42	22
9	3	35	14	32	21	51	21
10	3	58	14	51	22	0	20
11	4	22	15	10	22	9	19
12	4	45	15	28	22	17	18
13	5	9	15	47	22	25	17
14	5	32	16	5	22	32	16
15	5	55	16	23	22	39	15
16	6	19	16	40	22	46	14
17	6	42	16	57	22	52	13
18	7	5	17	14	22	57	12
19	7	28	17	31	23	3	11
20	7	50	17	47	23	8	10
21	8	13	18	3	23	12	9
22	8	35	18	19	23	15	8
23	8	58	18	34	23	19	7
24	9	20	18	49	23	22	6
25	9	42	19	4	23	24	5
26	10	4	19	18	23	26	4
27	10	26	19	32	23	28	3
28	10	47	19	46	23	29	2
29	11	9	19	59	23	30	1
30	11	30	20	12	23	30	0
Sig- nes.	♓ ♍		♒ ♌		♑ ♋		Sig- nes.

whiche the Sunne shall be founde in that day, shall you seke in the front oz foote of the table. And yf it be in the front, you shal seke the nomber of the degrees on the left syde. And if it shal- bee at the foote of the table, you shall seke it on the right syde. Then aboue oz vnder the signe in the front of that degree of the sayde signz, you shal find two nubers: wher of the fyzst is of de- grees, and the se- conde of minutes: and those degrees & minutes of decli- natyon hathe the Sunne that daye. And this is vnder- stode without ha- uyng respect to the od minutes aboue the degree, whiche the true place of the Sunne hath.

And yf you de- syze to verifye this moze pzecyselye, note the declinati- on of that degree, & of the degree fo- lowyng:

XV.

Plate XV gives the third table involved in the calculation of the declination of the sun. Cortes gave the following example:

'In the yeare 1546 the tenth day of September, the Sunne shalbe in 26.D.38.M. of Virgo [1546 was not a leap-year]: and to the 26 D. presyse, shall corresponde 1 D. 36 M. of declination. And to veryfye the declination that commeth to 38 minutes, which is more of the 26 D. (which is one D. 36 M.) to the declination of 27 D. whiche is 1 D. 12 M. The difference is 24 D. Of these you must take such part as is 38 of 60 which are almost twoo terces. Then two terces of 24 are 16 which must be taken of one D. 36 M. which corresponde to the 26 D. of Virgo: because the declinations go decreasynge [the sun was approaching the equinoctial on its southerly, autumnal descent], and remayneth 1 D. 20 M. And if the declinations increase, you must adde thereto, as you take away when they decrease.'

Thus the declination was 1° 20′ N.

The signs of the Zodiac:

Aries	♈	Libra	♎
Taurus	♉	Scorpio	♏
Gemini	♊	Sagittarius	♐
Cancer	♋	Capricorn	♑
Leo	♌	Aquarius	♒
Virgo	♍	Pisces	♓

Declinacion del sol.

Año Segundo.

Abril			Mayo			Junio		
Dias	G	M	Dias	G	M	Dias	G	M
1	viij.	x vj.	1	x vij.	xl jx.	1	xx iij.	viij.
2	viij.	xxxviij	2	x vij.	vj.	2	xx iij.	x ij.
3	viij.	l ix.	3	x viij.	xx.	3	xx iij.	x vj.
4	ix.	xx j.	4	x viij.	xxx v.	4	xx vij.	xx.
5	ix.	xl ij.	5	x viij.	l.	5	xx iij.	xx iij.
6	x .j	iiij.	6	x ix.	iiij.	6	xx iij.	xx vj.
7	x.	xx v.	7	x jx.	x viij.	7	xx iij.	xx viij.
8	x.	xl vj.	8	x jx.	xxx j.	8	xx iij.	xx ix.
9	x j.	vij.	9	x ix.	xl iiij.	9	xx iij.	xxx j.
10	x j.	xx vij.	10	x ix.	xl vij.	10	xx iij.	xxx ij.
11	x j.	xl viij.	11	xx.	x.	11	xx iij.	xxx iij.
12	x ij.	ix.	12	xx.	xx ij.	12	xx iij.	xxxiiij.
13	x ij.	xx viij.	13	xx.	xxx iiij.	13	xx iij.	xxxiij.
14	x ij.	xl viij.	14	xx.	xl iiij.	14	xx. iij.	xxx ij.
15	x iij.	viij.	15	xx.	l vj.	15	xx iij.	xxx i.
16	x iij.	xx vij.	16	xx i.	vij.	16	xx iij.	xx ix.
17	x iij.	xl vj.	17	xx i.	x viij.	17	xx iij.	xx vij.
18	x iiij.	vj.	18	xx i.	xx viij.	18	xx iij.	xx v.
19	x iiij.	xx v.	19	xx i.	xxx vij.	19	xx iij.	xx iij.
20	x iiij.	xl iiij.	20	xx i.	xl vj.	20	xx iij.	x ix.
21	x v.	j.	21	xx i.	l v.	21	xx iij.	x vj.
22	x v.	x ix.	22	xx ii.	iiij.	22	xx iij.	x ij.
23	x v.	xxxvij.	23	xx ii.	x ij.	23	xx iij.	vij.
24	x v.	l v.	24	xx ii.	xx.	24	xx iij.	iij.
25	x vj.	x ij.	25	xx ii.	xx vij.	25	xx ii.	l viij.
26	x vj.	xx ix.	26	xx ii.	xxxiiij.	26	xx ii.	l iij.
27	x vj.	xl v.	27	xx ii.	xl j.	27	xx ii.	xl vij.
28	x vij.	iij.	28	xx ii.	xl viij.	28	xx ii.	xl.
29	x vij.	x ix.	29	xx iij.	l ij	29	xx ii.	xx iij.
30	x vij.	xxx iiij.	30	xx ij.	l viij.	30	xx ii.	xx vij.
			31	xx iiij	iiij			

XVI. DECLINATION TABLE FOR 'ABRIL-MAYO-JUNIO' 2ND YEAR AFTER A LEAP YEAR, 1545.

GVARDAS

Polo

NORTE

ORIZONTE

Libro tercero del altura del Norte.

XVII. Taking a Pole-Star Sight with a Cross-staff, 1552.

ORIZONTE

Libro segundo del altura del Sol.

XVIII. Taking a Meridian Altitude Observation of the Sun with an Astrolabe, 1552.

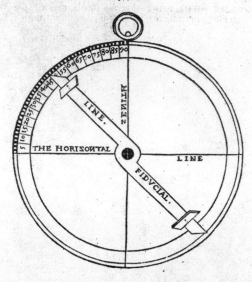

To take the altitude of the Sunne, hange vp the Astrolabie by the rynge: and set the Alhidada against the Sunne. And rayse it o2 put it downe in the quarter that is graduate, vntyll the beames of the Sunne enter in by the lyttle hole of the tablet o2 raysed plate, and p2ecysely by the other lyttle hole of the other tablet. Then looke vppon the lyne of confydence. And howe manye degrees it sheweth in the quarter that is graduate (begynnynge fro the Ho2izontall lyne)so many degrees of height hath the Sunne. In lyke maner shall you doe to take the altitude of any other Starre lookynge tho2ough the greate holes,

To take the altitude of the Sunne.

XIX(a). SPANISH SEA-ASTROLABE OF 1545.

XIX(b). Sea-Astrolabe, probably Portuguese, of 1555.

Here followeth the Mariners Quadrant.

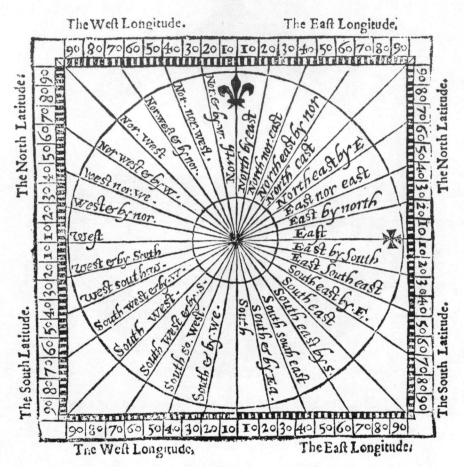

XX(a). THE SHIPMAN'S QUADRANT OR THE MARINER'S QUADRANT—
BLUNDEVILLE, 1636.

XX(b). The Shipman's Quadrant of Humphrey Cole's 2-ft. Astrolabe
of 1575.

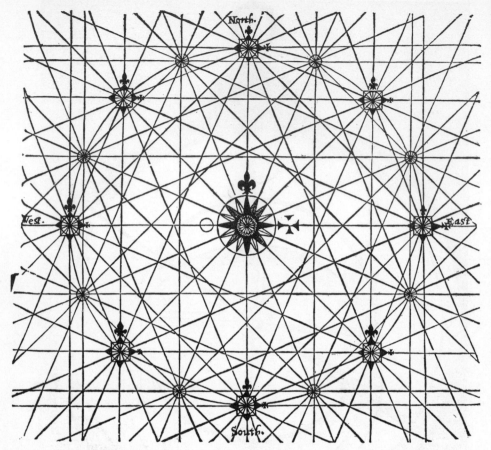

XXI. THE PLANE CHART'S LOXODROMES, 1636.

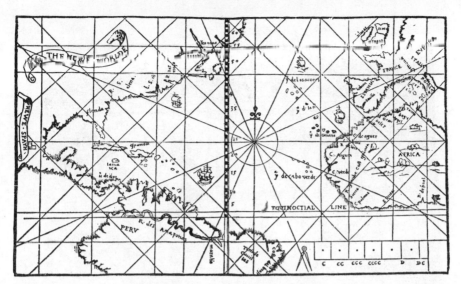

XXII. CHART OF 1561 OF THE ATLANTIC.

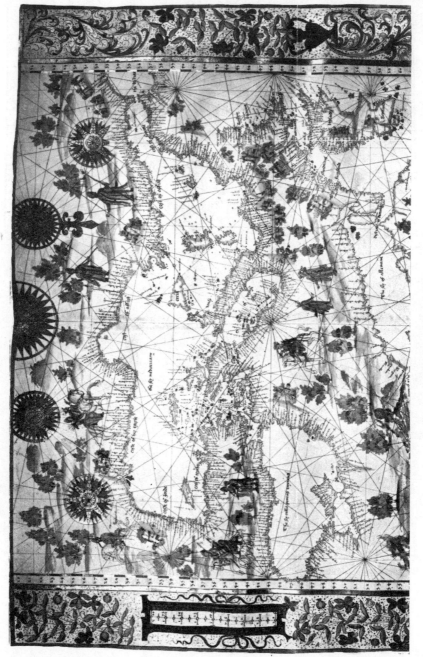

remainder being the elevation of the pole, the latitude. When the Cock's Foot was 30° above the horizon he knew he was on the equator. The charting of the heavens of the southern hemisphere, it may here be remarked, was a task the explorer-navigators of the fifteenth century were the first to tackle.[1]

The navigator shot the sun when the sky was clear by turning the astrolabe and its alidade until the spot of sunlight from the upper sun-sighting hole fell on the lower sun-sighting hole. He did not peer at the dazzling sun. If the sun was hazed or he was observing a star, it appears that assistants aided him in his observation, one holding the astrolabe, a second reading the index.

The original sea-astrolabe was not a very satisfactory instrument. The users found it impossible to take observations within 4°–5° 'however little the ship rolls'.[2] But the development of the cast brass model, completed by the middle of the sixteenth century, turned it into a useful instrument. Even so the navigator preferred to go on shore and use it there if he wanted to be sure of his latitude to within half a degree. In tropical waters, for lack of a better instrument, he had to use it, unless he could find a star suitable for a cross-staff morning or evening sight.

While the Portuguese explorations down the coast of Africa had raised the problem of latitude in an acute form, and had resulted in a solution by 1485, the rounding, two years later, of the Cape of Good Hope by Diaz, after he had struck boldly out into the ocean in order to clear the head winds off south-west Africa, had raised another problem, that of longitude. The daring voyage of Columbus in 1492, the partition of the world between Portugal and Spain a year later, and the triumphant voyage of Vasco da Gama in 1497 had made the solution of this problem more urgent.

---

[1] A sixteenth-century English writer on navigation (Blundeville, in his *Exercises*, 1594) observes:

'The ancient Astronomers ... did never describe any Starre to be more nigh with the South Pole, than that which is called *Canopus*, which is a faire bright starre of the first bignesse, and according to the Table of Copernicus, is distant from the South Pole 38 degrees and ¼. But those that have sailed in the South Seas of latter daies, have found out other stars unknowne to the ancient Astronomers.'

M. *BLUNDEVILE* His Exercises, containing sixe Treatises, the titles wherof are set down *in the next printed page*: *which Treatises are verie* necessarie to be read and learned of all young Gentl*emen that haue not bene exercised in such disciplines,* and yet are desirous to haue knowledge as well in Cos*mographie, Astronomie, and Geographie, as also in the* Arte of Nauig*ation,* in which Arte it is impossible to profite without the helpe of these, or such like instructions. To the furtherance of which Arte of Nauig*ation, the said* M. Blundeuile *speciallie wrote the* said Treatises and of meere good will doth *dedicate the same to all the young Gentlemen of this Realme,* London. *Printed by John Windet, dwelling at the signe of the crosse Keies, neere Paules wharffe, and are there to be solde.* 1594.

[2] The error of early astrolabe observations at sea is quoted from Cabral's voyage of 1500, in Prestage, E., *The Portuguese Pioneers* (1933), a valuable survey of early Portuguese achievements.

Unfortunately, owing to the revolution of the earth, there is no fixed celestial point of reference such as the pole or equator. How could navigators fix their position in an east and west direction, astronomically? It was realized that the essence of the problem, for which no practical solution was to be found for 300 years, was time. When the sun is overhead at any point on the earth's surface it is noon at that point and at all points along the meridian running through it. It is noon by local time. At any position east of it, towards the sun's rising, it is already past noon; west of it, it is not yet noon. If the difference in time could be found, could not this be used to find the position of these places with reference to the one where it was, say, already noon? As the earth in 24 hours rotates through 360°, in one hour it rotates through 15°, in one minute through 15'. Clearly position east and west could be found if time could be carried in a ship. This method, first proposed by Gemma Frisius in 1530, we find explained by William Cuningham, the first Englishman to write on cosmography, in his book, *The Cosmographical Glasse*, written in 1559.[1] But the watches he recommended ('such as are brought from Flanders, and we have them as excellently without Temple barre') were accurate to within only a quarter of an hour a day. To determine longitude to within half a degree at the end of a six weeks' voyage, the error must amount to not more than two minutes in all, or about three *seconds* a day!

Columbus had tried to find his longitude on his voyages of 1494 and 1504 by finding the difference in time between the occurrence of eclipses based on his observations and the times predicted, probably in Regiomontanus's *Calendarium*. But the difficulty in observing eclipses was to ensure that the same moment during the eclipse (which is a long drawn-out occurrence) was observed. Moreover, apart from the fact that eclipses are infrequent, lack of accurate instruments of observation and of a sufficiency of accurate observations over a period of time long enough to establish accurately the laws of the moon's motions rendered the lunar tables far from accurate. They were to remain so until the eighteenth century.

Another astronomical method for finding longitude attempted was that of the conjunction of the moon and a planet. It has been explained that the First Point of Aries was used as a datum point. Astronomically the half-meridian passing through it served just as the meridian of Greenwich does today for terrestrial longitude. By observing the position and time of transit of planets and stars at the equinoxes, their declination and right ascension, their angular distance measured in time from the First Point of Aries can be recorded in an almanac or plotted on a star map. This makes it possible to find longitude by the occultations of the planets by the moon's disc, that is by observations made when the declination and right ascension of the moon and a planet are identical.

---

[1] Cuningham, W., *The Cosmographical Glasse* (1559). The full title will be found on p. 98. See Pl. XII for Cuningham's illustration of the Ptolemaic system of the world.

William Cuningham gave an example of how he had looked up the positions of Regulus and of the moon, had observed their distance apart, and knowing the rate of change of bearing of the moon to be 35′ every hour, had found the difference in time to be 16 minutes, and so his position 4° W of Antwerp. But lunar distances, proposed by Werner in 1514 were, like all others, impracticable with the almanacs and instruments available.

Columbus, the Portuguese pilots, and later navigators also tried to determine longitude by observing the change in variation of the compass. From being easterly in the Mediterranean it diminished to zero in about St. Michael's in the Azores, and then became westerly, increasing in amount the farther westward they sailed. They attempted by means of this phenomenon to relate their position east or west in terms of longitude. The difficulty was to find the variation. At first this could only be done, and then only in the middle and lower latitudes, by taking the compass bearing of the Pole Star, rectifying it by the 'Rule of the North Star', and so finding the difference. Meantime the need for accurate direction-finding increased the urgency of determining the variation and by the first quarter of the sixteenth century special instruments and techniques had been evolved for observing the morning and evening amplitude of the sun. But none of these methods, nor of their later refinements, ever gave results sufficiently accurate to determine longitude, even when the longitude of a position of given variation was known. This position, of course, was known only by dead reckoning. The method suffered from fundamental limitations.

Besides wanting to find variation accurately in the hope of being able to solve the problem of longitude, the navigator crossing the oceans needed to be able to determine his true course. Since he found that variation constantly altered during his voyage, if he wished to keep to an observed latitude, he had to relate his direction accurately to true north. This he could do only by means of his compass, and then only if he could correct it for variation. Consequently in order to rectify his course he now found his variation whenever possible. He found it also in order to rectify his bearings when he was fixing his position by compass bearings. No longer could he afford to steer by compass course and fix his position by compass bearing as he had done hitherto, and as the mariners in the Mediterranean and north-west Europe continued to do. If he was to make his landfall successfully after an ocean passage, he had to steer by true and not magnetic courses. One result of this was that if he was wise, he now always aligned his compass needle with the north-south line of his fly. If he did not, on correcting for variation he got terribly confused as to his true course.

Lack of a means of finding longitude made it essential to compute accurately the distance run. The navigator still relied on estimation. To measure time he used a sand-glass or else repeated a series of words, twice if the ship was going slowly. This patter was supposed to be equivalent in time to that measured by a minute or half-minute glass. Gunners in the Navy still did this in the writer's youth at sea. When firing saluting guns they timed the firing of the salvoes by repeating rhyming lines beginning: 'If I wasn't a gunner I wouldn't be here. Fire One!'

To enable time to be found astronomically at other times besides noon, Gemma Frisius, the brilliant cosmographer to the Emperor, invented an astronomical ring-dial.[1] There were many subsequent variations of this instrument, all seeking to ensure greater accuracy, and they were very popular on shore until superseded by reliable watches in the eighteenth century. At sea, despite all the ingenuity of the designers, they ever remained of little practical value. A typical one consisted of a brass meridian ring with an adjustable shackle and ring to enable it to be suspended at the point equal to the latitude engraved on it. To the meridian ring was pivoted, so that it could be laid flat when not in use, an equatorial or hour ring. In the position of the polar axis was a metal plate with a long slot in it with a sliding pin-hole block adjustable for the sun's declination. This set, and the meridian ring hung in the plane of the meridian, the spot of sunlight fell on the hour on the equatorial circle. Martin Cortes devised a universal dial to meet the same purpose. It was to all intents and purposes a sun-dial and thus of little practical use at sea. Probably under the impetus of the nautical need for time-keeping the art of dialling developed to a high degree in the early sixteenth century, particularly in Germany and Flanders where the finest metal craftsmen and mathematicians lived in close communication with the navigators, cosmographers, and geographers of the rest of the Empire. But all time-instruments depending on the sun suffered from what were for seamen fundamental defects. They had to be aligned accurately, north and south, and set accurately, for latitude, and held stationary. Towards noon the sun's rapid rate of change of bearing made them particularly unreliable. The writer has never succeeded in reading the time more accurately than to within 15 minutes, using a universal ring-dial as a seaman had to do. However, by long practice navigators did estimate time and their speed sufficiently accurately to reach their destinations, though generally not when they expected to reach them.

It was one thing to steer a course, quite another to 'make good' that course. The sixteenth-century ships were very leewardly. No doubt the navigator did what the Dutch navigator Wagenaer recommended in his *Spieghel der Zeevaerdt* of 1585 should be done, and what continued to be done to modern times—he cast a line astern attached to a piece of lead-weighted wood with a pole in it, and measured the angle of leeway by means of a compass on the poop. As for currents, local ones might be known, though as we have seen their speed was not. The north-eastward drift of the Gulf Stream in the Atlantic was early recognized and later commented upon by the English navigator Frobisher in the course of his

---

[1] This consisted of three brass rings, one of them with sighting vanes. It is clearly depicted in the portrait of the great cosmographer reproduced in Stevenson, E. L., *Terrestrial and Celestial Globes* (1921), Vol. 1. The ring-dial could also be used for finding latitude.

voyages to the north-west, but again its speed was unknown. All that was known was that it was liable to set ships upon the coasts of Europe before their time.

In an endeavour to help navigators to compute their course between places of known, or at least recorded, latitude and longitude, Gemma Frisius in the 1540s designed a shipman's quadrant.[1] It seems to have been little used, possibly because of the cartographical error underlying it, probably because of the inexactitude of geographical positions and the lack of a settled prime or zero meridian. As for the prime meridian, some navigators took 'the westermost part of Africa', others 'St. Michael's in the Azores', others again 'the Canaries'. All differed, and none was definite. Even after years of experimental traverses, at the close of the sixteenth century the position of London, taking the extreme west of St. Michael's in the Azores for the prime meridian, was $6\frac{1}{2}°$ out, Madeira 4° 20', St. Vincent 6° too far west. As so often, the scientists produced instruments of exquisite accuracy, or theoretical solutions to problems, which were yet useless or little used for lack of the necessary data which would make them practical.

The shipman's quadrant consisted of a square divided into four equal parts or quadrants by two straight lines which crossed each other at right-angles in the centre and represented the prime meridian and the equator. They also represented the north and south, and east and west rhumbs of a compass fly centred upon their point of intersection, and whose perimeter represented the horizon. Two sides of the square were divided both above and below the equinoctial line into 90° representing north and south latitude, and the top and bottom sides were divided to right and left of the meridian into 90° representing east and west longitude. Knowing the latitude and longitude of the place where he was, the navigator was supposed to use the quadrant to find the course that should take him to a place of which also he knew the latitude and longitude. He was to find this by subtracting the lower latitude from the higher, and, if the destination lay north of him, stretching a thread (a favourite instrument) across the northern latitude scales at the point corresponding to the difference in latitude. He had then to subtract the lesser longitude from the greater (longitude being measured eastward from the prime meridian through 360°) and marked the difference by another thread stretched between the longitudes scales, using the left-hand scales if the destination lay to the east. Where the two threads crossed was supposed to be the position of the destination. The course to it was supposed to be indicated by the underlying rhumb. The fundamental error in using the instrument in this manner was that a given difference of longitude was treated as being of the same linear distance at different latitudes, whereas because of the convergence of the meridians towards the poles, it is not. Nor was correction practicable by means of the table of the length of a degree in different latitudes given in manuals such as Cortes's, consequently the course found was incorrect

[1] See Pl. XX.

As stated in the previous chapter, the Italian and Catalan pilots of the Mediterranean had for centuries used charts, now known as bearing and distance charts. The earliest surviving one, known as the *Carta Pisana*, was drawn *c.* 1275, and is remarkably accurate. By the sixteenth century the charts of Europe extended as far south as Morocco and sometimes the Congo, and as far north as the British Isles and Flanders. Farther north they did not go, as the Mediterranean seaman's trade routes ended there. Farther south they did not extend, as the Portuguese had kept secret since 1504 all their detailed charting south of the Congo, and continued to do so until King Philip II of Spain usurped the throne in 1580. The Italian and Catalan pilots had passed their cartographical skill to the Portuguese. In the century and a quarter after rounding Cape Bojador the latter surveyed and charted about 300 miles of new coast a year, basing much of their eastern information on the charts used by the Arabian seamen.[1] By 1509 they had a chart of surprising accuracy covering the Arabian Sea and the Indian Ocean between the Cape of Good Hope and India and Ceylon.[2] Portuguese pilots served Spain. Like the Italian pilots they taught the Spaniards the arts of pilotage, navigation, and hydrography.

In the fifteenth century the Casa de Guinea e India at Lisbon included an organization equivalent to a modern hydrographic office, at whose head was a cosmographer-in-chief. He was assisted by cosmographers whose business it was to draw and to correct charts and to compile books of sailing directions and, no doubt, as in the similar Spanish organization of the sixteenth century, to assist in the instruction of pilots. By 1508 the Spaniards had established as part of the Casa de Contratación at Seville—their equivalent of the Portuguese Casa de Guinea e India—what was virtually a national school of navigation. It was here that pilots were trained—initially chiefly by the Portuguese—in the new art of oceanic navigation, and, on graduating, were duly licensed. Here too charts were drawn, hydrographic information was accumulated, chart corrections were incorporated in master copies, and, in due course, manuals of navigation were compiled and published. The most distinguished navigators of the age served in its various offices, Amerigo Vespucci, de Solis, Vincente Pinzón, Juan de la Cosa, and Sebastian Cabot—who may have sailed with his father, John, when he sailed from Bristol in 1497 and discovered the New Found Land in the north-west — to name only a few. Several rose in succession to be pilot-major of the institution.[3] Although Martin Cortes was not the first Spanish author to publish a manual of navigation, yet as a

---

[1] Gernez, D., *Importance de l'œuvre hydrographique et de l'œuvre cartographique des Portugais au 15ème et au 16ème siècles* (1940).

[2] Uhden, R., 'The Oldest Portuguese Original Chart of the Indian Ocean, A.D. 1509', *Imago Mundi*, Vol. 3. See also the Canerio Chart of *c.* 1502–04, French Ministry of Marine, deposited in the Bibliothèque Nationale, Paris.

[3] Haring, C. H., *Trade and Navigation between Spain and the Indies* (1918), is a valuable study of the early colonial system of Spain, including the measures taken to ensure the safety of sea-borne goods, and the provision of navigators.

result of the teaching and research work of this officially sponsored and regulated nautical academy, his *Arte de Navegar*, published at Seville in 1551, is quite the best for fullness of content and clarity of exposition. It is from the pages of his manual that we learn how, amongst other things, the mariner's chart was made.

For making 'Cardes for the Sea . . . it shall bee requisite to knowe two things . . . the right position of places' and 'the distances that is from one place to another'. Position, Cortes explains, was shown by 'the windes', distance on 'the outline of the coasts'. The charts were drawn upon paper or parchment; if on parchment then usually on a whole sheep's, goat's, or calf's skin, the neck to the left. First the sheet was divided by two black lines in the centre at right-angles, giving length east and west, breadth north and south (but French pilots, like the Arabian ones and the old Romans, put south at the top).

Positions were ascertained by those who had travelled and had 'well paynted' patterns 'of the best and most approved to be true'. These were copied by the use of tracing paper, made from thin paper rubbed with linseed oil and dried, and carbon paper of paper 'smoked . . . with a lynke or with matches of pitche'. After the tracing was made it was pinned down on the ruled skin, the carbons were inserted and the outline was transferred to the skin by use of a steel bodkin. Tracing paper and carbon were then removed and the outline inked in. When dry, it was cleaned with breadcrumbs, and the names of ports, capes, and bays were added, those of ports in red ink, those of the rest in black. The chart was then garnished and beautified with cities, ships, banners, beasts, and compasses. The drawing in of the compasses was particularly important. From the centre of the skin a large 'hidden circle', which could easily be rubbed out with breadcrumbs, was drawn in with a piece of lead. The quadrants were bisected with black lines. The eight principal winds had thus been drawn in. These were divided into half-winds, using azure or green lines, and quarter-winds, using red lines. The 'mother compass', as the central one was called, was completed by being filled in with a flower or rose, in colours and gold; lines of different colours were used to differentiate the rhumbs of the winds, which were marked, the north one with a *fleur-de-lis*, the east one with a cross, and the remainder with their letters. Where the winds of the mother compass crossed the hidden circle were drawn sixteen other compasses; larger charts had thirty-two. These compasses had their radiating winds drawn in also, after which the hidden circle was rubbed out, and the chart was almost complete. At first glance it appeared to be covered with a medley of criss-cross lines, but as soon as the hidden circle had been distinguished the fact that each line was a rhumb or wind leapt to the eye.[1] They were in fact indispensable, for by means of them and a pair of compasses, or as we should say today, of dividers, the pilot read off his course. Parallel rulers were not invented until 1584 when the Frenchman,

[1] See Pl. XXI.

Mordente, devised them, but the lack of reference to them in subsequent works on navigation, the continued directions to take off the course by means of compasses or protractors, and the continued, though slowly diminishing, inclusion of loxodromes or rhumbs of the winds in charts into the eighteenth century show that the parallel ruler came only slowly into use at sea. The time-honoured, centuries-old 'rhumb and compass' method died hard. It was supplanted first by the use of the protractor, also an invention of the 1580s but an English one. The charts, even the earliest ones, were completed with a distance scale, distances being measured off with a pair of compasses. When in the fifteenth century the Portuguese began sailing far south and west in the Atlantic, the pilot, in order to find his position, had to know 'the true altitudes of the Pole, of certen principall capes, portes, and famous cities' and correlate these with the pattern of his original bearing and distance chart. A latitude scale was therefore added, being drawn in 'by the Islands of Azores' or 'wher the carde shall be lesse occupyed', and the graduation 'begun from sone one cape, whose altitude of the Pole is wel knowen'. Spanish pilots took Cape St. Vincent as their datum point, marking it correctly in 37° N; until the sixteenth century no longitude scale was drawn; even in the middle of the century Cortes's latitude scale, which was necessarily drawn on a meridian, was not used as a prime meridian.

According to the opinion of the roundness of the earth it was reckoned that either $16\frac{2}{3}$ leagues or $17\frac{1}{2}$ leagues equalled one degree. Accordingly the scale or 'Truncke' was drawn in 100 leagues in length 'and in the cardes that had XVII leagues and a halfe for a degree . . .' the roundness of the land and water were said to contain 'six thousand and three hundred leagues'. This vagueness about the size of the length of a degree was caused by the inability of the cosmographers to measure it accurately. It can be measured only by observing accurately the latitude of two places on a meridian, measuring the distance accurately between them (making allowances for all detours, dips, and rises on the way), and then, knowing the angular distance apart of the two places, computing the length of a degree. Until the pilots began navigating astronomically the length of a degree did not bother them. In northern waters they worked in kennings for measuring the distance between places; in the Mediterranean in miles and in leagues. Pilots used neither degrees of latitude nor longitude. When at the close of the fifteenth century they began to have to relate linear distance to angular distance on the earth's surface, the Portuguese and Spanish navigators generally counted 70 miles of 5,000 feet to the degree, or $17\frac{1}{2}$ leagues, four miles going to the league. Many navigators and cosmographers, however, took shorter miles or counted less miles to the degree, 60 of 5,000 feet. It was the latter which the English eventually adopted when they came to navigate. Mediterranean pilots, however, did not trouble about latitude or longitude until the eighteenth century. They traversed or caped their way about that sea. The result of the different values outlined above was that the length of the mile, and of the circumference of the earth, varied from

0·66 to 0·86 of what we know to be their true measurement.[1] On the north-south route along the West African coast, where position could be frequently checked by observations of latitude, this shortening of the mile did not matter and errors arising from it were attributed to currents. The trouble started with east to west voyages in different latitudes, when at first the length of a degree of longitude was charted as being in all latitudes the same as the length of a degree of latitude. As the latitude of a place is the angular distance between the line joining it to the centre of the earth and the plane of the equator, the length of a degree of latitude never varies, but the length of a degree of longitude does. This is because, unlike parallels of latitude, meridians of longitude are not parallel. As Martin Cortes pointed out, they converge from the equator towards the poles, where they meet in a point. The consequence is that the length of a degree of longitude varies as the cosine of the latitude. As it happens the cosine of 35° is 0·8, and the east-west axis of the Mediterranean lies roughly along the parallel of 35° N. Thus in practice the Mediterranean hydrographers did correlate their distances east and west with their longitude fairly accurately. But as the Iberian cosmographers transferred the value of the length of a degree of longitude in 35° N to the length of a degree of latitude, and to the length of a degree of longitude, *on the equator*, their distances were always less than actuality

---

[1] Nordenskiöld's *Periplus* contains a valuable analysis of the value of the portulan mile.

Taylor, E. G. R. (ed.), *Brief Summe of Geographie*, Hak. Soc., Series 2, Vol. 69, pp. xv and xvi and Appendix II, is valuable for the political and classical reasons underlying the different values of the length of a degree. At the beginning of the sixteenth century seamen took the length of a degree to be 70 Roman (Italian) miles of 5000 feet or $17\frac{1}{2}$ leagues of 4 Roman miles. The inspiration behind this was the ancient Greek astronomer Eratosthenes' measurement of the circumference of the earth—252,000 stadia, 10 sea stadia being taken as equal to 1 Roman mile. This was included in Sacrobosco's *Sphaera*, and thus made known to seamen through the Portuguese navigation manuals. By adopting the measurement of the earth's circumference laid down by Ptolemy, 180,000 stadia, the Spaniards were able to try to claim the Moluccas in the East Indies, in the early part of the sixteenth century, as being within their half-share of the world. 180,000 stadia gave 18,000 Roman miles. Thus a league 3 miles long gave the length of a degree as: as:

$$\frac{(18,000)}{3} \div 360 = 16\frac{2}{3} \text{ leagues}$$

The important point was that by taking Ptolemy's measurement the Portuguese half-sphere could be made to measure only 3000 leagues instead of 3150. The Spanish chances of successfully claiming the Moluccas were thus increased. Cosmographers got the value of $62\frac{1}{2}$ miles to a degree by taking Ptolemy's circumference of the earth and 8 stadia to the mile, while if Strabo's $8\frac{1}{3}$ stadia to the mile was taken, the result was 60 miles to a degree—20 leagues of 3 miles. This, probably because of the ease with which it would be divided into minutes, was the value taken by English seamen as soon as the art of navigation was acclimatized in the second half of the sixteenth century. Seamen of other nations, with a longer tradition of navigation according to Portuguese methods, generally adhered to the Portuguese 17½ leagues (of 4 miles) to a degree, = 64.4 English statute miles.

by about one-eighth. The resultant north-south errors the navigator could correct by celestial observations, as already stated, but he had no means of checking his position east and west. He could only calculate it by keeping a careful reckoning. Therefore he preferred his miles, or leagues, to be short, for by this means he avoided the danger of being ahead of his reckoning and making a landfall unexpectedly. So, although the length of a degree was recognized by many navigators to be demonstrably false, all preferred to keep it so rather than correct it. As it was expressed, they preferred to have 'their reckoning before their ship', and so 'to sight land after they sought it'.[1] Most navigators blamed the winds and the currents, leeway, and compass errors for the gross differences that frequently occurred between landfall and the expected hour of landfall. Many continued to do so until the close of the eighteenth century.

Besides the confusion about scale there were other and grave errors in the charts. The meridians were drawn in or counted as being equidistant vertical lines, and the parallels of latitude as equidistant horizontal lines. The charts were 'plane' charts (often spelt 'plain'), and 'The Pilottes and Maryners neyther use nor have knowledge to use other cardes then only these that are playne', wrote Cortes, adding, 'The which, because they are not globous, sphericall or rounde are imperfecte, and fayle to shewe the true distances.' Thus, as Cortes explained, whereas two ships 100 leagues apart on the equator which sailed due north to latitude 60° N finished up only 50 leagues apart, on the plane chart they appeared to be still 100 leagues apart. 'Besides these considerations', he went on only too truly, 'one errour bryngeth in an other: and so an other . . . whereof to speak any more here . . . shall . . . be an endlesse confusion', adding somewhat bitterly that to do so was in any case but 'to certen Pilottes . . . to paynt a house for blynd men.' As the Spanish and Portuguese pilots did almost all their navigating between the latitudes of 35° N and 35° S—the latitudes of Seville and Cape Hatteras and the Cape of Good Hope—they were not greatly affected by the inaccuracies of their plane charts induced by this defect in their compilation. It was in the higher latitudes that the error becomes pronounced. Scotland, for instance, in order to fit into the sea-charts, was drawn in twice as broad as it was, and the North American coast was stretched out in an east-west direction. This is clearly shown in the chart of the North Atlantic which Martin Cortes included in his *Arte de Navegar*.[2] Here it will be found that whereas the coastline of North America between the coast of Florida and New England has a NE by N trend, in the chart the trend is ENE. Nevertheless as a result of this distortion it will be found that latitudes and courses, though not distances, are tolerably correct when compared with those on a modern chart. Martin Cortes's chart was up-to-date at that time because it was drawn with true bearing 'and not by the wyndes that the compass sheweth'. However, in

1 Mainwaring's *The Seaman's Dictionary*, amongst other works, explains this. See N.R.S., Vol. 56.
2 See Pl. XXII.

'the Levant Sea (called Mare Mediterranean) and the Channel of Flanders (called the narrowe seas) it was not inconvenient for the Navigation, that the portes were marked in the cardes by the wyndes, which the compass shewed; forasmuch as they sayled not by the altitude of the Pole'—a point already discussed. Elsewhere, however, failure to correct for variation before delineating the chart led to distortions that made position by compass bearing and distance and position by latitude irreconcilable.

It was about 1500, when transoceanic navigation became common for exploration and trade with the New World and India, that a latitude scale became essential on many charts. 'The cardes that lack this ought to be corrected and amended by wyse and experte men', observed Cortes; and well he might, for it was no easy task, as the charts of the Mediterranean and Atlantic and New World of the time show. For instance, the effect of the easterly variation prevalent in the Mediterranean at the time of the plotting by compass bearing of the original charts, from which all others of the region appear to have been copied, had been to raise their eastern end through an angle of about 11°. In navigating by compass, provided the needle was set under the north point of the fly like that of the compass used in the plotting, this did not matter. The north shown was then the compass north, and the directions shown were compass directions. These were what interested the pilot, and, as a matter of fact, since he caped his way about the seas in the Mediterranean the pilot was not too careful about accuracy, and the inaccuracies arising, for instance, from the as yet unsuspected secular change of variation. The fact that its southern—the North African—coast was shown as lying ∧ and not ⌐ did not interest or affect him. But add for his use as a navigator a latitude scale, and it did. The first known chart to show latitude—one of 1502 of the Mediterranean —has only one latitude scale, and that is on the eastern end, and as the chart is twisted this scale is inevitably incorrect for places at the western end. A solution of this problem was found in the addition of a second latitude scale at the western end. A beautiful example of this is contained in a manuscript *Book of Hydrography*, prepared in 1542 by a Dieppois navigator in the service of the English Crown, Jean Rotz, for King Henry VIII.[1] Although in the Mediterranean chart Gibraltar and Alexandria are shown in the same horizontal line, the graduations on the latitude scale on the east start $5\frac{1}{2}°$ above those of the west—at $19\frac{1}{2}°$ N and 25° N respectively—so that the latitude of Alexandria reads correctly $30\frac{1}{2}°$ N when read from the eastern scale, that of Gibraltar 36° N when read from the western, the east-west axis being swung through 11° to the north.

The double latitude scale was still not a very satisfactory arrangement for a navigator wishing to plot his latitude in the central Mediterranean. It was even less satisfactory on ocean charts where the distances and changes in variation were greater, and hence where distortions in plotting

[1] Jean Rotz's *Book of Hydrography* (1542). 'This boke of Idrography Is made be me Johne Rotz sarvant to the kingis Mooste exellent Majeste. God saue his Majeste'. B.M. Royal 20. E.IX. See Pl. XXIII.

were greater too. In an attempt to counteract this, besides double latitude scales, double equators were often drawn in. In charts of the North Atlantic region recourse was also had to a twisted or 'oblique' meridian.[1] This was because in the north-west Atlantic the great westerly variation experienced resulted in the coast of Labrador appearing by compass bearings to run due north and south instead of to the NNW, its true direction. As in the charts the coastline was drawn in by compass bearings, the main latitude scale, usually drawn in the charts in mid-ocean, and of course in a

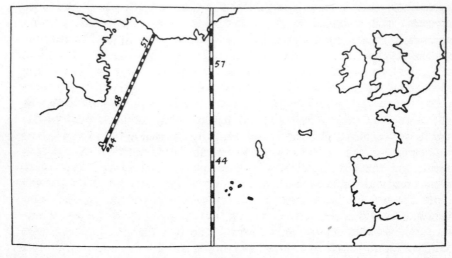

Fig. 8

THE OBLIQUE MERIDIAN

(After chart of the Atlantic of *c.* 1502 by Pedro Reinel)

The problem that faced the hydrographer in the early part of the sixteenth century was to reconcile the observed latitude of places with their position as plotted by observed compass bearings. The methods of determining magnetic variation were rudimentary; indeed, the very existence of variation was open to question, the navigator sailed by compass course often uncorrected for variation; when he surveyed and plotted new coasts by a combination of latitude observations and compass bearings he often left them uncorrected for variation. One solution was the oblique meridian. The chart was drawn on bearings uncorrected for variation. Then, in addition to the meridian line drawn in as the general magnetic meridian, a sloping meridian line was drawn in through a region where there was marked difference of variation. It acted as the *geographical meridian* for that area. Thus the navigator who saw the coast trending north by compass knew that its true direction was NNW.

Fig. 8 after Gernez, D., *Importance de l'œuvre hydrographique et de l'oeuvre cartographique des Portugais au 15ème et au 16ème siècles* (1940).

[1] Winter, H., 'The Pseudo-Labrador and the Oblique Meridian', *Imago Mundi*, Vol. 2, and Taylor, E. G. R., 'Hudson's Strait and the Oblique Meridian', *Imago Mundi*, Vol. 3. Both these scholars appear to have overlooked William Borough's explanation and condemnation of the oblique meridian in his *A Discours of the Variation*, London (1581), bound behind Robert Norman's *The newe Attractive*. The Portuguese chart of the North Atlantic, *c.* 1502, signed by Pedro Reinel is the earliest surviving chart with an oblique meridian. See Figs. 8, 9, 10, 11 and 12.

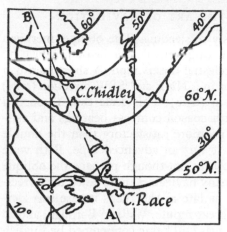

Fig. 9

THE NORTH-WEST REGION OF THE
ATLANTIC

Drawn according to the geographical and
not the magnetic meridian and showing
by isogonic lines—lines of equal variation
—the great westerly variation experienced
in the area (1937). In effect this chart is
drawn by compass bearing corrected for
variation. This became· increasingly common from the middle of the sixteenth
century as methods of finding variation
were developed.

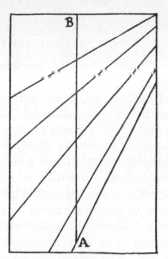

Fig. 10

THE OBLIQUE MERIDIAN

Corresponding to points
along the line A—B in Fig. 9
and indicating the amount of
variation experienced on them

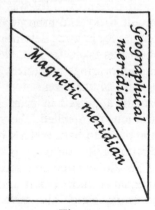

Fig. 11

THE MAGNETIC MERIDIAN
IN THE NORTH-WEST
REGION OF THE NORTH
ATLANTIC

Fig. 12

THE NORTH-WEST REGION OF THE
NORTH ATLANTIC

Shown in Fig. 9 replotted on a magnetic meridian as in the chart of Pedro
Reinel, and many another, that is, without
applying the corrections for variation.

Figs. 9, 10, 11 and 12 after Taylor, E. G. R., 'Hudson's Strait and the Oblique Meridian', *Imago Mundi*, Vol. 3.

north-south direction, was hopelessly misleading. The oblique meridian was an attempt to reconcile the conflicting claims of navigation by bearing and distance and of navigation by celestial observation. A short meridian was drawn on the chart off Labrador in a NNE and SSW direction (true) instead of in a north-south direction (true). This scale thus reconciled change of latitude in this region with coastal compass bearings and estimated distances. It was a solution no more satisfactory than the double latitude scale, of which, of course, it was an advanced type. Both were the source of much cartographical confusion, though perhaps the oblique meridian caused the most, because many navigators quite failed to appreciate its purpose. Nevertheless, since as late as the 1580s its use was condemned by an English navigator of great repute, William Borough, and in the early seventeenth century its use was still being condemned by English masters, it was clearly no short-lived device. Indeed some French navigators used it up to the close of the seventeenth century.

It was only when navigators really began to navigate by celestial observation that the conflicting hydrographical claims of bearing and distance and latitude and longitude were thrashed out. Gradually charts for navigation by latitude-finding carried the day. This meant that the land had to be drawn in with the bearings between places corrected for variation, so that they were true, and with distances which were, if possible, accurate. We have already seen that the leading navigators hoped to find a solution to the longitude problem by the use of compass variation. Nevertheless, many navigators steadily refused to believe in variation, holding that it was caused by the incorrect 'feeding' of the compass needle or by a fault in the making of the needle, or that it was an error arising from careless handling of the compass. They, therefore, preferred charts drawn by compass bearings, uncorrected for variation, and distances. This was partly because many a navigator in strange waters off rocky and inhospitable or verdant and seductive shores felt far safer relying for latitude determination on his compass, and a chart drawn from bearings taken from it, than on chancy sights and a chart drawn with compass bearings corrected for he knew not what uncertain and varying quantities of variation.

It was not until 1535 that a work (Spanish) appeared in print which described practical methods of finding variation, then called 'the northeasting of the needles', although Magellan appears to have taken a manuscript copy of it on his famous voyage of circumnavigation in 1519.[1]

In 1525 Felipe Guillen, an apothecary of Seville, devised an instrument for observing the shadows cast by the sun at equal altitudes before and after noon, and this was described in the 1535 work, which also gave three

---

[1] This was the extremely rare *Tractado del Esphera y del arte del marear: con el regimiēto de las alturas: cō algūas reglas nueuamēte ascritas muy necessarias* of Francisco Falero or Faleiro (1535). The whole problem is dealt with in Chapter 8, 'On the north-easting of the needles'. See the valuable papers by Harradon, H. D., 'Some early contributions to the History of Geomagnetism', *Terrestrial Magnetism and Atmospheric Electricity*, Vols. 48–50.

methods of variation finding: by the sun's noon shadow; by the amplitude of the sun at sunrise and sunset; and by the equal altitude method. Pedro Nuñez (Nonius), 1502–57, the gifted young Portuguese cosmographer to the King of Portugal, improved on the instrument by enabling the altitude of the sun to be taken by it, and the brilliant João de Castro used it most successfully on a voyage to India in 1538 to plot the variation of the compass on the route.

By the middle of the century most skilled navigators had some form of 'variation compass'. Jean Rotz presented one to King Henry VIII. Nevertheless, Pedro de Medina, who wrote an *Arte de Navegar*, published in 1545 at Valladolid, and much thought of on the Continent for many years, derided the existence of variation. Martin Cortes, on the other hand, firmly understood its existence, and was indeed the first writer to postulate that it was caused by terrestrial 'attraction', and to give the sum total of knowledge on the subject at the time; yet as regards its determination he merely said that 'an instrument to shewe the same by the sunne in the daye, and by the starres in the nyght' could be easily made. However, we see that he had been able to reproduce a map of the North Atlantic area corrected for variation by 1545, when he wrote his treatise. A Mediterranean chart of 1546 exists similarly corrected, but a still older example is the magnificent portulan chart of the world, in two parts, by Diego Ribeiro, dated 1529. It is notable also for its exquisite delineation of a sea-astrolabe and quadrant of the time.[1]

It was Pedro Nuñez who, in 1537, had first drawn attention to the cartographical faults of the plane chart in a work which also included observations on the art of navigation and on astronomy. One great contribution was the 'double altitude' observation of the sun. Provided the sights were taken over 40° apart it was possible by means of a terrestrial globe to fix latitude to within 1°. It would appear that 'double altitude' sights were not frequently taken, though they could be combined with variation finding by equal altitude and did free the navigator from being confined by day solely to a meridian altitude sight of the sun.

Pedro Nuñez, at the age of twenty-four, had first pointed out that the loxodromes or rhumb lines were not in reality straight lines but curved and, on a sphere, unless they were meridians or parallels of latitude, and thus one of the four principal rhumbs, were winding or spiral lines which twisted their way around the sphere towards the poles. He complained that globe-makers did not then know how to put them on their globes, but his representation was, in fact, incorrect.

A loxodrome is a line that makes the same angle with all successive meridians. When a ship sails along a loxodrome it crosses successive meridians at the same angle and maintains steadily the same ratio of northing or southing and easting or westing. Thus on a sphere a loxodrome, except when it lies along a parallel or meridian, because of the convergence

[1] The portulan world charts of Diego Ribeiro referred to are reproduced in Nordenskiöld's *Periplus*. See also p. 56, n. 1.

of the meridians, traces out a spiral.[1] To draw this on a sphere is no easy business, and Nuñez might well confess to being defeated by the task. Now on the plane chart, where the meridians were drawn as equal and parallel straight lines at right-angles to the equator, the latter was also drawn as a straight line. It was divided properly to scale. The remaining parallels were drawn equidistant from one another and also of the same length as the equator. This scale was true along the meridians and along the equator, but from the equator to the poles, since the convergence of the meridians was ignored, it was increasingly exaggerated along the parallels of latitude. This exaggeration was in the ratio of the secant of the latitude to unity. Thus, for instance, in latitude 60°, the secant of 60° being 2, the exaggeration will be found to be double.[2] The result was that on a plane chart drawn up in terms of latitude and longitude a course N 30° W appeared to the navigator to be a straight line, but in fact was a curved line which tended farther and farther round to the west the farther along it he sailed, and which would never bring him 'unto the haven where he would be'.[3] Moreover the farther north lay the latitude in which he started the voyage, the greater, over a given distance, was his error. It is no wonder therefore that, when they had to reconcile what appeared to be the true loxodrome on a globe with what also appeared to be the true loxodrome on the plane chart, the globe-makers were defeated.

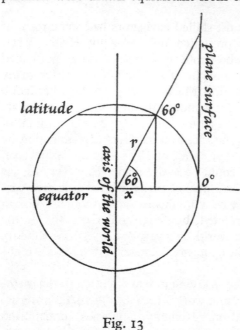

Fig. 13

PROJECTION OF A CURVED SURFACE ON TO
A PLANE ONE

If the curved surface of the earth be projected on to a plane surface with the meridians drawn as parallel straight lines equally spaced, the scale on the parallels of latitude is increasingly exaggerated as the equator is left behind and the poles are approached. The exaggeration is in the ratio of the secant to unity.

To pursue the shortcomings of the plane chart no further, the result of these and the other various faults already reviewed was that as often as not the plane chart was 'an inextricable labyrinth of error'. The wise navi-

    [1] See Pl. XXIV.
    [2] See Fig. 13.
    [3] For example a navigator steering NW from a position given on his plane chart in, say, latitude 40° N, longitude 0°, would expect to arrive in latitude 70° N, longitude 31° W. Actually he would arrive in latitude 70° N, longitude 55° W.

proach the Pole, and alſo goe round about it, but yet with un-
equall diſtance, ſo as he ſhall be nigher beyond it then on this ſide,
by meanes whereof he cannot returne to the place from whence
he came, as you may plainely perceive by this figure demon-
ſtrative here placed.

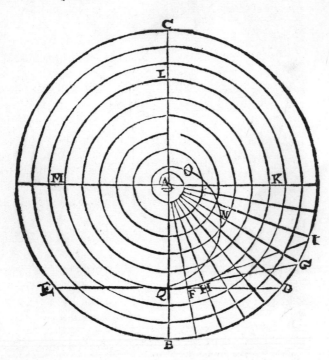

In which figure the letter A doth ſignifie the North Pole,
and the letters B C the Meridian paſſing through the Pole A,
then ſuppoſe your ſhip to be in Q, whereas the Pole is elevated
30 degrees: and Q to be your Zenith, and the right line E, Q D,
to be your right line of Eaſt and Weſt cutting the foreſaid meridian with right angles, and let D be the Eaſt point and E the
Weſt point.

Now you may ſaile from Q towards the North with a
South-winde, and from A you may ſaile againe South-ward

Pp 3   with

XXIV. THE RHUMB LINE A SPIRAL LINE, 1636.

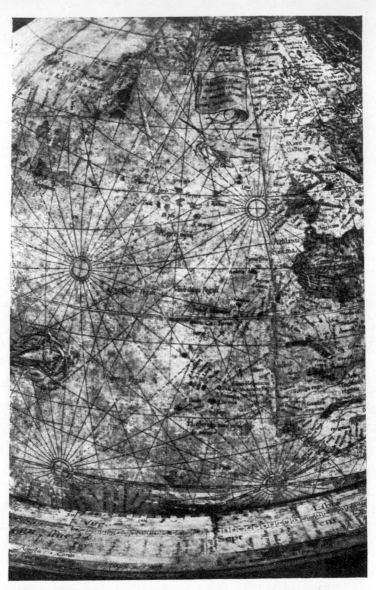

XXV. The North Atlantic and Part of the Horizon Ring
on Mercator's Terrestrial Globe of 1541.

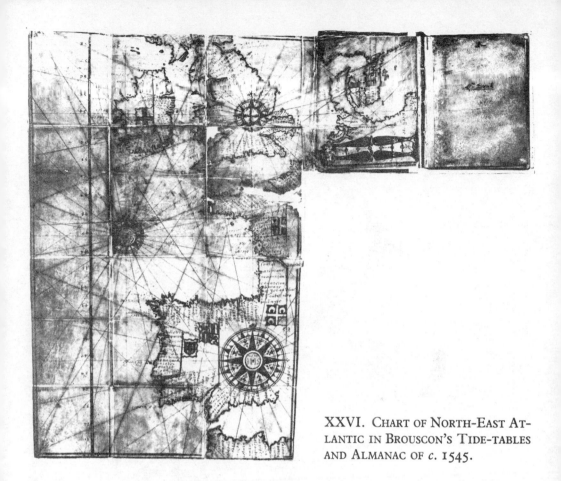

XXVI. Chart of North-East Atlantic in Brouscon's Tide-tables and Almanac of *c.* 1545.

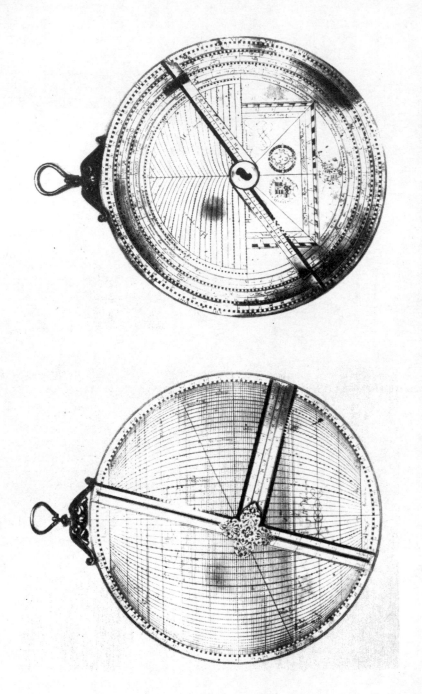

XXVII and XXVIII. The Front and Back of Thomas Gemini's Universal Planispheric Astrolabe of 1552.

gator used it with caution to supplement his far more reliable sailing directions. If he could afford it, by the middle of the sixteenth century he also took a globe to sea with him. On this he could plot his position with some certainty, and having his table showing the distance between meridians for every degree of latitude (Martin Cortes included an accurate one in his work) provided he had been sailing along a parallel of latitude, he could turn his departure—or distance run east or west—into degrees of longitude. Similarly he could measure on the globe the distances between places accurately (within the limits of the accuracy of their fixed position and the scale of the globe), and he could choose a series of courses along or close to a great circle, which demonstrably led him along the shortest track.[1] Up to the discovery of America, globes had been almost exclusively celestial, showing the positions of the stars, the equinoctial, ecliptic, zenith, and meridians. The Portuguese explorations down the African coast and of the Atlantic islands had inspired the city council of Nuremberg in 1490 to commission Martin Behaim (1459–1507) to construct what appears to be the earliest surviving terrestrial globe. On it the world was hand-drawn—on strips of parchment affixed to a hard core of composition fashioned over a mould. John Cabot (1450–98), discoverer of Newfoundland, used a globe, probably of parchment-covered wood, to mark his discoveries. With the discovery of the New World, a popular demand for terrestrial globes arose on the Continent. At first it could be ill satisfied, as globes were either hand-drawn as well as hand-made, or were hand-wrought in metal and then engraved—again by hand. However, in the first decade of the sixteenth century the printing of paper gores mathematically constructed to cover spheres accurately was devised in Germany, and the reproduction of globes in quantity became possible. But these globes were generally small. Nevertheless their popularity is vouched for by the number that have survived, and typical examples are those depicted in Holbein's famous painting of *The Ambassadors* (1536) in the National Gallery, London. While these globes were, of course, of value to navigators, what the latter really needed was a globe big enough to work out practical problems on, small enough to carry conveniently on board ship, cheap enough to buy, and last but by no means least showing rhumb lines correctly. A genius was to arise who was to satisfy their needs. Gerard Mercator (1512–94) was a native of east Flanders. He was born in a village close to the great port of Antwerp, whither the silks and spices of the east were brought in exchange for the fine cloths, fine printed books, exquisitely wrought instruments, and rich wines of Flanders and the Rhineland. Gemma Frisius, some of whose inventions we have already noticed, was a professor at Louvain University, at that time 'the fountain-head of learning'. Thither the young Mercator went in the year 1530—the year that Nuñez, ten years senior in age, left

---

[1] The shortest distance between two places on the earth's surface lies on the arc of a great circle—the arc of a circle on the earth's surface whose plane passes through the earth's centre. See Fig. 42, p. 483.

to take up the post of Portugal's Cosmographer Royal. It was the year too
in which Gemma Frisius produced his first terrestrial globe. Probably
at his prompting, Mercator turned to the making of instruments, globes,
and maps, and mastered the art of surveying. Seven years later appeared
Gemma Frisius's second terrestrial globe, and a companion celestial one.
Part of the engraving of the gores was the handiwork of Mercator. The
globes met with immediate popular approval. A feature of great interest
was that they showed a strait to the north of Newfoundland connecting
the Atlantic and the Pacific.[1] It was in 1541 that Gerard Mercator produced his own terrestrial globe. It excelled technically, the twelve gores
being designed with remarkable accuracy and terminated 20° from the
poles, in the now general manner, separate circular sections being drawn
for the polar regions. But what interested the navigator was that besides
having drawn upon it the equator, a prime meridian, through the Canaries,
meridians at 15° intervals, parallels of latitude at 10° intervals, the ecliptic,
tropics, polar circles, and various scales, the Spanish one being 18 Spanish
leagues to an equatorial degree, the sea surface was additionally laced with
numerous wind roses and rhumbs. Moreover it was fitted with a flexible
and adjustable quarter circle which enabled courses to be read off or laid
off accurately on its curved surface.[2] The size, too, of the globe (41 cm.—
16 inches—in diameter) was ample enough for accuracy, yet handy enough
for shipboard use. Furthermore, in various localities stars were represented, including the Pole Star and Ursa Major. Thus orientation and
latitude finding at night were simplified. The globes gradually supplanted
Frisius's amongst the educated. Cheap as well as expensive models were
sold, and many must quickly have found their way to sea. As we shall see,
they held their popularity in England and amongst seamen till the close
of the century. In 1551 Mercator produced a companion celestial globe.
With this and an almanac, compass, and astrolabe the competent navigator
could fix his position, tell the time and find the compass variation with considerable accuracy. With these two globes to supplement his rutter, plane
charts, compasses, sea-compass, and azimuth compass, ring-dial, nocturnal,
astrolabe, cross-staff, and quadrant, his shipman's quadrant and his hour
glass, traverse board, lodestone, journal, abacus and almanac, the navigator
could be sure that he had provided himself with the best available equipment. If his voyage was one of exploration, he would also have 'a Geographicall plaine sphere' (really 'plane' sphere) 'to describe a country'.[3]
This was the precursor of the theodolite. It consisted of a horizontal compass dial with an alidade and, inset in the face of the dial, usually eccentric-

[1] Taylor, E. G. R., *Tudor Geography*, 1485–1583 (1930), reviews the developments in geographical knowledge, theory and surveying in the sixteenth century.
There is a valuable bibliography.

[2] Blundeville, *Exercises* (1594). See Pl. XXV.

[3] William Cuningham illustrates 'The Geographicall plaine sphere' as 'an
Instrument serving the use to describe a country' on fol. 136 of his *Cosmographical
Glasse* (1559).

ally, a magnetic compass. By means of this instrument, and perhaps a plane table (now coming into use), he surveyed his discoveries, using the modern method, known as triangulation, devised by Gemma Frisius and first described by him in 1533. If, in addition, the navigator had a copy of Martin Cortes's *Arte de Navegar* of 1551, he had the very latest comprehensive navigation manual in existence, one which really did explain 'the way of a ship in the sea'. Much of its contents we have already drawn upon in describing the navigator's instruments.

The manual is divided into three parts. The first part describes the cosmos, and discusses its movements, rejecting absolutely the Pythagorean hypothesis that the earth itself revolved, 'for circular motion is proper to the heavens' (fol. ix.). The various divisions of the sphere—the horizon, meridian, zodiac, etc.—are defined, the size of the earth discussed, and its division into geographical climates explained.

The second part deals thoroughly with the course of the sun and of the moon, with the seasons, the use of sun-dials and nocturnals, and ends with the calculation of the tides and with weather lore.

The third part continues the practical note on which the preceding part closes. It deals exclusively with the ways and means available to the mariner to take his ship safely from port to port. The exact description of how to draw and use a sea-card is followed by shorter chapters on the characteristics and manufacture of the compass, and on the manufacture and use of both the astrolabe and the cross-staff, each process being described in detail, with clear drawings of the instrument under discussion, and finally on the manner of plotting or 'pricking' a position upon the chart. Wise admonitions on errors, omissions, and false estimates to be avoided conclude the work.

The navigator, explained Cortes, in the sixth chapter of the third part, must know two things which the sea-card would show him—his course, by 'the lynes of the sayling carde'—and distance 'by the scale or trunke of the leagues'.[1] Taking 'with a compasse the distance of two places' he then 'directed his foreshyppe to the selfe same wynde' as his card showed to be the right one. As for 'the distance he ought to know how muche the shyppe goeth dayly; well consyderyng . . . all suche thynges as may be with hym or against hym'. According to his reckoning, 'he should knowe how muche he hath gone' and so the distance he had still to go. 'And because this estimation . . . cannot be . . . exacte', particularly on long voyages or over a long time, Martin Cortes advised that he should 'rectifie . . . it . . . by the altitude of the pole', either by a Pole Star sight or a meridian sun sight according to the rules given in his manual.

Plotting the ship's position was termed 'setting or making a pricke in the card', to do which, Cortes explained, the navigator had to 'knowe from what degree or how many degrees of the altitude of the Pole he had departed, and with what wynde he had sayled'. If on taking his sight he

[1] See Pl. XXVI. The quotations are from Eden's translation (1561) of Cortes.

found his latitude unchanged, he knew he had made good an east-west course, in which event 'what he hath gonne can not bee knowen but by the judgement of a wyse and expert man'. If, however, the navigator found himself in a higher or a lower latitude, he took two pairs of compasses, placing a point of one in the place where he reckoned his ship was, its other point on 'the lyne or wynde' along which he reckoned he had sailed. Similarly he put one point of the other compass on the graduation on the latitude scale of his observed latitude, the other point on the nearest east-west line where it met the latitude scale. 'And so he drew both the compasses, the one in one hande, the other in the other hande' together. Where the points of observed latitude and estimated course met, there was his position. From this position henceforward he kept his 'accounte'.

It was no doubt already common for navigators to practise latitude sailing. The favourite method—which Columbus had used—was to steer a course which would bring the ship on to the latitude, but either well eastward or well to the westward, of the intended landfall, and then to steer along the latitude until the expected landfall was made. By this means the inevitable errors in estimation were at least largely eliminated in a north-south direction. As for those in an east-west direction, there was nothing for mariners to do except to navigate with care by day, and at night to avoid standing in towards the shore, if it was reckoned to be very close. To facilitate latitude sailing, Martin Cortes included a diagram showing the distance in leagues (of $17\frac{1}{2}$ to a degree) and in degrees and minutes that had to be run on a wind to raise or lower latitude by $1°$, and the distance run east or west in so doing. It was a more accurate version of the type of traverse table already referred to.[1] It was essentially one designed for 'latitude sailing'.

In keeping his daily reckoning at sea the navigator when out of sight of land used the astronomer's 'natural day'. In other words he kept his reckoning 'from the myddaye or noone, and ended it the next noone folowynge'. By this calendar the tenth day of a month ended 'the same daye at noone. And the houres that roen from that noonetyde forwarde, were of the eleventh daye'.

Although Cortes also included in his manual, as already remarked, an accurate table showing the value in minutes (angular) of a degree of longitude in every degree of latitude, nowhere did he touch upon the method by which departure should be turned into difference of longitude. In truth there was little point in doing so while the plane chart was the navigator's guide. Also, although 'the Nauigation or course from one place to another [according to the cosmographers] ought to be by the arcke of the greater circle: for that . . . shall be the shortest course', great circle sailing was a method of navigation far too ambitious to be explained. Indeed it could only be done with the aid of a terrestrial globe, since a great circle course could not be found from a plane chart; and until globes big enough for

[1] See Pl. XI.

navigational use were manufactured, great circle sailing was no more than a cosmographer's theory. Mercator's terrestrial globe of 1541 appears to have been the first globe offered for sale that could have been used by navigators for great circle sailing, for, in addition to the rhumb lines for ordinary sailing, it had the *quarta altitudo*, or adjustable flexible quarter-circle, which enabled great circle courses between places to be determined. The small size, however, of the globe must have rendered its navigational value low. The first brief, and by no means explicit description in English of great circle sailing by the aid of a globe is found in William Bourne's *Rules of Navigation* of 1567. The lack of reference to the *quarta altitudo*, and of rhumb lines, implies that he had not Mercator's globe in mind. It was not until over twenty years later that great circle sailing was clearly explained in print, or its practice recorded in an English journal, and it is significant that this was shortly after the appearance of an English globe much larger than Mercator's.[1]

[1] Davis, J., *The Seamans Secrets*, London (1595), contains the explanation; and *The Voyage of Robert Dudley to the West Indies*, in 1594, Hak. Soc., Ser. 2, Vol. 3, contains the record of great circle sailing.

Chapter Three

THE AWAKENING OF THE ENGLISH TO THE NEED FOR NAVIGATION

'Master John Cabot has his mind set upon even greater things, because he expects to keep more and more towards the east . . . where he believes that all the spices of the world have their origin, as well as the jewels . . . by means of this they hope to make London a more important mart for spices than Alexandria.'

Raimondo de Raimondi de Soncino, reporting the Cabots' discovery of Newfoundland to the Duke of Milan, 18 December 1497.

'the marchauntes of London . . . also divers noble men and gentelmen as well as the [Privy] council as other . . . have furnysshed and sent furth certeyne shyppes for the discovering of . . . landes and regions . . . unknowen, [and] have herein deserved immortall fame, for . . . they have shewed no small liberalitie upon uncerteyne hope of gayne . . . and . . . the two chiefe capitaynes of the same . . . Syr Hugh Wylloby and the excellent pilotte Rycharde Chaunceler who have therein adventured theyr lyves for the commoditie of theyr countrey are men doubtless woorthye for theyr noble attemptes to bee made Knightes of the Ocean or otherwyse preferred if ever God sende them home ageyne. . . . For as suche have obteyned absolute glory that have brought great thynges to passe so have they deserved immortall fame which have only attempted the same. . . .'

Richard Eden's *Preface to the Reader* in his translation of *The Decades of the newe worlde* of *Peter Martyr* (1455–1526) (the third book on America to be printed in English). Londini, *In aedibus Guilhelmi Powell. Anno. 1555.*
Sir Hugh Willoughby perished on this voyage, Richard Chancellor on the succeeding one.

WHEN King Henry VIII died in January 1547 not more than a few score Englishmen were interested in the practice of oceanic navigation. Probably fewer could practise it. In company with the more numerous Bretons and Normans, a few hardy fishermen made the annual trip to the cod-banks and to the inhospitable shores of Newfoundland, there to cure their catch for the return. But they were not navigators.

Roger Barlow, whose three brothers were in the Church, and who was himself a Bristol merchant, trading in Seville, had voyaged to Morocco. In 1526, with Henry Latimer, he had participated in Sebastian Cabot's intended voyage to the Moluccas by way of the Magellan Strait that, after the loss of the flagship, had finished up by exploring the River Plate in the hope that it would lead to the still fabulous treasures of Peru. Both Englishmen had become competent navigators during the two years of the expedition. But Henry Latimer, if not dead, must now, like Roger Barlow, have been close on sixty. Though one account has it that Henry VIII's death put an end to an intended voyage of 'discovery of the northern passage to the East Indies, with three of His Majesty's ships from Milford Haven' by Roger Barlow, the voyaging days of both must have been over. In the 1530s old William Hawkins of Plymouth and a few others had voyaged to Brazil and brought back dye-wood, but it seems certain that they all engaged foreign pilots to take them there and that the French wars put an end to their activities. We can say then that at the time of Henry VIII's death few Englishmen could navigate a merchant or a royal ship across the great ocean to a known landfall.[1] None could navigate to the East—to India, the Moluccas, Cathay. Nor had any Englishman penetrated the vast spaces of the Pacific Ocean—of the Great South Sea.

Most Englishmen, if not entirely ignorant of the New World, discovered almost a lifetime before by Columbus, were not in the least interested in it. Some might recall that Sebastian Cabot, now Pilot-Major of Spain, said he had sailed west in Bristol-manned ships with his father, John, some fifty years since and that it was they who had at last discovered the New Found Land and its cod-banks. Since then there had been a few voyages of discovery to the north-west planned and even attempted, but they had come to nought.

Although the study of geography was being advised in England by a few scholars from the 1530s, there was no popular work in print in English that described the wonders and possibilities of the New World or of the Orient now being discovered and exploited by the Spaniards and the Portuguese; indeed there was only one English book—little better than a pamphlet—that even mentioned America, and that had been printed in Antwerp and dated from 1511.[2] There was no popular demand for one. Except

[1] (a) See *A Brief Summe of Geographie*, Hak. Soc., Ser. 2, Vol. 69. See also Levillier, R., 'A Roger Barlow Map in Florence?', *Imago Mundi*, Vol. 8, where an English chart of Guinea and Brazil of *c.* 1536, signed 'R.B.' is reproduced.

(b) An action in the High Court of Admiralty in 1533 concerning the loss of John a Borough's sea chests (Public Record Office, High Court of Admiralty File 5, large bundle, *John a Borough contra John Andrewes*) shows that Borough had a cross-staff, quadrant, lodestone, running glass, a Portuguese Ephemerides, a Spanish rutter, an English rutter compiled by himself, two Spanish compasses, two other compasses, two charts, one being of the Mediterranean.

[2] *Of the newe landes and of ye people founde by the messengers of the Kynge of portyngale named Emanuel. Of the X dyuers nacyons crystened. Of pope Johan and his landes and of the costely keyes and wonders melodyes that in that lande is.* Antwerp, John of Doesborowe. [1511?]

See Arber, E., *The First Three English Books on America* (1885). *A new interlude and a mery of the nature of the iiij elementes etc.* A play of 1519 described the New World in a dialogue between *Experyence* and *Studyous desire*. Arber reproduces the relevant dialogue.

for one brief manuscript with charts by a Dieppois pilot in English service, in the Royal Library,[1] possibly two or three more elsewhere, like Roger Barlow's *Brief Summe of Geography* (though only one comparable to Jean Rotz's has survived, in Italy), not a single work existed in English on the art of navigation. The purely practical art of transoceanic navigation was of no interest to the English while they still got their oriental and tropical wares from the marts of Flanders, Portugal, and Spain.

The ignorance and indifference of the English of the middle of the sixteenth century to the geographical discoveries that were changing the whole conception and economy of the world were largely the result of force of circumstances, just as it was to be circumstances which were to oblige them ere long to take a practical interest in the discoveries. It was no 'spirit of romance' that inspired the Elizabethans. It was, in its crudest form, lust for gold; in its direst, lack of bread; in its noblest, love of country; in its sublimest, love of God—not a few died at sea 'in defence of the realm' and of 'established religion'; in its most honest form, love of commerce. What is remarkable is not that the English took no part in and no interest in the great discoveries of the fifteenth and early sixteenth centuries but that, awakening in the latter half of the sixteenth century to the reality of the discoveries, they mastered the art of oceanic navigation that made them possible so rapidly and so effectually that within thirty years they had defeated the leading maritime state in battle at sea, and within half a century had planted colonies of their own overseas, and were trading regularly round the Cape to India and the Far East, and making original contributions of fundamental importance to the art of navigation. It was not through love of fame but by force of circumstances that when Elizabeth ascended the throne the English also grasped that 'To be master of the sea is an abridgement of a monarchy', and 'that he that commands the sea is at great liberty, and may take as much and as little of the war as he will'.

It was not long before they concluded, again in Bacon's words, that 'the wealth of both Indies seems in great part but an accessory to the command of the seas'. The English were at once practical and imaginative. They went to the root of the problem of oceanic navigation, they built ships 'sufficient' for the ocean seas, and they trained men 'sufficient' for the task of navigating and, if necessary, fighting them.

It was King Henry VII who had made the naval interests of the English for the first time part of a deliberate, settled policy. If he had been unresponsive to Columbus, he had at least rectified his error by his reception of the Cabots. That their discoveries had not been further exploited was because they had found neither a way to Cathay nor to an inhabited land offering prospects of trade. Henry VII could not afford to seek elsewhere. He had had to fight to get his throne. He had now to retain it by diplomacy and wise economic policies. Men did not think of the north-east as a

[1] Rotz, J., *The Book of Hydrography* (1542).

possible route to Cathay. To seek 'elsewhere' meant trespassing upon the territories of either Spain or Portugal, for the Bull of 1493 had divided the New World between these powers; and by the Treaty of Tordesillas, a year later, they had agreed upon a line 370 leagues west of Cape Verde in Africa as the dividing line. It seems certain, although the wording is ambiguous, that the divisions applied only 'towards the South and West' of the latitudes of Lisbon and Madrid, since the English explorations north were never called in question.[1] As these appeared to be impractical, Henry VII had to be content to build up the traditional home trade between Portugal, Spain, France, and the Netherlands and to seek to establish new European markets in the Baltic and the Levant. He cut his coat according to his cloth. He built up a modest 'narrow seas' navy of ships able to guard his shores and convoy his merchants' ships in troublous times safely along the routes between the North Sea and Biscay ports. In quiet times they were available at attractive rates to enterprising merchants for voyages into the Mediterranean. Their armament was an important feature in their favour.[2] Henry VII could not foresee that the diplomatically brilliant match of his son with a Spanish princess would later embitter relations with Spain to the point of war, and in so doing bring the English out on to the high seas of the world.

Henry VIII succeeded his father in 1509. He was ambitious, brilliant, forceful, and deeply interested in the sea. Because of his continental ambitions he built up a powerful 'narrow seas' royal navy and allied himself with the Empire and with the Spaniards, in three wars against the French (1511–14, 1522–5, 1540–6). In short, he continued the policy of not trespassing upon the new realms of Spain. In return English merchants long settled in Seville were allowed to continue their trading with the Atlantic islands of Spain, and even to have factors in the New World, like the Thornes, who were contemporaries and friends of Roger Barlow. One of the effects of the divorce of Catherine of Aragon in 1530 seems, however, to have been to lead to the suppression of such factors. Unlike the Portuguese, the Spaniards did not keep their achievements in the New World secret, though they did prohibit trade between their colonies and any other port than Seville, and did insist that it should be confined to Spain. To enforce this they licensed, with few exceptions, only Spanish pilots to undertake the voyage. Consequently, the English could learn of the New

---

[1] The wording of the Bull reads: ' . . . by the fulnesse of Apostolycall power, doo gyue, graunt, and assigne to yowe, youre heyres and successours, al the firme landes and Ilandes found or to be found, discouered or to be discouered toward the West and South, drawyng a line from the pole Artike to the pole Antartike from the North to the South: Conteynygne in the donation, what so euer firme landes or Ilandes are founde or to bee founde towarde *India*, or towards any other parte what so euer it bee, beinge distant from, or without the fore sayd lyne drawen a hundreth leagues towardes the Weste and South from any of the Ilandes which are commonly cauled *De los Azores* and Cabo Verde . . . ' Reproduced in Richard Eden's *The Decades of the newe worlde*, London (1555), and in Arber, E. *op. cit.*

[2] See *Documents and Inventories of Henry VII*, N.R.S., Vol. 8.

World only from the merchants in Seville and its port of San Lucar. Detailed knowledge was lacking and navigational experience, though it could be acquired openly up to the 1530s, was discouraged by the English Government from wider motives. The Portuguese on the other hand ruthlessly kept secret all their discoveries along the route to the East Indies. Sufficient information was released for the maps of the world to be kept corrected, but the rutters and charts were rigorously protected by law from falling into foreign hands. Pilots experienced on the routes were closely watched. Henry VIII had none of the scruples over Portuguese possessions that he had with the Spanish ones; there were, too, pilots who had fled from Portuguese service for fear of persecution on the grounds that they had betrayed their knowledge, or for gain, and Henry had no qualms about employing them. Such pilots had probably guided old William Hawkins on his three voyages to Guinea and Brazil—there to get ivory and Brazil wood for cloth dyes.

Since 1528 the French in their wars with the Empire had had no scruples in preying upon the Spanish possessions and trade in the Caribbean and Gulf of Mexico. Soon religious passions were to add stimulus to their raids. The French had quickly mastered the art of navigation as practised by the Portuguese and Spaniards. As is evident from the early rutters, they had always been the link between the mariner of the Mediterranean and the North. They were soon called upon to aid the English.[1]

In building up his royal navy Henry gave it of the best—Italian shipwrights, French pilots, and German gunfounders.[2] He gave it also, as already mentioned, permanent administrative organizations—the Navy Board and Trinity House—to see to the maintenance of the ships and docks and of navigational aids, and to the provision of seamen. And he gave it officers drawn from the nobility and gentry. During his reign English shipwrights and gunfounders became second to none. The gunfounders cast fine cannon designed, and for the first time mounted, for shipboard use. The shipwrights built ships specially designed for the cannon's efficient use.

[1] Nicolas de Nicolai, at one time in the service of Henry VIII as hydrographer and pilot, later Premier Cosmographer of France, who stole various English charts for the French in 1546–7, translated Medina's *Arte de Navegar* of 1545, as early as 1549 or 1550. It was printed as Pierre de Medina, *L'Art de Naviguer*, at Paris in 1554. The Dieppois hydrographers of the early sixteenth century learnt their art from the Portuguese. This is unmistakably reflected in their surviving charts. Moreover, some illustrious Portuguese cartographers such as André Homem and Bartolome Velho stayed in France. The traditional link between France and Portugal was the wine trade between Rouen, the port of Paris, Nantes, Bordeaux, and the Portuguese ports. (Information provided by the late D. Gernez). For the dependence of Englishmen upon French pilots for the Brazil trade of the 1530s and 1540s, see Appendix 2. As late as 1577 the Spanish President of the Council of the Indies reported 'All the pilots who go on these English and French Armadas [i.e. to raid Spanish shipping] are Portuguese,' quoted in Taylor, E. G. R. 'Instructions to a Colonial Surveyor in 1582', *M.M.*, Vol. 37.

[2] See Taylor, E. G. R. *Tudor Geography*, 1485–1583 (1930), for the contribution of French pilots to the navy of Henry VIII.

Under the tutelage of French pilots and the supervision of the Brethren of Trinity House the English finally became independent of foreign pilots in European waters, so that in the closing years of Henry's reign they were able successfully to conduct their fleet unaided against that of the French. But the Reformation, combined with the new wealth pouring into Europe from the Portuguese and Spanish empires, sadly upset the economic web of English trade, while the dissolution of the monasteries, the breaking up of the church lands, and the creation of new estates dislocated the domestic economy. By the time of Henry's death in 1547 English 'merchants perceived the commodities and wares of England were in small request . . . and that those merchandises, which strangers in the times and memory of our ancestors had earnestly sought and desired, were now neglected and the price thereof abated, although they were carried to their own parts'.[1] New 'vents' had to be found for English farms and looms. If England could find new markets in northern latitudes as well as a northern route to Cathay, she could both sell her staple products and corner the world's spice market. In an age when vegetables were few, and meat poor, when most men's beer was thin, and wine sour, spices were less of a luxury than a necessity in most households. The spice market was better than a gold-mine. But the discovery and exploitation of such a route involved two matters quite strange to the English—the economics of an exploratory commercial expedition and the art of navigation.

While indifference to the great discoveries was characteristic of the English as a whole, it was not so of a few individual Englishmen. They were a varied lot—some merchants, like Roger Barlow; a few of the nobility like John Dudley, Lord Lisle, the Lord High Admiral; some officials in London; one or two scholars, such as Richard Eden—young men chiefly.[2] They were few but their influence was now increasingly effective. Henry VIII's successor, Edward VI, was a child of nine, so that it was the Privy Council that was to rule the realm in the king's name. To do this successfully they were dependent, if not upon popular support, at least upon the support of the commercial classes. This could be assured only by a sound economic policy. Such was the state of the traditional overseas markets that this meant successful overseas enterprise. Their first business therefore was to arrange for Englishmen to learn the techniques of navigation, of exploration, and of the financial and commercial organization necessary to exploit them. The Privy Council acted swiftly. Sebastian Cabot, as Pilot-Major of Spain, was familiar with all the navigational secrets of Spain and of her empire. He not only knew all the latest navigational charts, instruments and practices, and all the leading navigators of the day—he

---

[1] Hakluyt's *Principal Navigations*, Hak. Soc., Extra Ser., Vol. I, p. 243.

[2] On the ignorance of the English about the geographical discoveries of the fifteenth and first half of the sixteenth century there is ample evidence. Taylor's *Tudor Geography, 1485–1583* (1930), deals with it in detail, and a valuable review is contained in the opening chapters of Parks, G. B., *Richard Hakluyt and the English Voyages* (1928). It has a valuable bibliography.

was himself one of the most illustrious. He was experienced in exploration, and thoroughly conversant with the economic structure of the colonial empire of Spain, and with the methods used in financing expeditions. Moreover he claimed to be English. His loyalty to the Emperor was known to be not above question. Indeed there were some in England who knew of earlier negotiations with Cabot. He was approached and the bribe was accepted. Early in 1548 Sebastian Cabot on leave of absence from Spain reached England, never to leave again. There he remained till his death some ten years later, a royal pensioner, teaching the English all they sought to learn.[1]

It seems clear that Lord Lisle, the Lord High Admiral, was the power behind Cabot. In February 1547, one month after King Henry's death, Sir Thomas Seymour, brother of Edward, Duke of Somerset, the Protector, had been created Lord Seymour of Sudeley, and had supplanted Lord Lisle as Lord High Admiral. In January 1549 Seymour's intrigues had led to his deprivation of office and two months later to his death by beheading. In October Lord Lisle, who had been created Earl of Warwick, had been reappointed Lord High Admiral and Cabot, who had retired to Bristol during Seymour's tenure of office, had at once been summoned to London. It is perhaps significant that Roger Barlow had been appointed

---

[1] See Appendix 4. 'Sebastian Cabot filled in Spain the office first of Crown pilot, from 15 August 1515, and then of Pilot-Major from 5 February 1518, until 25 October 1525 (when he went on the voyage of discovery of 1526), and from 1533 until at least October 1547. Nor should we omit to state that not only was Sebastian by virtue of his office supervisor of the Chair of Cosmography in the *Casa de Contratación*, and filled the professorship of nautical and cosmographic science in the institution, but he was a member of the commission of pilots and geographers who in 1515 were required by King Ferdinand to make a general revision of all maps and charts.' Harrisse, H., *John & Sebastian Cabot* (1896) p. 73. This is the standard authority on the Cabots, but Williamson, J. A., *The Voyages of the Cabots*, (1929) is the most recent authority. This is a scholarly work reviewing also earlier ideas on, and attempts to explore, the Atlantic, particularly by the West-Country-men of England. The Portuguese hydrographer Diogo Homem, who had been banished to Africa for a year in 1545 for murder, was in England in 1547. In July he was given permission to return to Portugal to employ 'his knowledge of cosmography and his art of navigation'. It is not known when he left England. It seems clear he did not go to Portugal, but eventually to Italy. In April 1547 he had a law-suit over 'a certain great new chart or map' containing, as he asserted, 'a description of the land and provinces of the entire world and all the discovered navigations of sea, constructed and painted, as it appeared, in eight great rolls or sheets of parchment . . .'. To confirm its value, which was very great in England because of 'the wante and lack of expert learned men in that faculte of makyng cartes or mappes, and the scarcyte . . . of such cartes withein this realm of England . . .', he called as witnesses 'Peter Poll, Italyen, beyng experte in shipmen's occupacyon, born in the isle of Corsica, of the age of xxx^{tye} or thereabowte . . .' experienced 'in conductyng of shyppes by the seas and cuntreys specyfied in the said carte . . ., also Ferdynande Gonsalaez, ship master, beyng lernyd in cosmographe or descrycyon of the world, borne in Lushborne in the realme of Portuguale, of the age of xl yerys . . .'. Blake, J. W., 'New Light on Diogo Homem, Portuguese Cartographer.' *M.M.*, Vol. 28.

Vice-Admiral of the Coast of Pembrokeshire. Cabot had doubtless been discussing plans in the West Country, and Barlow had probably been influential in obtaining his services. Was it in recompense for his part in obtaining the services of Cabot that he was appointed Vice-Admiral? It could be a lucrative post.

The first navigators were soon trained. Within a year Sebastian Cabot seems to have organized a training ship—the bark *Aucher*—and a training cruise to Chios. The voyage was made under the command of one Roger Bodenham, who, it is not surprising to learn, was a Bristol captain. Its success may be gauged by the statement Roger Bodenham made years later to Richard Hakluyt: 'All those Mariners that were in my sayde shippe which were, besides boyes, three score and tenne, for the most part were within five or six years after, able to take charge, and did.'[1] One of these 'Mariners' was Richard Chancellor—'the incomparable Richard Chancellor' as in later years, and long after his death, Dr. John Dee was to call him—a brilliant mathematician and astronomer, and soon to prove himself gifted as a sea-captain and skilful as a navigator.

While Sebastian Cabot was training navigators he was also organizing in London the preparation of charts, ephemerides and instruments and the economic backing essential to provide the ships, men, and wares for a trading venture into unknown seas and lands.[2] By 1553 'The Merchant Adventurers of England for the discovery of lands, territories, isles, dominions and signories unknown' had the first expedition ready. It sailed that year under the command of an Englishman, Sir Hugh Willoughby, in the ship *Bona Esperanza*, 120 tons, with, as chief pilot, Richard Chancellor in the *Edward Bonaventure*, 160 tons, of which ship Stephen Borough was the master. A third ship, the *Bona Confidentia*, 90 tons, completed this, the first all-English expedition of discovery. The destination was Cathay, the aim, old John Cabot's. He, in 1497, discovering new land to the west, had supposed it to be a part of Asia and, it was reported, 'had his mind set upon even greater things, because he proposed to keep . . . more and more towards

---

[1] Roger Bodenham was the captain of the bark *Aucher*. The master was one William Sherwood. Bodenham 'provided a skilful pilot to carry over Land's End', and recounts, 'I had in my ship a Spanish pilot, called Nobiczia, which I took in at Cadiz at my coming forth. He went with me all this voyage into the Levant without wages, of good will that he bare me and the ship. He stood me in good stead until I came back again to Cadiz; and then I needed no pilot. And so from thence I came to London with the ship and goods in safety: God be praised!

'And all those mariners that were in my said ship—which were, besides boys, three score and ten—for the most part were within five or six years after, able to take charge of ships, and did.

'Richard Chancellor, who first discovered Russia was with me in that voyage; and Matthew Baker, who afterwards became the Queen's Majesty's Chief Shipwright.' Hakluyt's *Principal Navigations*, Hak. Soc. Extra Ser., Vol. 5, p. 76. It will be noted that even for the Mediterranean voyage a Spanish pilot was essential.

[2] See Pls. XXVII and XXVIII.

the east . . . where he believed that all the spices of the world had their origin, as well as the jewels. . . . By means of this they hoped to make London a more important mart for spices than Alexandria.'[1]

It was this that inspired the Merchant Adventurers who financed the voyage of discovery towards Cathay in 1553, as it had inspired Robert Thorne in 1526, and Roger Barlow in 1547. The preparation for the voyage brought out (in June 1553) the first book in English to treat at any length of the newfound lands, and the second to mention America, Richard Eden's translation from the Latin of Sebastian Munster's *A treatyse of the newe India, with other new founde landes . . . as well eastwarde as westwarde . . . of* 1536.[2] Born in about 1521, Richard Eden had received a good education, and had gone up to Cambridge. There he had studied for ten years, from 1535 to 1544. Then had followed years in official service, either in the Treasury or in the service of Sir William Cecil, later Lord Burghley, and already one of the Secretaries of State and a Privy Counsellor. Eden dedicated his work to the Duke of Northumberland, fated to be beheaded in the August after Mary's accession, but still the virtual ruler of the country, and a driving force behind the voyage of discovery.

The aim of the voyage was not realized. The expedition was scattered by a storm, and Sir Hugh Willoughby and his men were frozen to death.[3] Richard Chancellor, however, survived. At Vardo he met Scotsmen who had heard of the rigours of the Arctic winter, and would have had him turn back, but he pressed on, 'persuading himself that a man of valour could not commit a more dishonourable part than, for fear of danger, to avoid and shun great attempts'. He, too, was ultimately held by the ice, but he made his way by the White Sea to Moscow, and out of his negotiations developed the Russian trade. He returned in 1554, and in 1555 a trading company, the Muscovy Company, was chartered by the new queen, Mary, and her consort Philip II of Spain.

At the time the fruits of the 1553 expedition—the Russian trade—must have seemed small, such richer ones had been hoped for; particularly as in 1555 had appeared *The Decades of the newe worlde or west India. . . . Wrytten in the Latine tounge by Peter Martyr of Angleria and translated into Englysshe by Rycharde Eden'*. It was the first collection of voyages printed in English, and the first work to contain narratives of English voyages. To encourage the furthering of other enterprises Eden contri-

---

[1] John Cabot's aim is quoted from the letter of Raimondo de Raimondi de Soncino to the Duke of Milan, 18 Dec. 1497. From the Archives of Milan. Printed in Williamson, J. A., *The Voyages of the Cabots* (1929).

[2] A treatyse of the newe India, with other new founde landes and Ilandes, as well eastwarde as westwarde, as they are knowen and found in these oure dayes, after the descripcion of Sebastian Munster in his boke of universall Cosmographie: wherein the diligent reader may see the good successe and rewarde of noble and honest enterpryses, by the which not only worldly ryches are obtayned, but also God is glorified, & the Christian fayth enlarged. Translated out of Latin into Englishe. By Rycharde Eden. [London, 1553].

[3] See Pl. XXIX and Appendix 5.

buted a lengthy preface on the noble nature of honourable exploration and enterprise by sea.[1]

By the time the book was published it was, of course, known that Sir Hugh Willoughby was dead. But the book must have been a revelation of the New World he was attempting to reach, an inspiration second only to that of his example. Moreover, for over a quarter of a century it proved to be the English source-book of geographical and navigational knowledge. As such it was to be of the utmost value to men like Hawkins and Drake. Here were Peter Martyr's descriptions of 1511 of 'the Ocean'; of 1516 of 'the supposed continent', America; 'the discovery of the Pacific'; and 'Cabots' voyages'; his description of 1521 of the discovery of Yucatan and Mexico; Oviedo's *Natural History of the West Indies*, first printed in 1526; Pigafetta's *The First Circumnavigation of the Globe*, also first printed in 1526; a treatise *Of the Pole Antarctic, and the stars about the same* from Amerigo Vespucci's narrative of his voyage to Brazil in 1501; and Andreas de Corsali's *Voyage to the East Indies*.

Richard Eden was a shrewd editor. He not only adorned his tale with these descriptive works of hitherto unimagined isles and peoples, voyages, and adventures to excite the English imagination but he pointed the moral. Of Vespucci's narrative he carefully included the portion containing the description and illustration of the Southern Cross, and of the world in relation to the zenith of travellers 90° apart in latitude, and Vespucci's explanation that he could observe such things 'hauynge knowledge of geometrie', and could successfully undertake such a voyage 'in suche daungerous places wanderynge in vnknowen coastes' only because he had 'byn skylfull in the science of Cosmographie'.

Further descriptions—of Muscovy, Cathay, and the North Regions, and of the Indies—followed, and then the first printed English treatise on the compass, the first description of 'What degrees are', and 'A demonstration of the roundnesse of the Earth', with an account, too, of Gemma Frisius's methods of finding the longitude. At the end of the book Eden added a section on metals, the first work of its kind printed in English, for the benefit of explorers and prospectors; and at the very last came accounts of the first two voyages out of England into Guinea.

Richard Chancellor, who had returned to England in 1554 to establish the Muscovy Company, had sailed again in 1555 with factors who were

[1] The Decades of the newe worlde or west India, Conteynyng the nauigations and conquestes of the Spanyardes, with the particular description of the most ryche and large landes and Ilandes lately founde in the west Ocean perteynyng to the inheritaunce of the kinges of Spayne. In the which the diligent reader may not only consyder what commoditie may hereby chaunce to the hole christian world in tyme to come, but also learne many secreates touchynge the lande, the sea, and the starres, very necessarie to be knowē to al such as shal attempte any nauigations, or otherwise haue delite to beholde the strange and woonderfull woorkes of God and nature. Wrytten in the Latine tounge by Peter Martyr of Angleria, and translated into Englysshe by Rycharde Eden. Londini. In aedibus Guilhelmi Powell. Anno. 1555.

to live in Russia and collect the Russian goods for transport to England. Returning in 1556 with the two ships of Sir Hugh Willoughby's lost squadron which the Russians had found frozen in the ice, Chancellor had met with a series of great storms. Of his four ships all save one foundered or were cast away. He himself perished on the Scottish coast, while attempting to save the life of the first Russian ambassador to the Court of St. James's. However, in that year three of the Muscovy Company's ships sailed for Russia. One of them, the pinnace *Searchthrift* (her commander, Stephen Borough), pushed eastwards along the Siberian coast in search of the route to Cathay, but at the island of Vaigats turned back in the face of approaching winter; and thereafter for over twenty years exploration in this direction ceased. The company, though vested with the rights of exploration, was content to exploit the Russian trade.

Modest as the success of the Cathay venture was, it was yet of prime importance in the development of English maritime enterprise and navigational skill. The immediate gains were important. The principal Russian products were naval stores—pitch, hemp, and timber. Hitherto these had come from the Baltic through the medium of the Hansa League, who could thus control the English navy and merchant marine. The Russian trade broke this monopoly, and placed a lever in the hands of the English with which they could prise open a way into the Baltic trade. This they soon did, as the ships of the realm had been made free of dependence upon the Hansa for their moorings, rigging, and spars. Moreover, the commercial organization, the joint-stock company, created to finance the trade that arose from the discoveries, proved so sound that it was adopted with equal success as a means of financing later trading, colonizing, and raiding ventures otherwise quite beyond the means of individual merchants or captains or even of the Government. Chancellor and Willoughby had not given their lives in vain.

While the English, under the expert guidance of Sebastian Cabot, were opening new markets in the north-east, an old one was closing up in the south-east. Since 1458, when Robert Sturmy of Bristol had first ventured into the Levant in search of wines and spices, English merchants had occasionally traded to the Levant for the wines of Chios and the currants of Greece. Henry VII and Henry VIII had fostered the trade, and individual merchants, despite the hazards of the voyage, which took a year, made fortunes. But in the face of the advancing Turks the risks mounted. The voyages, never very frequent, declined and, despite the bark *Aucher's* voyage of 1550, the last recorded voyage for a quarter of a century was made in 1553. But another and perhaps more lucrative source of trade was now being tapped. Cabot had with him John Alday, who described himself as his servant and 'a man of knowledge in the Arte of Navigation and Cosmographie', whom Cabot had prevented at the last from sailing as master of the bark *Aucher* in 1550. The reason is not clear, but it may have been that, as the voyage was likely to take a year, and he had a venture in a different region of the world on hand, he needed a man of Alday's abilities to conduct it. John Alday claimed that it was on his suggestion that 'the first voyage of traffique into the Kingdom of *Morocco in Barbarie*, [was] begun in the yeare 1551, with a tall ship called the *Lion of London*, of 150 tons'. It is more probable that it came from discussion between Cabot and leading English merchants in the Spanish and Levantine trade. He may well have talked over with Roger Barlow the latter's voyages to Madeira and the Azores, made in the course of his trading at Seville, and the business journey, probably in search of sugar and dates, he had made to Santa Cruz in Morocco, the modern Agadir. Moreover, Cabot was related by marriage to William Ostrich, eventually Governor of the English merchants resident in Spain and deeply engaged in the Levant trade.[1] It was in Cabot's interests to further those of Ostrich, and he must have known the Levant trade was becoming too risky. However that may be, John Alday should have sailed as master of the first English voyage to Morocco but was prevented by 'the sweating sickness', which broke out in London and which several of the promoters also caught. Nevertheless the *Lion* sailed. She left Portsmouth under the command of Thomas Wyndham, before, as the luckless John Alday put it, 'I was able to stand upon my feet'. Two Moors accompanied Thomas Wyndham 'whereof one was of the King's blood'; perhaps the other knew the coasts. Thomas Wyndham had served in the navy against the French, rising to the command of vice-admiral in the campaign of 1547. The settlement with France in 1550, which had followed the wresting of Boulogne from the English, had left him conveniently free. He was clearly a competent, and probably French-trained, pilot, and he would have had the observations of Roger Barlow on the route. Wyndham returned from Barbary before the year was out, with sugar, dates, almonds, and molasses—luxuries the English longed for. Already they were beginning to benefit from Sebastian Cabot's guidance. A second equally successful voyage, but with three ships, followed in 1552, and included a call, apparently for the first time by an English ship, at the Canary Islands. The Portuguese viewed these voyages with anger and 'gave out in England by their merchants, that if they tooke us in these partes, they would use us as their mortall enemies'. But as they had withdrawn their garrisons from Safi and Santa Cruz in 1541, they were powerless to prevent the trade. Indeed, for them worse was to follow. A Portuguese, Anthony Pinteado, falling into company with Wyndham, agreed with another Portuguese pilot, Francisco Rodrigues, to pilot Wyndham to the Guinea coast for ivory and gold. On 12 August 1553, three months after the first expedition for the discovery of Cathay by the north-east route sailed from London, the *Primrose* and the *Lion*, with the pinnace *Moon*, sailed from Portsmouth for the Guinea coast. After avoiding a Portuguese warship at Madeira, Wyndham came out in his true colours. He quarrelled with Pinteado, usurping his command and thrusting him amongst the sailors with opprobrious words. Nevertheless

---

[1] Taylor, E. G. R. (ed.), *A Brief Summe of Geography*, Hak. Soc., Ser. 2. Vol. 69, p. xxiii.

he saw to it that Pinteado piloted them to the Guinea coast. There they loaded 150 lb. of gold. Success assured thereby and the season growing late, Pinteado advised that the return voyage be started. But Wyndham would have none of it. By threats and insults he forced Pinteado and Rodrigues to pilot him eastward along the coast of Benin to the delta of the Niger, there to load pepper. It was his undoing. The crews, unaccustomed to the tropical fruits and climate, fell ill and died. Wyndham himself died. The men remaining fell upon Pinteado with bitter reproaches for leading them to such a place and forced him to sail for home leaving merchants on shore. Then Pinteado too died. Of all that company 'of seven score men came home to Plymmouwth scarcely fortye, and of them many dyed'. It was a sorry tale for all its golden ending, ignorance and covetousness competing against knowledge and prudence.[1]

The absence of such contentions over the Russian trade speaks much for the wisdom of Sebastian Cabot's guidance when it could be exercised personally. He had carefully drawn up 'Ordinances, Instructions, and Advertisements' for the proper regulation of the voyage of discovery to the north-east and for any subsequent trade.[2] For us, following the development of the art of navigation, the seventh instruction is of particular interest. It reads as follows:

> 7. Item, that the merchants, and other skilful persons in writing shall daily write, describe, and put in memorie the navigation of each day and night, with the points, the observations of the lands, tides, elements, altitude of the sunne, course of the moon and starres, and the same so noted by the Master and Pilot of every ship to be put in writing, the Captain-Generall assembling the masters together once every weeke . . . to put the same into a common leger, to remain a record for the company: the like order to be kept in proportioning of the Cardes, Astrolabes, and other instruments prepared for the voyage.

Here were the essentials for subsequent successful voyages over the same route. So sound were they that they became an integral part of every subsequent English voyage of repute.

Despite the mortality of the first Guinea voyage, despite the protestations of Portugal, sustained by Philip, other voyages followed. The Portuguese Pinteado (whose defection, after failing to get him extradited, the King of Portugal had tried to prevent by a belated pardon) had taught too well the secrets of the wind system and the currents off the Guinea coast. Besides, Rodrigues survived to impart to others the knowledge, lack of which made voyaging there a desperate venture of dead calms or head-

---

[1] Arber, E., *The First Three English Books on America* (1885); and *Europeans in West Africa* 1450–1560, Vol. II, Hak. Soc., Ser. 2, Vol. 87. This has a good map of the West African and Guinea Coasts showing the prevailing currents and typical courses sailed on outward and homeward voyages. Ignorance of the currents often prolonged the homeward voyages as much as the fickle winds.

[2] See Appendix 4 for other of Cabot's ordinances.

winds and unaccountable drifting. The bitter lessons, too, of Wyndham's shipboard quarrelling instilled a better sense of discipline and hygiene into the English seamen. John Lok commanded the second venture, of 1554 to 1555, and Richard Eden, by including in his *Decades of the newe worlde* a journal of the voyage, printed, in effect, the first English rutter for Atlantic, but not, of course, transatlantic, voyaging. It should be remarked that by including Oviedo's *Of the ordinary nauygation from Spayne to the West Indies* he gave a good idea of the transatlantic routes used. The three ships Lok took on the second Guinea venture were again very small—the *Trinity* of 140 tons, the *Bartholomew* of 90 tons, and the *John Evangelist* of 140 tons. Sailing from the Thames they called at Dover, Rye, and Dartmouth. 'The fyrst day of November at IX of the clocke at nyght departynge from the coast of Englande, we sette of the stert [Start Point] bearynge southwest all that nyght in the sea, and the nexte day all day, and the next nyght after untyll the thyrde daye of the sayde moneth about noone, makynge our way good, dyd runne 60 leagues. Item from xii of the clocke the thyrde daye tyll xii of the clocke the iiii day of the sayde mooneth, makyng our way good southeast, dyd runne every three houres twoo leagues, which amounteth to xvi leagues the hole [for the day's run].'

It will be seen that the point and time of departure were carefully noted, and that the way or course 'made good', that is to say, the courses steered and the estimated speed, corrected by means of the traverse board and checking of the leeway, were recorded from noon to noon. Each day the journal or rutter recorded the daily run. Then on 'the xix day at XII of the clocke, we had syght of the Ile of Palmes and Teneriffa and the Canaries', the rutter went on. The means of recognizing these by the landfall followed: 'The Isle of Palme ryseth rounde and lyeth southeaste and northweste, and the northweste parte is lowest. In the south, is a rounde hyll over the hedde lande, and another rounde hyll above that in the lande. . . . This Ile of Palme lyeth in the XXIX degrees [in latitude 29° N] . . . Teneriffa is a hygh lande and a greate hyghe picke lyke a sugar lofe. And upon the sayde picke is snowe throughout all the hole year . . . it maye be knowen above all other Ilandes, . . .' It was to become a familiar sight to Englishmen. In careful detail, giving land-marks, latitudes, soundings and the nature of the sea-bed in safe anchorages, the appearance of headlands, the lie of the land and the distances covered, the rutter carried on to the Guinea coast. It told what and where the ships traded. It was rich in casually thrown out hints and wonders. The pilot who wrote it was a friend of Richard Eden. He, though a scholar, could yet record 'sum of oure men . . . affirme ernestly that in the nyght season they felt a sensible heate to coomme from the beames of the moone' as credulously as the fact 'that in certeyne places of the sea, they sawe certeyne stremes of water which they carle spoutes saulynge owt of the ayer into the sea. And that sum of these are as bygge as the great pyllers of churches'. The English now found for themselves and for the first time recorded that 'the keles of theyr shyppes were marvelously overgrowen with certen shells of ii ynches length and more, as thycke as they could stande', which greatly hindered their sailing, and that 'Theyr shyppes were also in many places eaten with . . . woormes . . .', to prevent which one of the ships of the 1553 expedition to the north-east had been sheathed with lead after the Spanish fashion—thanks to Cabot.[1]

'Amonge other thynges that chaunced . . . it is woorthy to be noted', the account ran, 'that whereas they sayled thether in seven weeks, they coulde returne in no lesse space than xx weekes.' This was explained by the prevailing easterly winds off Cape Verde 'by reason whereof they were inforced to sayle farre oute of theyr course into the mayne Ocean to fynde the wynde at the west to bring them home. . . . It was also woorthy to be noted that . . . they overtooke [for the first recorded time in English voyaging] the course of the Soone, that they had it north from them at noone the xiiii day of Marche'.

It was Cape Verde, 'the green cape', he explained, 'to the whiche the Portugales fyrst directe theyr course when they sayle to America or the lande of Brasile . . . departynge from thence, they turne to the ryght hande to warde the quarter of the wynde . . . betweene the west and south . . .'. But that was forbidden territory, and these English ships made their sweep out into the ocean for home. They checked their latitude frequently, but guessed their bearing and distance, to begin with from the Cape Verde Islands, later as they progressed north 'from the Azores untyll we came in xlii degrees, where we set our course east northeast, judginge the Ile of Corvo south and by west of us and xxxvi leagues distant from us'. And so they came home bringing 'foure hundreth pounde weyght and odde of golde . . . and about two hundreth and fiftie elephantes teeth . . .'. Also they brought 'certeyne black slaves . . .'.

An incident occurred during a voyage to Guinea undertaken by William Towerson in 1558 which fortunately has been recorded by the faithful Hakluyt.[2] It affords a good insight into voyages made in time of war, in the middle of the sixteenth century, into the superior sailing qualities of English ships, and into the arms and instruments of navigation carried by a ship—in this instance, a Danzig 'hulk'—trading to Bordeaux. The Marian government had declared war on France on 7 June 1557, in accord-

---

[1] The Spanish had tried sheathing their ships with thin sheets of lead as a protection against the worms which could rapidly reduce a ship's bottom to a honeycomb condition. This proved too expensive for normal use; also its weight made it fall away from the bottom. It also set up an electrolytic action with the iron bottom fastenings. In addition to the worms rendering the bottom unsafe, weeds and barnacles grew upon it and could take knots off a ship's speed. Frequent beaching and breaming (burning off the weeds with brushwood fires) and careening (stranding the ship or hauling it over in sheltered waters for scraping, recaulking and coating the bottom with preservatives) were essential to seaworthiness. It was an Englishman, John Hawkins, probably in the 1560s, who first devised a practical form of wooden sheathing that combined cheapness with fair efficiency. It remained in use until copper sheathing was adopted in the 1780s.

[2] Hakluyt's *Principal Navigations*, Hak. Soc., Extra Ser., Vol. 6, pp. 251-252.

ance with the wishes of Spain. On 8 January 1558 French forces occupied Calais. At the end of that month Towerson's expedition left Plymouth Sound. On the day of their departure 'they met with two hulks of Dantzick, the one called the *Rose*, a ship of foare hundred tunnes, and the other called the *Unicorne*, of an hundred and fifty tunnes . . . both laden at Bordeaux, and for the most part with wines'. On examination it was found that their 'charter-parties' were false, and it was suspected that they were laden with French goods. These suspicions were quickly found to be correct, for on opening the 'bils of lading', which were directed in Dutch to Hamburg, it was found that their contents were entered in French. As French goods were lawful prize, a conference was held to decide what was to be done, whether to carry the ships into Spain or whether to take what they could then and there, and proceed on their way. After much altercation from the crews of the English ships, and some quiet authoritative arguments by Towerson, it was decided not 'to cary them into Spaine, seeing they sailed so ill that, having all their sailes abroad, we kept them company onely with our foresailes and without any toppe sailes abroad, so that in every two dayes sailing they would have hindered us more than one'.

The trouble was that Towerson dared not delay if he was to make a successful trading voyage to Guinea. He would miss the season, suffer calms, head-winds, sickness, scurvy, death.

'All these things considered', they all paused in their disputes while the Danzigers looked on with troubled eyes, fearful of what the heated words might mean. At the last it was determined 'that every man should take out of the hulks so much as he could well bestow for necessaries', and that they should then proceed. So they took for the ships a small hawser for ties for the yards and six double bases with their chambers—twin-barrelled breech-loading guns for rapid, close-range firing during boarding. Meanwhile the men helped themselves. They 'broke up the hulks' chests, and tooke out their compasses and running glasses, the sounding leade and line, and candles'; indeed they despoiled the crews of the *Rose* and the *Unicorne* of so much that Towerson and others of his type gave them, out of pity, 'a compasse, a running glasse, a lead and a line, certain bread and candles, and what apparell of theirs we coulde finde in their ship . . .'. The French pilot, whom the Danzigers had been unable to set ashore after the passage down 'the river of Bordeaux', they ransomed; ' . . . in fine we agreed to let them depart, and gave them the rest of the wine belonging to the Frenchmen for the fraight of that which we had taken . . .'. They then went on their way to make, as it proved, a very profitable third voyage to Guinea. It will be remarked that neither quadrant, astrolabe, cross-staff, nor chart was mentioned as being amongst the navigational instruments seized, perhaps because if carried they would have been the personal property of the pilot.

While English seamen were becoming more adventurous and obtaining their first experiences of navigation, the way to surer and swifter progress was being made by Englishmen in other walks of life.

When in 1558 Elizabeth came to the throne, not only was Chancellor 'the incomparable' dead, but the venerable and sagacious Sebastian Cabot, too. Chancellor had trained Stephen Borough to succeed him, and he in his turn had brought his young brother, William, to sea. By now the latter was a skilled hydrographer, and the elder Borough was privy to the instructional system of the navigation school at Seville, first described to Englishmen by Richard Eden. Moreover, a brilliant young Welshman, John Dee, had already established a reputation as a mathematician. With Chancellor he had made and used instruments for observing data and making calculations for the astronomical tables for the voyages to the north-east. He was in touch with, and the respected friend of, Gemma Frisius, now Cosmographer to the Emperor, of Pedro Nuñez, now Cosmographer Royal of Portugal and professor of mathematics at Coimbra, and of Gerard Mercator, now settled at Duisburg, cosmographer, globe-maker, instrument maker, and the leading cartographer in the world. John Dee took the place of Cabot as the technical adviser on navigational problems to the Muscovy Company, and tutor to their sea-captains.

Although there were as yet no chairs of mathematics at either of the English universities, and mathematics was not part of the ordinary schooling, there was a small but slowly growing number of students and teachers of that subject in England. Throughout the sixteenth and early seventeenth centuries the very language of mathematics—the symbols and abbreviations used—was still being evolved by individual scholars, so that original work in mathematics called for high intellectual powers. We have seen in the extracts from the Guinea voyage that pilots still used roman numerals. In these calculation is possible only with the aid of an abacus. The first printed work on arithmetic in English had appeared only in 1542. If we appreciate that 'arts' included what we should now term 'science', the title of the work, *The Ground of Artes*, was singularly appropriate.[1] In 1551 the same teacher, Dr. Robert Recorde, published a similar popular textbook on geometry and the use of the quadrant. Again it was the first of its kind in English. This book he called *The Pathway to Knowledge*—also a felicitous title.[2] As a knowledge of geometry was essential to the practice of navigation, we can be fairly sure that these later works were

[1] [Recorde, R.], *The groūd of artes* teachyng the worke and practise of Arithmetike, moch necessary for all states of men. After a more easyer & exacter sorte, then any lyke hath hytherto ben set forth : with dyuers newe additions, as by the table doth partly appeare. [1543. B.M. copy].

[2] The pathway to KNOWLEDG, CONTAINING THE FIRST PRINciples of Geometrie, as they may moste aptly be applied vnto practise, bothe for vse of instrumentes Geometricall, and astronomicall and also for proiection of plattes in euerye kinde, and therefore much necessary for all sortes of men.

> Geometries Verdicte
> All fresshe fine wittes by me are filed,
> All grosse dull wittes wishe me exiled,
> Thoughe no mannes witte reiect will I,
> Yet as they be, I wyll them trye.   [1551]

intended to aid navigation in England, for *The Castle of Knowledge*, a treatise on the sphere, was written and specifically printed in 1556 for the use of the Muscovy Company's navigators[1]; while *The Whetstone of Witte*, another elementary mathematical text-book, was dedicated in 1557 to the Governors of the Muscovy Company.[2] Robert Recorde's work may have been popular, elementary, instructional, but it was invaluable for just that reason. It brought mathematics out of the scholar's closet into the merchant's counting-house and into the sea-captain's cabin. 'He made Arithmetic plainer than it had ever been before. He taught Astrology and expounded Cosmography, he illuminated Geometry . . .', it was later said. No doubt he would have done the same to navigation as a whole, but he died before his promised work on that art could be completed.[3]

When the gifted young John Dee, who had gone to Louvain University to complete his studies, had returned in 1547, he had brought with him, besides 'sea-compasses of divers sortes', what were comparative novelties in England, 'rare and exquisitely made instruments Mathematical', 'two great globes of Gerardus Mercator's making', and astronomical instruments. These he had given to Trinity College, Cambridge, for 'the use of the Fellows and Scholars'.[4] Two years later, by the time Cabot was in England, the study of the classical geographers—Mela, Pliny, Strabo, and the great Ptolemy—had been instituted as a branch of mathematics.

While Dee was essentially a mathematician with a bent for astrology,

---

[1] [Recorde, R.], *The Castle of Knowledge.* [1556]
[2] *The Whetstone of Witte*, whiche is the second parte of Arithmetike: containyng the extraction of Rootes: The *Cossike* practise, with the rule of *Equation*: and the woorkes of *Surde Nombers*.

> *Though many stones doe beare greate price,*
> *The* whetstone *is for exersice*
> *As neadefull, and in woorke as straunge:*
> *Dulle thinges and harde it will so chaunge,*
> *And make them sharpe, to right good vse:*
> *All artesmen knowe, thei can not chuse,*
> *But vse his helpe: yet as men see,*
> *Noe sharpenesse semeth in it to bee.*
>
> *The* grounde *of artes did brede this stone;*
> *His vse is great and moare then one.*
> *Here if you list your wittes to whette,*
> *Moche sharpenesse therby shall you gette*
> *Dull wittes hereby doe greately mende,*
> *Sharp wittes are fined to their fulle ende.*
> *Now proue, and praise, as you doe finde,*
> *And to your self be not vnkinde.*

These Bookes are to bee solde, at the Weste doore of Poules, by Ihon Kyngstone. [1557]

[3] See Taylor, E. G. R., *Tudor Geography, 1485–1583* (1930), for an appreciation of his work.
[4] *Ibid.*

astronomy, and navigation, the practitioners of other arts flourishing in England were now to make their contribution to the growth of the art of navigation. These were the astronomer, the astrologer, the almanac-writer, and the surveyor. The instruments and techniques of the latter, so necessary to the good charting of new lands, were developed on the Continent in the early sixteenth century, largely as a result of the demands of siege warfare with cast cannon. The discovery of the art of casting cannon, made at the end of the fifteenth century, had made bombardment at unprecedented ranges possible, and thus called for the means of siting cannon correctly, and of aiming and of elevating them accurately. In England a professional army, such as was to be found in every continental country, did not exist. The Crown strictly controlled the armed forces, and prohibited private ones. Under Henry VIII the Royal Navy attracted many of the nobility desirous of a martial career; moreover, England was still not fully conscious of having changed from being on the periphery of the world to being nearer to its hub. Siege warfare did not loom large in the military curriculum. Technical advice, when needed, was given by foreign experts. Indeed, the first English book on the art of gunnery was not printed before 1578, and then it was taken, lock, stock, and barrel, from a continental text-book of many years' standing. What chiefly stimulated surveying in England was the break-up of the Church lands, and the creation of new properties, at the end of Henry's reign. The arts of the land-meter and the steward took on a new importance. So it was in the 1550s that the first up-to-date English text-book on surveying appeared. It was based, of course, on the mathematical methods developed on the Continent; nevertheless it marked an important addition to English intellectual life and professional practice, as the author, Leonard Digges, claimed. *A Book named Tectonicon* came out in 1556. Leonard Digges was a landed gentleman of Kent with a passion for practical knowledge, who spent some time on the Continent where, like the studious John Dee, he mastered the latest scientific ideas and practices. So it was that Digges's book placed before the English the latest astronomical and geometrical surveying methods develped on the Continent. Like John Dee, Leonard Digges was also an almanac-writer, and an astrologer. Dee's *Astronomicall and Logisticall Rules*, designed for use on the voyage of 1553, were matched by an almanac, no longer extant, by Leonard Digges.[1] It is possible that it, too, was intended to aid the first English navigators. A printed edition appeared in 1555, and was dedicated to Sir Edward Fiennes, Lord Clinton and Saye, and later Lord High Admiral of England until his death in 1585. This was probably the first English almanac covering a period of years to include tide-tables. Leonard Digges, and from 1570 his son Thomas, regularly produced new editions of the *Prognostication*, the last appearing as late as 1635. The fulsome title of the 1555 edition gives a good

---

[1] Dee, J., *Astronomicall and Logisticall Rules*; see Taylor, E. G. R., *Tudor Geography*, 1485–1583 (1930), p. 172 and Bosanquet, E. F., *English Printed Almanacs and Prognostications* (1917).

indication of their contents when written by Leonard Digges.[1] To many, the first part of the *Prognostication*, with its propitious days for various activities, was of little less importance than the succeeding astronomical and tide-tables or the instructions on how to make a sun-dial and use it for finding the time at night by the aid of the moon or the two stars Aldebaran and Abramech.[2]

That the practical and superstitious should be blended in one book was typical of men's minds at that time. But though they might be ignorant of the causes of natural events and even credulous, they were yet, for practical purposes, observing and reducing to order certain common phenomena; astrologers of the better sort were reputable physicians, mathematicians, or astronomers, and were among the first to respond to the ever-growing demand for more accurate astronomical tables for navigation based upon accurate observations of the celestial bodies.

Astrologers, astronomers, and, soon, seamen, needed instruments, wrought in metal, accurately balanced, graduated, mounted. Thanks to Henry VIII's introduction of skilled gunfounders and gunsmiths, and to the developments made by them in the art of gunnery, the skilled metal-workers were already in England. They were already making surveyors', astronomers', and gun-layers' instruments that, under the tutelage of religious refugees from Flanders, were soon to reach a high degree of perfection. The craftsmanship of Thomas Gemini (*fl.* 1550–60), and of Humphrey Cole (*fl.* 1560–80), for instance, is quite remarkable for its beauty, balance, and accuracy. Nor must the printers and publishers of books be forgotten. It is significant that it was from this time, in the reign of Philip and Mary, that the Company of Stationers received its first charter. Many of its members, too, were foreigners who brought with them, and demanded of the English, the advanced standards of the Continent in book production. They called for finely engraved illustrations, and so fostered the training of such men as Augustine Ryther, who towards the end of the century engraved amongst others the lovely charts illustrating Lord Howard's Armada dispatch. The handiwork of these men, many of them of humble origin, was, we must recall, to be indispensable to the seaman who aspired to be a navigator.

While these craftsmen played their part, no less important were the theorists, like John Dee and Leonard and Thomas Digges. William Borough

---

[1] *A PROGNOSTICATION OF RIGHT GOOD* effect, fructfully augmented, contayninge *playne, briefe, pleasant, chosen* rules, to iudge the wether for euer, by the *Sunne, Moone, Sterres, Cometes, Raynbowe, Thunder, Cloudes,* with other Extraordinarie tokens, not omitting the *Aspects* of *Planetes,* with a brefe Iudgemente for euer, of *Plentie, Lacke, Sickenes, Death, Warres &c.* Openinge also many *naturall causes,* woorthy to be knowē. To these and others, now at the last are adioyned, *diuers generall pleasaunte Tables*: for euer manyfolde wayes profitable, to al maner men of vnderstanding: therfore agayne publisshed by *Leonard Dygges Gentylman,* in the yeare of oure Lorde. 1555.

Imprynted at London, within the blacke Fryars, by Thomas Gemini. 1555.

[2] See Pl. XXX.

complained to the Queen in 1578 of their lack of practical experience, but, although there was some justification for his complaint, the theorists kept the problems of navigation before the intellectual strata of society. Keen wits amongst them were to take Borough's doctrine of 'practice at sea' to heart. Thomas Digges, for instance, spent three months at sea in order to demonstrate to seamen the truth of his mathematical proofs. He was only the first of many mathematicians to go to sea. Thereafter it did not take long for the value of mathematics in navigation to be grasped by the English. The contributions of scholars then became welcome along with those of the craftsmen. For instance it was William Barlow, an archdeacon of the Church—who loathed the sea—who was to improve the mariner's compass. On the other hand it was Edward Wright, a university scholar, who combined practical experience at sea with mathematical ability of the first order, who was to solve the greatest cartographical problem of the age. This was the representation of the earth's curved surface upon a plane surface in such a manner that courses and distances could be accurately plotted by the navigator.

As yet, however, it is unlikely that any English seaman had crossed the ocean unaided. But the English had this much at hand: the elements of the necessary knowledge, the men to teach it, and, thanks largely to Richard Eden, the beginnings of the desire to learn.

In the very first year of Elizabeth's reign, at Norwich on 18 July 1559, William Cuningham, doctor in physic, and since 1553 editor of an annual almanac, set out for readers 'the dignitie and ample use of Cosmographie' in the preface of his *The Cosmographical Glasse*, the first treatise exclusively on cosmography printed in English.[1]

By cosmography, Cuningham pointed out, America, the fourth part of the world '(unknowne in all ages before our time)' had been discovered, likewise the Indies in the East. And he advocated its study both on grounds of its practical value to seamen and its educative value to the man of affairs who was unable to travel abroad.

The Cosmographical Glasse has been criticized as being of no originality, not up to date, and soon superseded; and by another as being beyond the mental powers of anyone who had not had a university education. The book may have had these faults, but it must be remembered the author laid no claim to originality. If by being not up to date is meant that there was no mention of the Copernican theory of the cosmos, this applies equally to

---

[1] THE COSMOGRAPHIcal Glasse, conteinyng the pleasant Principles of Cosmographie, geographie, Hydrographie, or Nauigation. Compiled by William Cuningham Doctor in Physicke. *Excussum Londini in officina Ioan. Daij Typographi*. Anno. 1559.

In this glasse if you will beholde
The Sterry Skie, and Pearth so wide,
The Seas also, with windes so colde,
Yea and thy selfe all these to guide:
What this Type meane first learne a right,
So shall the gayne thy trauaill qnight.

standard books on the subject written a century later; while as to its being quickly superseded, it is to be remarked that it was one of very few books forming the library of Martin Frobisher's expedition to find a North-West passage to Cathay in 1576. But just as it was a supreme mental achievement to develop mathematics in this era, so was it hardly less of an achievement to compose in English a book on a novel technical subject in language which can still be appreciated for its lucidity and nobility.

Whatever its faults, William Cuningham's book did for cosmography, and to some extent for navigation, what Robert Recorde's books had done for mathematics; it brought the subject from the recesses of the scholar's closet to the shelves of the gentry and the desks of the merchants. Within ten years of its publication, many Englishmen guided by it had learnt to 'like, love, get and use Maps, Charts, and geographical globes'.[1] The seed sown by John Dee's gift of astronomical instruments to Cambridge University, and cultivated by a physician, sprang up and brought forth good fruit in many Englishmen's minds—a desire for geographical knowledge. This in its turn was a stimulant for nautical enterprise, which generated in Englishmen an interest in navigational problems and their solution that still survives.

[1] Dee, J., Preface to Billingsley's *Euclid* (1570).

Chapter Four

THE INITIATION OF THE ENGLISH INTO THE ART OF NAVIGATION

*' . . . how indigent and destitute this Realm is of excellent and expert
Pilottes. . . . But as touching Stephen A. Brough, the chiefe Pylote of your
voyages of discovery . . . he is neither malicious nor envious of his arte and
science . . . he desireth ye same for the comon profite to be comen to al mē:
And for the same intent was the fyrst that moved certen worshypfull of your
company . . . to have this worke translated into the Englyshe tongue . . . knowe
therefore this worke of the art of Navigation, beying publyshed in our vulgar
tongue, you may be assured to have more store of skylful Pilotes . . . such
as by their honest behaviour and conditions joyned with arte and experience,
may doe you honest and true service . . .'*
Richard Eden's The Preface to *The Arte of Navigation,* 1561.

WHEN Elizabeth I came to the throne English trade, which had
been bad for twenty years, was getting steadily worse. The sale
of woollen goods was becoming ever more difficult in the face of
increasing competition from coutries whose products, if not of superior
finish—as they often were—could be bought more cheaply. An end had
been put to the Mediterranean trade five years since by the ruthless advance of the Turks; and on the Guinea coast trading ventures had become increasingly hazardous by reason of increased Portuguese armed
intervention. In only one direction had new markets been established,
in the north-east, but here the market for woollen goods was limited,
and the rigours of the north Russian climate seemed to place a bar upon
further expansion in that direction. England was still smarting from the
loss of Calais, her continental possession, lost in 1558 by Mary, in the
interests of whose Spanish husband, Philip II of Spain, the country had
rashly gone to war. Rashly, because the navy had been unready to go to
the succour of the beleaguered garrison of Calais, which had been forced
to capitulate. Englishmen looked back upon the Spanish interlude of
Mary's unhappy, persecution-ridden reign with loathing and resentment.
There had been no material gains, only losses and frustrations. Besides
the culminating insult of the loss of Calais, they had been refused a share
in the lucrative trade with the colonial empire of Spain. This had continued
to be the absolute monopoly of the merchants and officials of the Casa de
Contratación at Seville. Furthermore, the English merchants now long
established in Spain, in Seville, Cadiz, and San Lucar, and in the Atlantic
islands, the Madeiras and Canaries, had been looked upon with increasing

suspicion as heretics, and as legitimate subjects for the Inquisition. Philip, as Mary's consort, had done his best to suppress the Guinea trade, and had granted the charter to the Muscovy Company only because he was farsighted enough to allow an outlet to English energies by legitimizing a trade that clearly lay beyond the confines of Spain's sphere of interest.

In losing Calais the English had lost their chief export market or 'staple' for wool—an important though dwindling export—and experience was soon to prove this loss irreparable. Staples set up in the Low Countries never flourished. The loss of Calais did more than cause resentment and damage trade; unperceived it had this merit: it tended to divert the flow of Englishmen's ambitions at the very moment that the precariousness of England's European markets demanded it. Its most immediate effect, however, had been to make clear the fate likely to befall an island country lacking an adequate navy. England was only part of an island; Wales formed a part of the realm, but Scotland was an independent kingdom under French influence, and France was hostile and had a Scottish queen. Philip, Spain, the Spanish Empire, were Catholic; Elizabeth, and hence England, heretic and Protestant. Common prudence exacted the creation of an efficient navy and the prosecution of a policy designed both to restore the economy of the country, and to guide its feet into the way of peace.

It is impossible to dissociate the name of Sir William Cecil, later Lord Burghley, from the history of English maritime achievements. It is not too much to say that he was the presiding and directing genius behind them from the first day of Elizabeth's reign until his death in its closing years. Without his guidance, without his directing and controlling will behind the technical advisers of the Crown on maritime affairs, the rapid rise of Englishmen to fame on the high seas could never have occurred. Just how rapid that rise was can be gauged by the fact that in 1558 probably not one, as late as 1568 probably only one, English seaman was capable of navigating to the West Indies without the aid of Portuguese, French, or Spanish pilots. Yet, by the time of the Armada, a mere score of years later, Englishmen had gained 'the reputation of being, above all Western nations, expert and active in all naval operations, and great sea dogs'.[1]

Right from the start of Elizabeth's reign the policy of England was to keep a navy 'ever in readiness against all evil haps', and to ground this healthily upon a mercantile navy of well-manned, well-found ships—well armed too, if need be—conned by experienced pilots.[2] In this the people,

[1] Cal. S.P., Venetian, Ven. Ambassador in France, 8 April 1588.

[2] See Waters, D. W., 'The Elizabethan Navy and the Armada Campaign' in *M.M.*, Vol. 35. A source-book of great value is E. M. Tenison's *Elizabethan England*, a magnificent production, profusely illustrated and covering every aspect of Elizabethan activity. Anglo-Spanish relations and culture are particularly well illustrated. The work is indispensable. The first eight volumes (issued between 1933 and 1947) cover the period 1553 to 1589. Naturally, however, no one can afford to neglect Conyers Reade's *Bibliography of Tudor History*, which is the standard work, though much subsequent research on maritime matters has been published since its issue. Extraordinarily it omits Tenison's great work.

the merchants, Parliament, and, as important as any, the patrons of science and art, the nobility, were at one. While Burghley may thus be credited with being the able interpreter and executor of their policy, his minutes leave no doubt that he was the initiator as well as the planner and contriver of ways and means of a mercantile policy designed to support a strong, self-sufficient fleet by means of wide-flung seaborne trade and native fisheries. Nor is this surprising in view of his mental calibre, for it will not be forgotten that he must have been nurtured on Richard Eden's translations of the maritime achievements of Spain.

In numerous Acts passed during the reign, in the charters of new companies, will be found wording such as 'for the maintenance of the Navy' or 'for the maintenance and increase of the Navy and mariners'.[1] An idea of the tenacity with which the English pursued their aim can be got by a brief citation of some of the most important early enactments. The sale of ships to foreigners was forbidden in the first year of the reign; besides subsidies to encourage the building of larger vessels, the small coastwise vessels were forbidden to partake in the foreign trade, so that the building of larger ships for this was obligatory; in 1562, by an 'Act touching certain Politic Constitutions made for the Maintenance of the Navy', the English coasting trade was confined to English ships and the wine trade, which for the last eighty years had been confined to English ships 'the greater part of the crew of which were English', was confined exclusively to English ships *with English masters*: it was further enacted that fishermen and 'Mariners haunting the Sea as Fishermen or Mariners', should not be compelled to serve as soldiers upon land or at sea, except as mariners, and shipwrights and shipowners were empowered to take apprentices; and in an attempt to encourage the fisheries, fish-eating days were instituted, and the landing of English-caught fish was made duty-free.[2] It was three years later, in 1565, that, it will be recalled, the Trinity House of Deptford had its powers increased to include the setting up of beacons and sea-marks anywhere necessary on the coasts of England and to prevent the removal of land-marks, such as well-known buildings, towers, steeples, or trees, and to ensure their maintenance in good order. In 1571, in an endeavour to encourage the building of larger vessels, the carriage of fish was confined to 'cross-sail' vessels.[3] These are only some of the earliest measures

[1] Cunningham, W., *The Growth of English Commerce and Industry in Modern Times* (1903) is the standard work on the subject, and a fascinating source-book.

[2] 5 Elizabeth cap. 5 (1562). *An Act touching certain Politic Constitutions made for the Maintenance of the Navy.*

[3] This was one of the measures advocated by John Montgomery in a treatise he wrote in 1570 'On the Maintenance of the navy', which he dedicated to the Earl of Leicester (B.M. Add. MS. 18,035). John Montgomery was one of the young men trained in navigation during the voyage to Chios in the bark *Aucher*, in 1551. His treatise came to the notice of Stephen Borough and was used by him to strengthen his arguments in support of measures designed to increase the mercantile marine and the standard of navigation. After the Armada, 1588, Montgomery added to his treatise, embodying various naval 'lessons learnt'. His MSS.

of the reign, but they suffice to give the tenor of its economic legislation and to illustrate the argument that the English, once forced to take to the sea, became competent seamen as a result of a deliberate national policy. As early as 1540 Henry VIII had framed a Navigation Act 'For the Maintenance of the navy of England . . .' whose preamble admirably sets forth the case for the advancement of navigation.[1]

Now, united as never before in the last quarter of a century by the firm handling of the religious issue by Elizabeth, and by antipathy to Spain and Catholicism, and guided by the unobtrusive genius of Sir William Cecil, the English were at last taking whole-hearted measures to maintain and increase their navy, navigation, and seamen. The necessary supplies of timber and naval stores were being safeguarded, and the shipyards and shipwrights for ship-building encouraged; a sufficiency of seamen and masters to man the ships, and of pilots to conduct them in and out of port and overseas, was being assured; better sea-marks, surer land-marks, safer ports for lading and discharging cargoes—all were being legislated for, and, as we shall see, the legislation was being made effective through the medium of the Trinity Houses.

The man behind the initiation of this important legislation and the increased activities of the Trinity Houses was Stephen Borough. One inestimable gain the English had won from the Spanish marriage was this: in 1558 Stephen Borough, who had succeeded Richard Chancellor as Chief Pilot of the Muscovy Company, had been admitted to the Casa de Contratación at Seville as an honoured guest. There he had been shown the system of training which for the last half-century had been turning out pilots and navigators qualified to conduct ships on the various routes laid down to and from and in the Spanish Indies. He had been shown the instruments and manuals used and the process of examination. He had returned filled with admiration for an establishment where knowledge was so well organized and so well taught, and with a shrewd insight into the power that competence in navigation conferred on a nation.

Borough had returned impressed also with the depth of knowledge and the high degree of skill required for successful navigation. He appreciated that knowledge and skill could only be acquired by a combination of good teaching and practice. This he was determined English seamen should have. He brought back with him the best means for teaching his fellow-seamen the art of navigation that was possible—a standard manual of navigation used by the Spaniards themselves—Martin Cortes's *Arte de Navegar*. It did not take a great deal of persuasion to convince the Muscovy Company that it would be an action no less profitable than public-spirited to have it translated into English and published for the general public

on these matters in the B.M. are Add. MS. 18,035 (1570) cited above, Add. MS. 20,042; Arundel MS. 22; Lansdowne MS. 1225 (1588). Large portions of the treatise of 1570 and 1588 are reproduced in Brydges, Sir S. E., *Censura Literaria* (1807) Vol. V.

[1] 32 Henry VIII cap. 14 (1540) is reprinted in full in Hunter, H. C., *How England got its Merchant Marine* (1935).

as well as for the use of its own servants. An able translator was at hand, and indeed already in the company's service. Richard Eden was concerned in the compilation of its records. He readily undertook the task of translation, and in 1561 the resultant work, *The Arte of Navigation*, appeared. It is probably not too much to say that this was one of the most decisive books ever printed in the English language. It held the key to the mastery of the sea.

It is true that William Cuningham's *Cosmographical Glasse* had preceded Richard Eden's *The Arte of Navigation* by two years, but it was altogether a different work. Cuningham claimed no more for it than that it was 'a compilation', designed (though it had a section on navigation and included examples of his own methods of longitude-finding and of determining the length of a degree) for the study. Eden's book on the other hand was a manual of navigation designed from the start and written throughout for the instruction and use of practical seamen. The handy size of the English edition made it particularly suitable for use at sea, while its detailed directions on the making of charts and instruments, as well as on the solution of navigational problems, provided just the sort of information needed by a seaman mastering the art, and hitherto denied it either by the ignorance of his instructors or the jealousy of the initiated. Stephen Borough was far from being satisfied with this production of an English version of a standard Spanish manual of navigation. To ensure a supply of competent navigators something more was needed, and Borough was convinced that, as in Spain and other countries famous for the navigational skill of their seamen, only positive action by the Crown could bring this to pass. Accordingly, in 1562, the year following the publication of *The Arte of Navigation*, Borough petitioned the Crown to appoint and authorize 'a learned and a skilfull man in the arte of navigacion to teache and instructe' English seamen in that art. The office of pilot-major in Spain and elsewhere, averred Borough in the preamble to his petition, turned ignorant seamen into competent navigators, who thereby benefited the country by the wealth and honour that their skill brought and by the avoidance of losses through bad seamanship and shipwreck. The rest of his petition was an expansion of this theme. In Spain no young seaman, he pointed out, was permitted to take charge of any warship or large merchant ship or of any ship engaged upon a rich voyage who had not first been examined and approved as competent by the pilot-major. Nor could he call himself a pilot or master until he had a certificate stamped by the pilot-major entitling him to do so. Furthermore, whereas the English recognized only men and boys, in Spain and elsewhere there were established grades of seamen, as pilot, master, mariner, grommett, page, and boy, each having his scale of pay, and a man or boy had to be certified as being in one or other grade. In English ships, on the other hand, as soon as a youngster grew to 'any reasonable stature, he will loke for his Age and not for his knowledge to have the name of a man and also of a mariner', Borough complained.[1]

[1] See Appendix 6A.

The superiority of the Spanish system was daily manifested, he pointed out, both by the wealth of overseas commodities brought in, by the number of 'skilfull men in those regions', and by the ability of Spain to undertake voyages of discovery, unlike the English, without the help of expert navigators from other countries. He claimed, too, that losses and wrecks caused by ignorance were avoided under the Spanish system. Borough then pointed out that only very few English mariners practised or tried to learn the new methods, the greatest number contenting themselves with the old and erroneous rules. Nevertheless, some, he added, would gladly learn if they had a teacher. The trouble was that those who knew more than the common sort of pilot or master 'wold not gladly teach other, for hinderinge of their oune lyvinge', while those who would learn if they could were either ashamed to admit it because for appearance's sake they already took navigational instruments to sea with them, though ignorant of their use, and so had already acquired 'the name of and preferment of a master or pilott', or else had learnt a little about navigation and thought they knew everything about it. These he complained were the chief causes of the many recent losses amongst English ships trading to Spain. Some had perished upon the Andalusian coast, others upon Cape Finisterre, and others upon Ushant and the Brittany coast; and, Borough concluded, most of these losses had been due to ignorance. It seems clear that the important Act of 1562 'touching the Maintenance of the Navy' was the immediate official response to Borough's petition. But there were further reactions. In January 1564 Elizabeth proposed to appoint, as recommended by Borough, a 'Cheyffe Pilote of this owr realme of Englande', and drew up a commission to appoint Stephen Borough himself to hold the office during his natural life.[1] On the commission being granted he, or his deputy, or deputies, was to have the examination and appointing of all such mariners as from that time forward took the charge of any ship of 40 tons burden and upwards either as pilot or master. Furthermore, from henceforth no man was to be signed on as a mariner before being 'examyned, allowed, and aucthorysed' as a competent mariner by the Chief Pilot or his deputies (upon pain of forfeit of twenty shillings, half to be paid to the Chief Pilot and half to the Lord Admiral). As evidence of his competence every mariner satisfactorily examined was to have the signed testimony of the Chief Pilot or his deputy. Nor was any man without a mariner's certificate to be allowed to take on the office of boatswain, quartermaster, or master's mate nor to test another's ability to fill those offices nor those of 'boye, page or grommett', upon pain of forfeit of forty shillings, half to be paid to the Lord Admiral and half to the Chief Pilot. Moreover, in contradistinction to previous English practice, no mariner was to be admitted to the offices of boatswain, quartermaster, and master's mate except by the Chief Pilot or his deputy.

[1] See Appendix 6B. Both Taylor and Parks, *Richard Hakluyt and the English Voyages* (1928), ascribe it to 1563; Oppenheim, M. *The Administration of the Royal Navy*, 1509–1660 (1896), a very meticulous authority, ascribes it to January 1564.

Lastly, the Chief Pilot, both at the admission and approbation of the mariner, and also of the pilot or master, was 'to geve rules and Instructions towching the poyntes of navigacion and at all other tymes to be redye to enforme theim that seke knowleg at his handes'. So much for the intention. It was never fulfilled.[1] Borough's commission as Chief Pilot was never completed. He was, however, appointed 'one of the fowre masters' of the Queen's ships in the Medway.

In failing to confirm Borough's appointment as Chief Pilot and in confirming his appointment to one of the four new posts of 'masters of the Queen's ships in the Medway', the Crown knew exactly what it was doing, what it wanted done, and how it was to be done. Briefly, it decided to foster the art of navigation amongst its seafaring men and to ensure the material efficiency of the ships of the Royal Navy with the administrative machinery already at hand.

As one of the four masters of the Queen's ships Stephen Borough had the responsible task of 'the kepyng and over syght of owr shipps'. But he had, as well as to 'direct and oversee the Boatswains and Shipkeepers who were allowed in harbour, to perform the ordinary maintenance service of the ships . . . also to carry in and out of the River such ships as happened to be prepared for the seas, and to see them rigged and fitted completely'.[2] Whom more competent could the Crown have appointed to discharge these responsible tasks—and the Medway and the Thames estuary are notoriously tricky waters of pilotage—than Stephen Borough? The post might be unadventurous, but it was fundamental to the fighting efficiency and activity of the navy. As a master of the Queen's ships he personally examined and recommended pilots and masters for the royal ships besides overseeing the ships themselves and piloting them up or down the Medway and Thames. Monson, who fought against the Armada and whose writings have already been noticed, specifically states that 'A master' of a royal ship 'is to be chosen by the election of the Trinity House . . . upon commendations from them to the four principal Officers of the Navy', upon

---

[1] There is ample evidence to prove this. The annual sum to be paid to the Chief Pilot is left blank in the commission, and there are no references subsequently, or on Borough's epitaph in Chatham Church, to his having been Chief Pilot of the Realm.

[2] *Boteler's Dialogues*, N.R.S., Vol. 65, contains a dissertation upon the duties of the pilot and the master of a ship; and in the course of it a footnote, based on a contemporary MS., defines the duties of the four Masters of England. Nathaniel Boteler (?1577–?1643), the author, was a member of the Council for Virginia (1619), Governor of Bermuda (1619–1622) and a commissioner of the Crown Colony of Virginia (?1624), and commanded a hired merchantman on the Cadiz (1625) and Ile de Ré (1627) expeditions and a royal ship at La Rochelle (1628). From 1638–?1640 he was Governor of Providence Island. His *Dialogues*—discussions between an Admiral and a Captain—were probably written between 1634 and 1639. They contain little original material of his own, but are of great value as they conveniently collect together a variety of authorities who wrote on nautical matters of the time, such as Mainwaring and Raleigh. Like Raleigh, Boteler was no practical seaman.

which he was 'to receive warrant for taking charge of the ships of the Crown', and this, it may be remarked, was still the practice in the eighteenth century.[1] The Trinity House (of Deptford Strand), it will be noticed, was thus directly concerned with the navigational competence of the masters and pilots of the Royal Navy. So Borough, who was a member of that corporation, and its master ten years later, when it was granted its coat of arms, was doubly implicated in ensuring the navigational proficiency of the pilots and masters of the royal ships.[2] Certain it is that he discharged his duties well. The navy got competent pilots and masters without having to go to Spain or France, as heretofore. In Elizabeth's reign no royal ships were cast away or lost by stress of weather, faulty handling, or careless pilotage. It is equally certain that, although the Crown created no office of Chief Pilot to supervise and enforce the training of the masters, pilots, and mariners of the merchant ships in the latest navigational practices, in the late 1560s and early 1570s Englishmen in rapidly increasing numbers did master them and did reap the benefits that Borough said would accrue therefrom; and it was through the agency of the Trinity Houses of the Realm and of the Trinity House of Deptford Strand in particular that this was achieved. There can be little doubt that the opposition to the appointment of Stephen Borough to the post of Chief Pilot of the Realm—and there must have been opposition for his prepared commission to have remained incomplete—came primarily from the master, wardens, and assistants of the Trinity House of Deptford Strand. No doubt they quoted their original charter of 1514 and pointed out that upon her accession Elizabeth had confirmed this charter; that their powers had been consistently upheld by the Admiralty Court; that to create a Chief Pilot of the Realm could only result in the usurpation of their authority and privileges; in short, that the Crown had already the

---

[1] *Monson's Tracts*, Vol. 4., N.R.S., Vol. 45, p. 22. 8 Elizabeth cap. 12 (1565) *concerning sea-marks and Mariners* is reprinted in part by Hunter, *How England got its Merchant Marine* (1935), and in full in Cotton, J., *Memoir on Trinity House* (1818).

(Anon.), *The Laws, Ordinances, and Institutions of the Admiralty of Great Britain, Civil and Military*, (1746) contains in Vol. 2, p. 449, 'An Account of the Trinity-Corporation' and states: 'The Ends and Intents of this Foundation were for the Encrease and Encouragement of Navigation, for the good Government of the Seamen, and the better Security of Merchant Ships. And a Power is granted them in their Charter, to make By-Laws for the said good and useful Purposes.

'They examine and report to the Navy Board, if desir'd, the fitness of Masters for the King's Ships; and Certify what Rate the Ships are that they take Charge of; and give Certificates and Testimonials to the said Masters, under the Masters and Wardens Hands.

'They examine, authorize and appoint all Pilots under the Seal of the Corporation, as well for taking Charge of the Royal Navy, as other Merchant Ships . . .

'They bind and enrol Apprentices to the Sea; though many, or most are bound elsewhere nowadays.'

[2] This grant, with comments on the earlier seal of the corporation, is reproduced in Cotton, J., *op. cit.*

necessary machinery for implementing those recommendations for improving the navigational knowledge and skill of English seamen made by Borough.

The creation and functions of the Trinity Houses of the Realm has already been briefly mentioned in the opening chapter. It was on 19 March 1513, during the middle of Henry VIII's first war with France, that the Thames ship-masters petitioned the king to empower them to reform the management of shipping in the River Thames and other places.[1] They complained that whereas in times past only experienced English ship-masters and pilots, well acquainted with the dangers of the Thames and other places, had been allowed to handle shipping—and had done so with marked success—now young and inexperienced men, foreigners among them, were meddling in the business. Not only were many ships damaged or lost but the 'ancient mariners' who could no longer work at sea, because of 'bruises and maimings' incurred in the king's service, were being forced out of employment. More serious, too, and dangerous, was the knowledge of the estuary which was being picked up by potential enemies of the realm. From his petition it is clear that Borough, when he petitioned for the creation of the office of Chief Pilot forty years later, had read the original petition of the Trinity House to which he belonged and had framed his petition for improved navigational skill—as distinct from skill in pilotage—along its lines. On 20 May 1514, when Henry VIII had returned with the army from France and peace negotiations were under way, the Trinity House of Deptford Strand had received its first charter. This re-established the guild as the fraternity of 'the shipmen or mariners of this our realme of England', and empowered it, while maintaining almshouses for aged and maimed sailors, also to hold lands and tenements and to perform acts of piety, to meet regularly in order to secure the sound government of the guild, the conservation and good state of 'the science or art of mariners', and to make 'laws and ordinances, and statutes amongst themselves, for the relief, increase and augmentation of the shipping of this our realm of England'.[2]

One master, four wardens, and eight assistants might be elected annually, who might 'admit and accept whatsoever persons our natural subjects only to be born within this our Realm of England, and other places under our allegiance, and not others . . . as brethren'.

Thus was established the machinery for controlling the shipmen, pilots, and mariners not only of the Thames but, it should be noted, of the whole realm.

The first master, Thomas Spert, lately successively master of the *Mary*

[1] The Trinity House petition of 1513 is given in full in Ruddock, A. A., 'The Trinity House at Deptford in the Sixteenth Century', *E.H.R.*, Vol. 65. The original is given as 'Chancery warrants for the Great Seal, file 388, No. 36'. This otherwise valuable study underestimates the authority of the Trinity Houses in naval navigational affairs and national navigational affairs.

[2] The Latin original is reproduced in Ruddock, A. A., *op. cit.*, and an English translation in Cotton, J., *Memoir on Trinity House* (1818), Appendix 1.

Rose and *Henry Grace à Dieu*, two of the king's finest ships, wasted no time in promulgating by-laws to bring pilotage in the Thames under the control of Trinity House. Indeed he drew them up before the charter was granted, for, on 10 May, it was ordained 'that no maner persone shall take uppon hym to be a lodesman wythin the said River of Thamys withowte he be a Brother of the said Fraternitie'. The only exceptions were the brethren of the Trinity House of Dover, an uncharted 'Court of Lodesmanage' of the Cinque ports, and pilots of the estuarine ports such as Harwich and Orwell, bringing ships from their own ports to the Thames. For this privilege the pilots paid a fee to the Deptford Trinity House, which in fact claimed the monopoly of the pilotage of all ships passing between London and the sea.[1]

By 1529 Thomas Spert had been knighted for his services to the Crown, was controller of the king's ships, and a wealthy Thames shipowner. Enforcement of the authority of Trinity House over all pilots and ship-masters had proved impossible with the powers granted by the charter of 1514; accordingly, in 1536, probably through Sir Thomas's personal intervention with the Lord High Admiral, who had granted him the 'ballastage' of Thames shipping, a warrant was issued in the Admiralty Court for the arrest of pilots and ship-masters refusing to pay the Trinity House dues, and ordering them to be brought to the Admiralty Court at Orton Keys to explain their conduct. Henceforward by payment of an annual fee on Trinity Sunday to the Judge of the Admiralty Court a general warrant was obtained upholding the Trinity House's rights for the ensuing twelve months. By this means its authority over all shipmen of the realm became undisputed.[2]

This action of the Trinity House of Deptford evidently inspired the Guild of Masters, Pilots, and Mariners of Newcastle upon Tyne to apply for a similar charter for the port of Tynemouth. Accordingly on 5 October 1536 it too received a charter empowering it to create a Fraternity of the Holy and Undivided Trinity of Newcastle upon Tyne. This Trinity House could set up a master and four wardens to govern the fraternity and admit brethren (and sisters). Property could be owned and meetings held to further the objects of the guild, which was also empowered to levy a due to set up and maintain two towers, one on either side of the port entrance 'with a perpetual light, to be nightly maintained'—the first lighthouses of England.[3] By 1538 this Trinity House, too, was applying for and receiving an annual Admiralty Court warrant to enforce its powers.[3] Early in their reigns Edward VI, Mary, and Elizabeth I confirmed the original Newcastle upon Tyne, as they confirmed the original Deptford, charter.

[1] Ruddock, A. A., *op. cit.*

[2] Ruddock, A. A., *op. cit.* reproduces the Latin original of the High Court of Admiralty warrant of 1536.

[3] Whormby, J., *An Account of Trinity House and of Sea Marks* (1746), (ed. of 1861), reproduces in translation much of this first charter.

The Hull Guild of Trinity House originated from a religious guild founded in 1369, and changed in 1456 into a guild exclusively of ship-masters supporting a chantry in Holy Trinity Church and an almshouse for the maintenance of maimed or aged seamen. The necessary funds were raised by the payment of 'lowage and stowage' (later known as 'primage'), the payment for loading and unloading cargo customarily made in certain trades and ports in addition to the voyage wages. In 1505 this agreement—which had received royal sanction in 1457—was renewed, and seven years later the mayor and aldermen of Hull agreed that only members of the guild should have the right to bring ships up and down the Humber. It was not until 1541 that this guild received a royal charter, and it is significant that this should have been the year in which Henry VIII visited the port and by tradition was piloted up the Humber by a Scot until he ordered his replacement by an Englishman. Within a short time of becoming by charter 'The Wardens or Masters, Mariners and Brethren and Sisters of the Fraternity or Guild of the Holy Trinity of Kingston upon Hull', this corporation also was petitioning for a warrant under Admiralty seal similar to that granted to Deptford and Newcastle upon Tyne.

This charter, too, was renewed by Edward VI, Mary, and Elizabeth I, upon their accession to the throne.

Thus, although the three incorporated Trinity Houses of Deptford, Newcastle upon Tyne, and Hull, and the unincorporated one of Dover, were distinct and independent one from another within what may be termed their parochial bounds, that of Deptford Strand was by far the most consider-able, and exercised authoritative influence over the others by virtue of its being a fraternity of 'the shipmen or Mariners' of the whole realm empowered to treat of 'all and singular articles' concerning the ships of the realm and the craft of the seamen of the realm. It is clear too that by 1563 Trinity House was failing in its responsibilities to ensure that English seamen should have an up-to-date knowledge of 'the science or art of mariners' and did not grasp that it was thereby failing to ensure 'the relief, increase, and augmentation of the shipping' of the realm. What is quite certain is that Borough's petition and the provisional commission appoint-ing him Chief Pilot aroused the Trinity House to a full sense of its current navigational responsibilities. In Henry VIII's time its main tasks had been to ensure a supply of English pilots competent to act as port pilots and of English masters competent to conduct ships safely on the then almost exclusively coastal voyages undertaken, also to deny to foreigners the opportunity to become acquainted with the secrets of our port channels by acting as local pilots and so to expose the realm to the risk of invasion in time of war. As we have seen, the merchants' trade and the naval opera-tions of the time had demanded no more. Now times had changed. Mere pilotage no longer sufficed. Trinity House must now ensure the competence of masters and pilots to undertake protracted overseas, indeed oceanic, voyages, and, if the Act of 1562 'in the Favour of Fishermen and Mariners haunting the Sea' which freed such men from military service was not to be abused and was really to assure to the Crown a supply of mariners, would have to certify mariners as such. There was, in fact, no denying the soundness of Borough's contentions. Trinity House took action. We can see reflected in the Act of 1565 'Concerning sea-marks and Mariners,' already referred to in the opening chapter, something of the struggle for power, some of the heart-searchings that must have gone on, and some of the results. This Act it will be recalled, in order to reduce shipping losses, authorized the Trinity House of Deptford Strand 'being a company of the chiefest and most expert masters and governors of ships', to set up and maintain beacons and sea-marks anywhere on the coasts of England, and to prevent the destruction of existing natural aids such as conspicuous trees, towers, and steeples.

This Act is important as marking the first practical action by the Crown —no doubt on Borough's prompting—to reduce on a national scale by means of navigational aids the risk of shipwreck round the coasts. But it is important from yet another aspect. Besides being concerned with 'sea-marks', it was also concerned, it will be recalled from its title, with 'mariners'. In effect it confirmed that, as recommended by Borough, stipulated in his provisional commission as Chief Pilot, and rendered necessary by the act of 1562, seafaring men who were mariners were to receive a certificate of competence from the Master, Wardens, and Assistants of Trinity House. They might then ply their own or hired boats upon the Thames for their own pleasure or for hire. The fact that the Act referred only to men dwelling beside the Thames is accounted for by the privilege of wherrying being granted only to Thames-side mariners. One result of this registering of seamen was that the Government from now on was better able to keep check of the numbers of masters (for we shall see that masters had also to be licensed as such), mariners, and fishermen in the realm, and periodically did so, together with the numbers and tonnages of the shipping of the realm. By this means it was enabled to check the effects of its maritime legislation and its readiness for war. Thus a muster of ships and mariners throughout England taken in 1582 showed that there were some 1,600 merchant vessels—of which only 250 were above 80 tons—and about 16,500 mariners of all sorts, some 6,500 being fishermen.[1]

The Trinity House of Deptford Strand never received a new charter from Elizabeth, but the charter granted to it by James I, in 1604, after his accession to the throne, was a redrafted one and not a replica of the original. For the first time a distinction was made between Elder and Younger Brethren, there being thirty-one of the former, from whom were elected the Master, Wardens, and Assistants, 'all the rest of the seamen and mariners' of the guild being Younger Brethren. This charter clearly stated

[1] Monson's *Tracts*, Vol. 3, N.R.S., Vol. 43. The masters, mariners, and fishermen are not always specified separately under the county headings in which they are arranged. The masters probably numbered between 1,600 and 2,000.

that the corporation was to consult 'of and upon the Conservation, good Estate and wholesome Government, maintenance and increase of the Navigation of this Realm, and of all mariners and seafaring men within the same', and of 'the cunning, knowledge, or science of seamen and pilots'. It empowered the corporation to make and enforce the necessary by-laws.[1] The Trinity Houses of Newcastle upon Tyne and of Hull, however, did receive new charters from Elizabeth I. Hull's original charter had been renewed by each successive sovereign, including Elizabeth, upon accession; and in 1580 Elizabeth granted it a modernized and amplified one, distinguishing between Elder and Younger Brethren and embodying amongst other powers—and from a purely navigational point of view this is most significant—the certification of masters, pilots, and mariners.[2] For instance, concerning the masters and pilots, the Master and Wardens of the Trinity House of Hull were authorized to forbid any mariner to sail from the port of Hull whom they had not certified as competent. They could limit his licence according to the degree of his competence, noting the ports to which he was entitled to sail. In the early eighteenth century a tablet was hanging in the Hull Trinity House with Elizabethan by-laws reputed to date from 1570 painted upon it. Amongst these was one to the effect that outward bound masters were to give to the Trinity House an account of the number of their mariners, and, on their return, of their behaviour on the voyage, and that straggling seamen from other ports were not to be employed without certificates.[3] The mid-seventeenth-century oath book of the corporation shows that mariners applying to become masters or pilots were examined, that incompetent candidates were failed and that successful ones were admitted, the ports to which they were authorized to sail being entered against their names.[4]

In 1582 the Newcastle upon Tyne Trinity House also obtained a similar new charter creating Elder and Younger Brethren, but it lasted for only seven years, when the town of Newcastle upon Tyne asserted its prior rights of judicature. The Trinity House therefore reverted to its original charter, and the Deptford Trinity House intervened when special maritime powers were needed.[5]

Unhappily a series of disastrous fires has resulted in the destruction of many of the records of the Trinity House of Deptford Strand, but,

[1] Whormby, J., *op. cit.*, gives these essential features of the charter.

[2] Ruddock, A. A., *op. cit.* and Brooks, F. W., *The First Order Book of the Hull Trinity House, 1632–1665* (1942) and 'A Wage Scale for Seamen, 1546', *E.H.R.* Vol. 60.

Whormby, J., *op. cit.*, reproduces in translation most of the charter of 1541, and a précis of that of 1580.

[3] Whormby, J., *op. cit.*, where the charter is reproduced in some detail and the by-laws are summarized.

[4] Brooks, F. W., *The First Order Book of the Hull Trinity House* (1942).

[5] Whormby, J., *op. cit.*, reproduces much of the 1582 charter, and illustrates its revocation and the intervention of the Deptford Trinity House.

from the evidence already quoted, to say nothing of the books on navigation in due course dedicated to or published by its Brethren, it is clear that henceforth, in Elizabeth I's day and in early Stuart times, it discharged its navigational duties towards the seamen of the realm as conscientiously as the Houses of Newcastle upon Tyne and Hull.

The decentralized method of navigational training outlined above, without any established school of navigation, sufficed the English in the 1560s, '70s, and early '80s, because it suited their still limited needs. The only chartered overseas trade was that of the Muscovy Company, of whom Stephen Borough was the distinguished Chief Pilot. As this company had a monopoly of the trade, the only pilots and masters engaged in it would be those in the service of the company. It could be only in the interests of the company to attend to the advice of their Chief Pilot in matters concerning the navigational skill of their servants, whom, despite his naval appointment, he could still easily supervise, since London was their port of departure and return. The only other overseas trade was that to Guinea, which was not the monopoly of a chartered company. Portugal, as we have seen, claimed exclusive trading rights here by virtue of first discovery, and so far as it was able took measures to prevent the activities of interlopers. If English Guinea activities had been known to have been legalized by charter by the English Crown, open hostilities must have ensued. What actually happened was that the Government, from the queen downwards, recognizing only the right of 'effective occupation', invested in the Guinea trading ventures of syndicates of merchants and even allowed them to hire royal vessels. Borough was one of the officials responsible for ensuring that these royal ships were furnished with pilots and masters who were as adequately trained as the ships were adequately armed. The success of the voyages speaks for the success of the system.

That no school of navigation of the continental pattern was established can also be attributed to the economic structure of the English overseas trade. Unlike that of Spain, it was not a monopoly from whose profits an actual school of navigation could be financed, nor was it extensive. To set up an institution to train masters for oceanic navigation when there was little of such navigation to be done, and small prospects of any without incurring conflict, would have been a measure as extravagant as it would have been provocative. As it was, the requisite standard of navigation, when the demand for many more oceanic navigators arose in the 1570s, was achieved by the English masters qualified by the Trinity Houses, employing, as the Spanish records show, French and Portuguese pilots to assist them. For a text-book on navigation Englishmen had Eden's translation of Cortes, and by the middle of the '70s their activities had called forth an English manual to supplement this. When internationally legitimate explorations to the north-west began to be undertaken from 1576, and navigational skill of the highest order was called for, the deficiency of public instruction in higher mathematics and navigational theory was made good by consultation with the navigational adviser to the

Muscovy Company, Dr. John Dee, whose preface to the first English *Euclid*, published in 1570, had stimulated intelligent interest in navigational problems to an unprecedented degree.

Such flexible arrangements also suited the independent spirit of the Elizabethan seamen, who were first and foremost individualists, conscious of nationhood, but impatient of governmental control and intolerant of officialdom. The secret of the success of the Tudors as rulers was that they could judge both the needs and the temper of their virile, restless, people with extraordinary insight. They had the ability of knowing how to satisfy their needs by the means most in harmony with their temper. Thus Elizabeth's Government, by listening to the best informed nautical advisers, by applying the apprentice system to seamen under the surveillance of revitalized Brotherhoods of Trinity House, assured itself early in the reign of an adequate 'store of skylful Pilotes'. After seeing to the provision of ships and seamen, this was its chief concern. By itself participating in overseas ventures, and by encouraging individual adventurers of outstanding merit, such as Hawkins, Drake, and Frobisher, to take well educated young gentlemen to sea with them to learn the art of navigation, the Crown began at the same time to ensure that there should also be a sufficiency of men qualified by navigational skill and experience as well as by birth and education to command its ships in the event of war.

Chapter Five

THE SPUR TO MASTERY

' . . . Cecil simply said the Pope had no authority to divide up the world . . .'
Bishop Alvaro de la Guadra, Spanish Ambassador to the Crown, London, 27 November 1561.

'Secretary Cecil sent to aske me to furnish them with a memorandum of the places where it is forbidden to trade without your Majesty's license. I sent it to him saying that the places were all the West Indies Continent and Islands. He sent to say the Council do not agree . . .'
Guzman da Silva, Spanish Ambassador to the Crown, London, October 1566.[1]

SOME ten years of Elizabeth's reign elapsed before the Government felt that the economic and political situation of the country justified the prosecution of a more aggressive mercantile policy than hitherto. After 1568 the whole emphasis changed. Partly it was in response to the growing awareness of Englishmen of the possibilities latent in oceanic exploration and trade. Partly it was because Englishmen were growing increasingly conscious of the religious and political issues at stake and that, despite the risks, these demanded action if vassalage to Spain was to be avoided. Partly it was because for the first time conditions both at home and abroad had become favourable for action. In 1568 Mary of Scotland had become a prisoner in England—the threat from over the border had ended —and a year later the crushing of the Rising of the North put an end to the Catholic threat in the north of England itself. In 1569 the third and most formidable of the wars of religion that since 1562 had been sapping the strength of France had broken out; La Rochelle had been established as the Huguenot headquarters, and Huguenot privateers had recommenced harrying all Catholic commerce in the Narrow Seas; in 1568, too, the embers of rebellion that since 1565 had been glowing in the Netherlands burst into flames. Though they were quickly stifled by Alva's army of Spain, 1569 saw the struggle transferred to the sea by the issuing of letters of marque by William, Prince of Orange, to seamen who were soon to become famous as the Beggars of the Sea. The same year saw an English expedition under John Hawkins sail to the succour of the garrison of La Rochelle. In short, the time had come to start curbing by all overt and indirect means 'the exorbitant power of Spain'. The spark which had fired the train of events that, in a few brief years, was to establish the fame of

[1] From *English voyages to the Caribbean*, Hak. Soc, Ser. 2, Vol. 62, p. 10. The first quotation is from a discussion upon English traffic to Guinea, the second is on Hawkins's voyages to the West Indies.

English seamen upon the seven seas had been struck late in 1568 by the Spaniards themselves in the little Mexican port of San Juan de Ulloa.

In the 1560s the Muscovy, North Sea, and Baltic trades were still primarily the concern of the merchants of the East Coast ports. London, though already the chief port of the realm, was still only on the way to its rapid rise as the undisputed economic centre of the country. The merchants of Southampton, Plymouth, and Bristol, whose ports faced south and west, had for long been the principal traders with the Biscayan and Peninsular ports and Atlantic Islands. It has already been mentioned that in the 1530s, aided by foreign pilots, they had started going farther afield. Hakluyt expresses it this way:

> Olde M. William Hawkins of Plimmouth, a man for his wisedom valure, experience and skill in sea causes much esteemed, and beloved of K. Henry the 8, and being one of the principall sea-captaines in the west parts of England in his time, not contented with the short voyages commonly then made onely to the knowne coaste of Europe, armed out a tall and goodly shippe of his owne of the burthen of 250 tunnes, called the *Paul of Plimmouth*, wherewith he made three long and famous voyages unto the coast of Brasil, a thing in those days very rare, especially for our nation. In the course of which voyages he touched upon the river of Sestos upon the coast of Guinea, where he traffiqued with the negroes, and tooke of them elephant's teeth. . . .[1]

There is clear evidence in the Plymouth port books that as late as 1540 the *Paul* was still plying the trade started in 1530. Certain duty was paid by William Hawkins on 24 February 1540 on an outward cargo of the *Paul* of knives, combs, hatchets, bracelets, cloth, copper, lead, and '19 dozen nightcappes'. On 20 October 1540 duty was also paid on an inward cargo of the *Paul*'s consisting of Brazil wood and '1 dozen elephant's teeth weighing 1 cwt'.[2]

Old William Hawkins had been born at Tavistock in Devon at about the time of the Cabot voyages. He lived until 1553 or 1554, and thus long enough to see the English Guinea trade, of which he had been the pioneer, revived, probably at the instigation of Cabot. Old William Hawkins left two sons to carry on his West Country shipping business; both were born at Plymouth, William in 1519, and John in 1532, the year of his father's third successful Brazil voyage. For a few years after their father's death the brothers carried on the family business together. Then they divided; William kept Plymouth his headquarters, made a number of voyages as a merchant for the Crown, and died in 1589. John, the younger, while keeping closely in touch with Plymouth, made London, not without good purpose, his headquarters. He had inherited his father's discontent with short voyages.

---

[1] Hakluyt, *Principal Navigations*, Hak. Soc., Extra Ser., Vol. 11, pp. 23–4.
[2] Hakluyt Society's Publication, *Europeans in West Africa*, 1450–1560, Vol. 2. Hak. Soc., Ser. 2, Vol. 87, pp. 300–01.

The right to explore and trade to the north, north-east, and north-west had been vested in the London Muscovy Company, of which Hawkins was not a member. Pope Alexander VI in his bull *Inter Caetera*, 1493, had given to Spain the New World within which lie the Caribbean coast and islands, and had forbidden 'all persons of no matter what rank, estate, degree, order or condition' to dare, without Spain's permit, 'to go for the sake of trade or any other reason whatsoever to the said islands and countries after they have been discovered'. Spain claimed upon the strength of this grant a threefold monopoly of the New World—political, commercial, and religious.[1] In West Africa, Portugal in the 1560s was making good her claim to the right of exclusive trade by sending more and better armed ships to guard the coasts. To make longer trading voyages legitimately would be no easy task for an Englishman, particularly as climatically the Spanish colonies did not promise to be particularly suitable marts for English cloth. Nevertheless, an enterprising trader might find a commodity that was in demand, and one so much in demand that the Spanish colonials might be prepared to juggle with the regulations about trade so that both trader and colonial buyer might make transactions to their mutual benefit. With suitable financial backing and suitable ships, and possibly with the connivance of the English Government, a breach might be made in the ramparts of Spanish colonial trade. The area was vast, Spanish defences were few and far between, and the needs of the colonists greater probably than their loyalty. So it was that in 1562,[2] having considered carefully the fact that the first of the revived Guinea voyages had brought back 'certain tall slaves', that the Portuguese were the chief suppliers of slaves to the West Indies and that, in order to keep the prices high, they had the habit of keeping the supply short; considering moreover that, since the Spaniards had exterminated the docile, and failed to exploit the intractable natives of the New World, manpower was the greatest need of the Spanish colonists, John Hawkins determined to attempt the trade. Therefore, early in the 1560s he formed a syndicate in London of merchants and officials willing to finance him. In the West Indies, whither he sailed late in 1562, touching at the Canaries, to pick up a Spanish pilot, and the Guinea coast to collect slaves, he found the colonists eager to trade, provided adequate safeguards were taken to ensure that though illegally engaged in trade with him they could not be punished from home. He hoped to become a *concessionaire* in the trade, and so render it legitimate as well as profitable.

John Hawkins was not, as it happens, the first English sea-captain to break into the isolation of the West Indies. Thirty-six years before there arrived off Santo Domingo in 1527

'a large three-masted ship belonging to the King of England . . . this ship, together with another, cleared perhaps nine months ago from England on

---

[1] *English Voyages to the Caribbean*, Hak. Soc., Ser. 2, Vol. 62.
[2] Hakluyt's *Principal Navigations*, Hak. Soc., Extra Ser., Vol. 10, p. 7.

order from their King, to make a certain exploration toward the north, between Labrador and Newfoundland, in the belief that in that region there was a strait through which to pass to Tartary. . . . They had sailed as far north as fifty and some degrees, where certain persons died of cold, the pilot had died: and one of the said vessels was lost. . . . For which reason they came to this land to take in water and subsistence and other things which they needed, and they asked for safe-conduct to enter this port which their honours extended to them in his Majesty's name, sending with them to the ship . . . pilots to bring the said ship into the harbour . . . today. . . . They boarded that said ship, when the Master received them well, and gave them to eat and drink abundantly indeed, and showed them certain linens, woollens and other merchandise which he carried for barter.

'And just when they had dropped anchor,' [off Santo Domingo], 'and the ship being anchored, all hands had begun to eat, with much pleasure and good humour, from the fortress of this city a lombard was fired, and the stone passed by the poop of the ship, very near to it.

'Whereupon the ship's Master turned colour, saying . . . it was a plot to betray them';

and at once raised anchor and made sail 'on a course for Castile.'[1] This ship (possibly the *Mary Guildford*, with Jean Rotz, the French pilot, as master) was the first English, the first interloper indeed of any nation, in the Indies. Though this visitation was brief, it had held a threat—expressed by some of the crew—and been an omen. The threat had been answered by the shot, and for thirty-six years that had sufficed the English. Not so the French, who had followed in ever-increasing numbers and boldness. Now, in the '60s, if old memories were not revived by Hawkins's voyages, at least the threat inherent in them was felt as keenly. The Spanish Government refused to legalize his ventures, either his first, or his second, made in 1564. In their eyes he was not only a law-breaker— for he was a foreigner and without a licence to pass to those parts, his goods had not been manifested at Seville, and he had traded without a trading licence—he was a threat to the very security of the Indies. Consequently they determined to nip his activities in the bud.

After his second voyage, and when Hawkins was known to be preparing a third, the Spanish Ambassador delivered an uncompromising ultimatum to Elizabeth. This was in October 1566. After the first voyage Spanish protestations had been met by assurances that Hawkins would 'do King Philip's subjects no harm'[2]; now Hawkins was forbidden by the queen 'to go to any of Philip's prohibited ports'.[3] His ships were stayed. Nevertheless he sailed them secretly on 9 November 1566 under the command of a deputy, John Lovell, and a young man, Francis Drake by name. Thus

[1] *English Voyages to the Caribbean*, Hak. Soc., Ser. 2., Vol. 62, p. 29.
[2] *Ibid.* p. 16, note 1.
[3] *Ibid.* p. 16.

Hawkins's ships reappeared in the West Indies with the Frenchman, Jean Bontompo, Juan Buontiompo or John Goodweather, who seems to have acted as confederate and probably as navigator on these later voyages. Lovell's expedition returned in September before Hawkins sailed on his fourth voyage—the third which the English Government had now countenanced his making. Indeed, as on the second voyage, he sailed not only with royal ships under his command but under the orders of the queen. Hawkins in fact was sailing as an official seeking to extend England's overseas trade and, it would appear from negotiations with da Silva, the Spanish ambassador, in an attempt to persuade Spain to hire the English ships for the defence of the Caribbean, as she hired Genoese warships to serve her in the Mediterranean against the Barbary pirates. On the Guinea coast Hawkins fell in with a French captain, and forced him to join the expedition—probably to aid him in his pilotage. Another joined him voluntarily before the Atlantic was crossed. Once again Hawkins's skill as a trader, negotiator, and leader led to satisfactory trading with the colonists eager for manpower. But on Friday, 17 September 1568, John Hawkins's fortune changed. He was anchored in the port of San Juan de Ulloa, driven there by stress of weather and lack of victuals, at the tail of the hurricane season, when in the offing were seen the sails of Spanish ships. It was the fleet from Seville, on board it the new Viceroy of Mexico. Hawkins was in a most unenviable position. There was no other port on the whole coast of the Mexican Gulf whither either he or the Spaniards could go. To exclude them might mean their destruction by storm; to admit them his own destruction by treachery. He did the only thing he could do. He admitted them on terms. They did what they deemed most expedient. For them the situation was galling. Indeed it was undignified as well as dangerous. The Englishman's impertinence was matched only by his effrontery as an interloper in forbidden territory and trade. So, while openly they accepted Hawkins's terms, secretly they planned his destruction by treachery. A week later, on the morning of Thursday, 23 September, some time before noon, suddenly a trumpet sounded in the Spanish flagship. The fight was on. Hawkins had two royal ships, the *Jesus of Lubeck* and the *Minion*; a 50-ton ship of Drake's, the *Judith*; two smaller ships, the *Angel* and *Swallow*; and a French caravel. Though he had prepared his squadron against treachery, only the *Judith* and the *Minion* escaped, Drake in the former, Hawkins in the latter. The tale was told in January 1569. It was the end of an epoch. Far from driving the English from the New World, by that act of treachery the Spaniards attracted Englishmen's attention to their New World possessions, and this they did at the very moment that the Narrow Seas were absorbing the activities of the French corsairs who hitherto had harried the Spanish Main and islands in the Caribbean Sea. If they had not known of it before, it was not long before the English learnt of the comparative defencelessness of the Spanish possessions.

Hawkins's disaster had been caused by his being forced to fight a pitched battle with the guard-ships of the Seville fleet, as a result of treachery. Nevertheless he had sunk the "capitana" and "almirante"—the flagship and second-in-command's flagship—and a third ship, and this was no mean feat. The Spaniards had had the fight by no means all their own way. Indeed, in the history of the Royal Navy that action at San Juan de Ulloa proved of singular importance. From the year in which it was fought the character of the Royal Navy changed. Hawkins's royal ships had been the customary high-charged ships designed for battle in the Narrow Seas by a combination of bombardment by cannon and cut-throat, hand-to-hand boarding. At San Juan de Ulloa he destroyed the three Spanish ships by cannon-fire, by relatively *long-range* cannon-fire, alone. The significance of this feat, and the unsuitability of the traditional type of warship for oceanic warfare, were immediately appreciated by the Navy Board. The new warships were designed, and the old ones reconstructed, on new lines and, before long, they were victualled, armed, and manned for long sea-voyages and battle far from home.[1] Equally surely from that action can be traced the rise of the English oceanic merchant marine, the development of the English merchant ship capable of trading over the oceans, and, concurrently, the appearance of a growing band of sea-captains capable of navigating them without the aid of foreign pilots. By the 1580s English sea-captains no longer subordinated themselves to Frenchmen in order to learn the ropes of navigation, though they might still bribe or abduct the foreign pilot, Portuguese or Spanish, to conduct their ships to a desired landfall in unfamiliar seas—the technique of Hawkins and Drake to their dying day. On the contrary, by the 1580s it was the English who were teaching the seamen of the world new-found secrets of the art of navigation.

The immediate economic lesson of San Juan de Ulloa for Englishmen was that if they wanted to trade with the Indies, they would have to fight for the right under one guise or another, and that the wealth of the Indies could be won only by hard endeavour on the high seas. Into the *mêlée* of the religious wars, lapping along the Channel coasts, in the 1570s, they ventured as privateers, or, to use the current expression, 'letters of marque' men: the more heartily from 1570 in that their queen had been excommunicated.

Deprived by his personal relations with the Government from gaining redress by his own actions, Hawkins dispatched privateers and illicit traders to the Caribbean on his own behalf. Others joined them. Of these Drake was the most successful. His exploits culminated in his classic voyage of circumnavigation of 1577–80, the first by an Englishman, and his return with the richest cargo yet brought by an Englishman into an English port. But the venture, it is important to remark, was still made possible only by Drake's practice of seizing competent pilots to aid him on his voyage—a Portuguese, Nuña da Silva, for the voyage to Brazil

---

[1] For a full discussion of the naval results of San Juan de Ulloa, see Waters, D. W., 'The Elizabethan Navy and the Armada Campaign', *M.M.*, Vol. 35.

... we gat the ...
... it until night, ...
... store to us, we gatt us into ...
... have Sea roome,

... of September, we saled to the Shore
having then sufficient wynd, and weather
... nere unto the Shore, and the Type ...
spent, we came to an Anker in 30 faddomes water
... 13th day) we came along the Cost w[ith]
... Northwest, and by west, and Southeast & by East
The 14th day) we came to an Anker w[ith]in 2
leags of the Shore having 60 faddomes, Therr
... went a shore with our Bote, and found ij or
... good harborowghs, the Land being Rocky, and
... But as for people this we se none.

The 15th day) runing still along the Cost untill
the 17th day), then the wynde being contrary) to
us, we thowght it best to returne unto the Harborow
w[hich] we had found before, and so we bare roome w[ith]
the same, Hereby, we cold not accomplish our
desire that day. The next day) being the 18th
of September we entred into the Haven, and there
came to an Anker at 6. faddomes, This Haven
runneth into the mayne about 2 leags, and is in
breadth half a leage, wherein were many seall fisshes
fisshes, and other great fisshes, And upon the
mayne we saw Bears, greate Dear, Foxes,
w[ith] divers strange Beasts, as Gulwomes, & suche
other, w[hich] were to us unknowen, and also wonder-
full. Thus remayning in this Haven the space of
a Sevennyght, seing the yere far spent, & also very
evill weather as frost, Snow, and hayle, as
thowgh it had bene the depe of winter, we thowght
it best to enter therin, wherefore we sent oute
                                                        iij men

XXIX. THE HAVEN OF DEATH, 1553.

Foy, Lin, Hüller, wermot, Dertm, Plimot.	Bristo.	Misso, Brig, water.	Portl, Peter, porte.	Age of the Moone.	Orion, Pole, Ors wel.	Disp, Lux, Lev, moys.	Boloig, Douer, Harwick, Yarmot.	Callice
F & S.	E & S.	EsE	SEbE		SE	SEbS	SSE	SbE
H. M.	H. M.	H. M.	H. M.	☽	H. M.	H. M.	H. M.	H. M.
4	57	5	18	3	48	10	33	11	18	12	3
7	36	8	2	9	6	3	9	36	11	9	12	6	12	3
8	24	9	9	9	54	10	39	11	24	12	9	54	1	39
9	12	9	57	10	42	11	27	12	12	57	1	42	2	27
10	0	10	45	11	30	12	15	4	1	0	45	1	30	3	15
10	48	11	33	12	18	1	3	5	1	48	2	33	3	18	4	3
11	36	12	21	6	1	51	6	2	21	3	6	3	51	4	51
12	24	1	9	54	2	39	7	2	24	3	9	54	4	39	5	39
1	12	1	57	2	42	3	27	8	4	12	5	7	5	9	27
2	0	2	45	3	30	4	15	9	5	0	45	4	16	30	7	15
2	48	3	33	4	18	5	11	5	48	6	33	5	17	19	8	51
3	36	4	21	6	51	6	36	7	2	19	6	8	51
4	24	5	9	54	6	39	7	2	48	9	8	54	9	39
5	12	5	57	6	42	7	27	14	12	8	17	9	8	42	10	27
6	0	6	45	3	30	8	15	6	0	9	45	10	30	11	15
6	48	7	33	8	18	9	16	48	9	33	10	33	12	3
7	36	8	21	9	54	17	36	10	36	11	18	12	51
8	24	9	57	10	42	18	2	24	5	9	12	54	1	39
9	12	9	57	10	42	11	27	19	12	12	57	1	42	2	27
10	0	10	45	11	30	15	20	0	1	0	45	1	30	3	15
11	36	12	21	3	1	21	36	1	21	3	6	3	51	4	3
1	12	1	9	54	2	39	23	24	2	36	3	3	54	4	39
1	12	1	57	2	42	3	27	24	12	4	12	1	57	4	42	5	27
2	48	2	33	4	19	5	25	1	0	4	16	3	17	30	7	15
2	48	3	33	4	18	5	26	5	48	6	33	2	19	3	18	4	3
3	36	4	21	6	51	27	6	36	7	2	19	6	8	51
4	24	5	9	54	6	39	28	2	48	9	8	54	9	39
5	12	5	57	6	42	7	29	36	9	8	17	9	42	10	27
6	0	6	45	3	30	8	15	30	9	0	9	45	10	30	11	15
WVeſt.	wbn	wbſw			new	nwbw	nw	45 nw	nbw

The use of these Tables.

VVHen you wyll knowe the full sea, seke out the name of the place, where you desyre the full water, in the head of the tables: Or learne the poyntes of the co-pas there noted: Or if you luste know of some Ma-riner, what Moone maketh a full sea there: a South west or South Moone, &c. When the age of the Moone founde under the place or poynt of the compasse, sheweth in right oppe the houre & Minute of the full water. The clif, then is manifest.

Ensample.

I desyre to knowe the full water at London bridge, the yeare of our Lorde 1555, the fyrst daye of Februarie, the yeare before put forth, the 6 daye of Februarie, the yeare aforesayde, the Moone to be 14 daies olde. I see also under the title where London is S w, whiche letters fignifie that a South west Moone maketh a full sea there: and that is at 2 of the clocke, and 12 minutes past. Thus is well pertcained in the first Table before put fourth, if you trine down to the 14 Day of the age of the Moone, under London title.

A Note of the houre of the daye and nyght.

THe ingenious may gather here about the houre of the daye & nyght, by the Moone: &c. consideration had of the poyntes in those Table of types before noted, For the houre is openly put un-der the poyndes of the compasse.

Euery parte or poincte contayninge 11 Degrees and ¾: this com-pase is well figured here about the Center in the instrument fol-lowyng for the nyght towre, because ye may by it haue a delectable large use of these type tables.

How by the first of the tide tables, ye may readily knowe when the Moone com meth unto the south, when she riseth and setteth: with her continuance on the earth.

SEke the age of the Moone (as is opened) then resorte to the first Tide table loking out that age there: loo under the South point in right opposite, the houre appeareth, when she cometh unto the South. The which the spent half that arche that the Sunne woulde haue had in that Sygne, whiche pulled away, sheweth the rising: that half ar the also added to her coming unto the South declareth her going downe. The arche then that the Sunne woulde haue had in the Sygne, is her continuance on the earth.

A Table at all times plainly and briefly declaring, The breke of the daye: the houre and minute of the Sunne rysing, the iust length of the daye: the length of the nyght also: the very minute of the Sunne setting and the Twylight.

Of Ebbyng an Flowyng.

XXX and XXXI. TIDE-TABLES AND RULES FOR THEIR USE IN LEONARD DIGGES'S *A Prognostication everlasting* . . . (1556).

and down the South American coast—two Spanish pilots, or at least, since they refused to accompany him, their charts and rutters, for the passage across the Pacific. In the British Museum there lies today a manuscript manual of navigation of 1577 incorporating a rutter covering the trade routes followed by the English at that time, those from England (Orfordness) to St. Nicholas in North Russia, to Barbary and the Guinea coast. Significantly, it includes two detailed Portuguese rutters of the Brazilian coast, one of them continuing with the route down the South American coast to the Strait of Magellan, and up the coasts of Chile and Peru to Panama. The probability is that Drake made a copy of it for his voyage of circumnavigation.[1]

Drake's venture had official backing. Two of its main objects were to exploit the Southern Continent—*Terra Australis Incognita*—shown on the new map of 1570 of Abraham Ortelius, the great Flemish cartographer, and to find the Strait of Anian. This strait was believed to run from the Pacific, in the latitude of California, whose coastline was still unexplored, to the Atlantic, either in the region of Chesapeake Bay or (shades of the 1527 voyage!) north of Newfoundland, neither region being as yet explored. Drake's mere achievement in sailing round the world has pushed this aim of exploration into the background of history, but it is of importance because the discovery of the Strait of Anian continued into the seventeenth century to be a motive in English exploits in North America. It lay behind the Frobisher voyages of 1576-7-8 to the north-west, of the Davis voyages of 1585-6-7, and the voyages in the early seventeenth century of Hudson, Button, Baffin, James, and Foxe. It formed also an element (and a disruptive one) in the plans of the early colonists in Virginia. But for us its interest lies in the fact that it was the preoccupation of the English with northern navigation that made them tackle the hardest problems in navigation, because the hardest problems are met with in northern waters.

Once war was joined with Spain openly, in Europe as well as in the West Indies, as it was in 1585, further navigational problems had to be solved. The problems inherent in the successful interception of ships on the high seas brought home to the English sea-captain in command of a ship or squadron of the Royal Navy the vital need for accurate position-finding by celestial observation and accurately deduced reckoning and plotting. While the northern explorations by sea brought to the fore the problems associated with the magnetic compass and with chart projections in high latitudes, the voyages of reprisal and the naval operations in the latter part of the century, particularly around the Azores and in the approaches to Spain, underlined the universal nature of these problems. They led to what was probably the greatest advance ever made in marine cartography. This was the so-called Mercator's projection. Charts on this projection are those most generally used by seamen today. It was evolved by the

---

[1] Harleian MSS. 167. See also *A Brief Summe of Geographie*, Hak. Soc., Ser. 2, Vol. 69, Appendix 1, and Taylor, E. G. R., 'The Dawn of Modern Navigation', *J.I.N.*, Vol. 1.

Cambridge mathematician Edward Wright probably as a result of a raiding voyage to the Azores and against Spanish treasure ships in which he took part in 1589. From this latter period, the 1590s, can be dated the introduction of the plotting board and protractor, and of trigonometrical tables, improvements in the mariner's compass and of the means of finding and plotting its errors, the general introduction of the log and line for measuring the distance run, and assiduous attempts to measure longitude accurately.

By then the world had been encompassed for the second time by an Englishman, Cavendish (1586–88), and, though the Spanish war put an end for twenty years to attempts to reach Cathay by the northern route, his voyage whetted men's appetites for eastern spices. John Davis, who had made his fame in the '80s, by his voyages in search of a North-West Passage to Cathay, passed the Strait of Magellan in an attempt to find it from the other side of America.[1] He was forced back through the Strait and had to abandon the attempt, but James Lancaster rounded the Cape of Good Hope in 1591, and reached the Indies that way—the first English navigator to do so. Though he was wrecked in the West Indies on his return voyage, he had blazed the trail which Davis was to follow. Enlisting as chief pilot in a Dutch expedition to the East Indies in 1598, Davis returned in mid-1600 in time to pilot the first voyage of the recently chartered East India Company which sailed from the Thames in 1601 under James Lancaster's command.

Navigation in low latitudes, like navigation in high latitudes, had its special problems; in particular that of observing the sun's altitude. It was doubtless his first voyage through equatorial waters which caused John Davis, who was an exceptional man in many ways, to develop his 'Back-Staff' for observing the sun's altitude. It was the greatest advance made towards accurate observations at sea until the sciences of optics and mechanics enabled Hadley to produce the reflecting quadrant with Vernier's scale adjustment a hundred and forty years later.

These voyages to the East Indies by the English, despite their mastery of the art of navigation, were possible only by reason of their possession of the necessary route books and charts. Those to the East, as we have seen, represented the work of two centuries of laborious exploration by the Portuguese and, on the final discovery of the route via the Cape of Good Hope, had been kept closely guarded secrets. But these secrets had passed into the possession of Spain when King Philip had seized the crown of Portugal in 1580. This act warned the English anew to prepare for the danger to come, for after the conquest of the Azores, in 1582, the Spanish captains had openly declared, 'Now that we have all Portugal, England is ours.' Not only had the English co-operated in the Portuguese defence of the Azores, in 1582, but they had given refuge to the displaced pretender, Dom Antonio, and his followers. In return they had gleaned invaluable information from them concerning the Indies. Above all, war with Spain once joined, the Portuguese carracks from the East Indies had become fair

[1] 1591–93.

game. The capture of one, the *San Felipe*, in 1587, and of another five years later had rendered up many secrets, including charts. Thus warfare and trade together played their part in making the English proficient at sea. By the end of the century ocean voyages were a part of the nation's daily life. The first decade of the new century found Englishmen trading regularly to the East Indies; and not only that, when the war ended in 1603 the English turned their energies to the realization of other schemes cherished for thirty years—the planting of colonies. Originally conceived as trading ports on the route to Cathay, or as advanced bases against Spain, as sites for gold prospectors or outlets for surplus population, colonies had come to be viewed as potential sources of natural products that, given time, would be valuable for trade, and provide another source of naval stores. A diversity of objectives, inexperience, and war had left of the first attempts, made in Virginia in the '80s, scarcely a trace. Now the object, even if experience in 'planting' was lacking or ignored, was at least not distracted from execution by war. It was the old object in new guise : to make England the richest storehouse and staple for merchandise in all Europe, old John Cabot's intention of 1497. But in earnest of this intention the Government, carrying on the Elizabethan practice, legislated to foster such shipping. The English colonies had by law to trade with the mother country, England, alone. Small ships were forbidden to make the ocean passage. Although by law transatlantic trade by Englishmen, in English ships navigated by English sea-captains, was assured, it was up to them to exploit it. The assumption implicit in such legislation, that Englishmen were competent to put it into effect, when tested, proved sound. By the time of Captain Smith's death in 1631 their trade routes laced the Atlantic and stretched between Murmansk and Madras.[1]

[1] An Elizabethan navigator pays tribute to Sir John Hawkins as a pioneer English navigator (Captain John Davis, *The Hydrographicall Discourse* (1595)):

The first Englishman that gave any attempt upon the coastes of West India, being parte of America, was syr John Hawkins, knight: who then and in that attempt, as in many others sithins, did and have proved himselfe to be a man of excellent capacity, great government, and perfect resolution. For before he attempted the same it was a matter doubtfull, and reported the extremist lymit of danger to sayle upon those coastes. So that it was generally in dread among us . . . howe then maye Syr John Hawkins bee esteemed . . .